MICROCOMPUTER DECISION
SUPPORT SYSTEMS:
Design, Implementation, and Evaluation

ALSO FROM QED®

MICROCOMPUTER DECISION SUPPORT SYSTEMS:
Design, Implementation, and Evaluation

Edited by
Stephen J. Andriole

QED® Information Sciences, Inc.
Wellesley, Massachusetts

MICROCOMPUTER DECISION SUPPORT SYSTEMS:
Design, Implementation, and Evaluation

Library of Congress Catalog Card Number: 85-63247
ISBN: 0-89435-173-7

Printed in the United States of America

For the new one, Katherine Leigh

ACKNOWLEDGEMENTS

All edited books are as good as their contributed chapters. In this case, the book owes its technical success to the authors who took time from incredibly busy schedules to document some of their insights and experiences. I would like to thank them all once again.

I would also like to acknowledge the support and encouragement of Edwin Kerr of Q.E.D., support and encouragement that became more meaningful when the deadlines began to slip.

Finally, I would like to thank Denise M. Andriole for her efforts to make this book a reality. Without her help it would not have emerged from the stacks that perpetually cover my desk.

Stephen J. Andriole
Marshall, Virginia

PREFACE

Perspective is critical to the design, development, and application of decision support systems. Some of us regard decision support as option generation and selection. Others regard it as structured data base management. Still others see it as a comprehensive set of integrated functions that support all phases of the decision-making process, ranging from information gathering to post-hoc evaluation.

Decision support vendors are not much help here. Their perspective is as wide as the marketplace, and just as volatile. Commercial definitions of decision support have changed as the vendors themselves have improved, removed, and introduced new products.

The most extreme perspective sees decision support as computer-based problem-solving of any kind, while the narrowest defines it as criteria-based decision option evaluation. The perspective adopted in this book is, I hope, balanced. We deliberately tried to include articles that represent several different, though by no means incompatible, approaches to the design, application, and evaluation of decision support systems. We have, however, also made an attempt to highlight *microcomputer-based* decision support systems.

Part I of the book develops the backdrop. The lead article by Andrew P. Sage covers a lot of conventional decision support territory, but also breaks new assessment ground. He identifies and evaluates no less than twenty of the most popular decision support systems, including TK!Solver, Knowledgeman, Harvard Project Manager, Decision Analyst, Lotus 1-2-3, and SuperCalc. Sage's article is practical and insightful, required reading for the serious decision support aficionado.

Janice Fain's article is much more philosophical, focusing on the role of decision support in the cognitive problem-solving process. She is concerned with problem structuring and the ideal role for the computer in that and related processes. She also examines the role of artificial intelligence in the computer-based problem-solving process, the optimal distribution of tasks between humans and computers, and the prospects for machine learning. Fain's article balances Sage's by forcing us to remember that TK!Solver and dBaseII are tools intended for human use, and that unless they satisfy specific cognitive tasks they should be ignored.

Part II of the book turns to design and development issues. Barth and Lehner discuss the role of artificial intelligence in the design and application of microcomputer-based decision support systems, while MacLean discusses the leverage that can be gained via the design of effective user-system interfaces. John Sutherland is concerned about how "feedforward" technology can enhance decision making and decision aiding in command and control, a specific problem-solving area in the military. Bennett Teates continues this theme by concentrating on how decision support systems technology can be brought to bear full force on the defense command and control system. My article in Part II looks at how several decision support systems could be used to solve corporate crisis management problems.

Part III of the book looks at a number of successful applications. The purpose of this part is to present a variety of case studies that crosscut the problem-solving worlds of industry and government. Phelps' article looks at the Army's use of decision support systems for intelligence analysis and production. Bessent, Bessent, Clark, and Elam examine a microcomputer decision support system for increasing managerial efficiency, and Allene Cormier describes how decision support systems can be "coaxed" into operational use.

Part IV of the book turns to evaluation. William B. Rouse leads Part IV with a discussion of some methods and techniques for structured evaluation. Adelman and Donnell continue with the evaluation problem and, together with Rouse, present a balanced and practical survey of the evaluation literature as it applies to decision support systems effectiveness. Gerald Hopple is cautiously pessimistic and warns against the misapplication of decision support systems. He develops a strong case for pre-planned compatibility assessment *before* systems are designed and evaluated. He also suggests that evaluations be structured around the right questions, that is, questions that spotlight how well (or badly) the system is handling the most recalcitrant human cognitive information processing problems.

You will note that throughout the book reference is made to *decision support systems, decision aids, decision-aiding technologies,* and *computer-based problem-solving systems.* No effort is made here to distinguish among the many definitions of essentially the same process: (micro)computer-based problem-solving.

You will also note that there are several references to *command and control, intelligence analysis,* and *tactical problem-solving.* What might appear as a disproportionate amount of attention to military problem solving is in reality vastly understated in the book, given that the U.S. Department of Defense spends well in excess of several billion dollars a year on computer-based problem-solving systems design and development. Many hundreds of millions of dollars of this total are directed at the design and development of decision support systems. The key distinction between private and public sector decision support systems design and development lies in the push—in the private sector—to design generic decision support systems capable of performing as many tasks as possible, whereas the public sector is much more dedicated to the design and development of special purpose decision support systems. The distinction is noted in several of the articles in the book.

Part V concludes the book with a blue sky look into the future. I wrote this last article in response to those who wonder why advanced technology has yet to exert an influence on decision support systems designers. Some of the ideas are not so new, yet uncirculated, while others are farily new yet well known. The really interesting ones in Part V are the ones that are completely new and uncirculated.

I hope that the articles in this book communicate some new ideas and reaffirm a growing recognition concerning the role that microcomputers can play in corporate and government problem solving. Here the reference is not to word processing or straight data base management, but to the use of microcomputers to structure problems, identify alternatives, make decisions, and improve effectiveness. It is to this end that this book is aimed.

CONTENTS

II
DECISION SUPPORT
SYSTEMS TECHNOLOGY

III
DECISION SUPPORT
SYSTEMS APPLICATIONS

IV
DESIGN, EVALUATION,
AND IMPLEMENTATION ISSUES

V
FUTURE DECISION SUPPORT
SYSTEMS TECHNOLOGY

I

THE DECISION
SUPPORT BACKDROP

INTRODUCTION

Decision support is a natural result of the evolution in data base management and in computer-based problem-solving. It is significant that there were a lot of *decision aids* around long before they were placed under the decision support systems umbrella. As suggested in the Preface, there are still many professionals who refuse to accept anything but the most rigid (i.e., option selection) definitions, just as there are many who readily accept any and all definitions.

The two articles in this part of the book are eclectic and interdisciplinary. The first article by Andrew P. Sage, now The First American Professor of Information Technology at George

Mason University, looks at decision support through practical eyes. He develops a category scheme for identifying decision support systems and then proceeds to describe the systems and the functions that they perform. The assessments are primarily descriptive, and therefore of great use to anyone who is thinking about purchasing one of the more popular packages. The key to Sage's definition of decision support lies in his focus on "ill-structured issues." Decision support, unlike the support available for accounting, invoicing, and record keeping, is flexible and adaptive to changing requirements.

Janice Fain's article, "The Use of Computers in Decision Making," provides counterpoint to Sage's article not in a strictly philosophical sense, but in its focus. Fain is concerned with the proper role of the computer in the otherwise human problem-solving process. Why use computers at all? How should we use them? How should the tasks be allocated? These are just some of the questions that Sage presumes you have already answered. As suggested some time ago by Michael L. Donnell, the coauthor of Chapter 12, decision-making models grounded in the discipline of decision analysis are *normative* models, not descriptive. Fain suggests that computers are best suited to the solving of routine, structured, value-free problems, and that unassisted humans should probably tackle the heavily value-laden tasks. These extreme positions are offered as food for thought, rather than as a prescription for decision support systems design: Fain herself has developed more than a few systems with a value content.

The Fain article is so valuable because it forces us to think first about the assumptions in Sage's excellent piece, and second about the whole decision support process. (Hopple returns to these issues in Chapter 13.)

1

An Overview of Contemporary Issues in the Design and Development of Microcomputer Decision Support Systems

Andrew P. Sage

INTRODUCTION AND TAXONOMIES OF DECISION PROBLEMS

Numerous disciplinary areas have contributed to the development of decision support systems. Computer science has provided the hardware and software tools necessary to implement decision support system design constructs. The field of management science/operations research has provided the theoretical framework in decision analysis that is necessary to design useful and relevant normative approaches to choice making. The area of management information systems has provided the data base design tools that are needed. The areas of organizational behavior, and behavioral and cognitive science, have provided rich sources of information concerning how humans and organizations process information and make judgements in a descriptive fashion. This is indeed an interdisciplinary area of inquiry.

There have been many attempts to classify different types of decisions. Articles on knowledge representation and decision rules discuss some of these. Among the classifications of particular interest here is the decision type taxonomy of Anthony (1965). He describes four types of decisions:

> *Strategic Planning Decisions*—decisions related to choosing highest level policies and objectives, and associated resource allocations;
>
> *Management Control Decisions*—decisions made for the purpose of assuring effectiveness in the acquisition and use of resources;
>
> *Operational Control Decisions*—decisions made for the purpose of assuring effectiveness in the performance of operations;
>
> *Operational Performance Decisions*—day-to-day decisions made while performing operations.

Simon (1960) has described decisions as structured or unstructured depending upon whether or not the decision-making process can be explicitly described prior to the time when it is necessary to make a decision. This taxonomy would seem to lead directly to that in which expert skills (holistic reasoning), rules (heuristics), or formal reasoning (holistic evaluation) are normatively used for judgement. Generally, operational performance decisions are more likely to be prestructured than are strategic planning decisions. Thus *expert systems* can usually be expected to be more appropriate for operational performance and operational control decisions than they are for strategic planning and management planning decisions. In a similar way, *decision support systems* will often be more appropriate for strategic planning and management control than they are for operational control and operational performance.

It is important to note that expertise is a relative term that depends upon familiarity with the task and the operational environment into which it is imbedded. Since decision environments do change, and since novices become experts through learning and feedback, it is clear that there should exist many areas in which the proper form of knowledge base support is a hybrid of an expert system and a decision support system. This suggests that there will be a variety of decision-making processes in practice and that an effective support system should support multiple decision processes. In a similar way, the information requirements for decision making can be expected to be highly varied, and an effective support system should support a variety of data base management needs.

There are a number of abilities that a decision support system should support. It should support the decision maker in the formulation or framing of the decision situation in the sense of recognizing needs, identifying appropriate objectives by which to measure successful resolution of an issue, and generating alternative courses of action that will resolve the needs and satisfy objectives. It should also provide support in enhancing the abilities of the decision maker to obtain the possible impacts on needs of the alternative courses of action. This analysis capability must be associated with enhancing the ability of the decision maker to provide an interpretation of these impacts in terms of objectives. This interpretation capability will lead to evaluation of the alternatives and selection of a preferred alternative option. Associated with these must be the ability to acquire, represent, and utilize information or knowledge, and the ability to implement the chosen alternative course of action. All of this must be accomplished with economic and technological rationality, organizational process rationality, incremental or bureaucratic politics rationality, and other forms of social, legal, or organizational rationality (Sage 1981).

There are many variables that will affect the information that is, or should be, obtained relative to any given decision situation. These variables are very clearly task dependent. Keen and Scott-Morton (1978) identify eight variables:

> *Inherent accuracy of available information*—Operational control situations will often deal with information that is relatively certain and precise. The information in strategic planning situations is often uncertain, imprecise, and incomplete.
> *Needed level of detail*—Very detailed information is often needed for operational type decisions. Highly aggregated information is

often desired for strategic decisions. There are many difficulties associated with information summarization that need attention.

Time horizon for information needed—Operational decisions are typically based on information over a short time horizon, and the nature of the control may be changed very frequently. Strategic decisions are based on information and predictions based on a long time horizon.

Frequency of use—Strategic decisions are made infrequently, although they are perhaps refined fairly often. Operational decisions are made quite frequently, and are relatively easily changed.

Internal or external information source—Operational decisions are often based upon information that is available internal to the organization, whereas strategic decisions are much more likely to be dependent upon information content that can only be obtained external to the organization.

Information scope—Operational decisions are generally made on the basis of narrow scope information related to well-defined events internal to the organization. Strategic decisions are based upon broad scope information and a wide range of factors that often cannot be fully anticipated prior to the need for the decision.

Information quantifiability—In strategic planning, information is likely to be highly qualitative, at least initially. For operational decisons, the available information is often highly quantified.

Information currency—In strategic planning, information is often rather old, and it is often difficult to obtain current information. For operational control decisions, very current information is often needed.

The extent to which a support system has the capacity to formulate, analyze, and interpret issues will depend upon whether the resulting system will be a management information system (MIS), a predictive management system (PMIS), or a decision support system (DSS). In a classical *management information system*, the user inputs a request for a report concerning some question, and the MIS supplies that report. When the user is able to pose a "what if" type question and the system is able to respond with an "If then . . ." type of response, then we have a *predictive management information system*. In each case there is some sort of formulation of the issue and this is accompanied by some capacity for analysis. The classic MIS need only be able to respond to queries with reports. Thus it would respond to a request for inputs concerning airline flights from Washington to Chicago on July 4 with a report of available flights on that date. Search of an electronic file cabinet, or perhaps a relational data base, would provide information from which a report generator could construct the desired report. In this case, the MIS would include the following capabilities: a focus on data processing and structured data flows at an operational level, and summary reports for the user.

Alternatively, we might desire a response to a what/if type question such as "What will likely happen if we drill for oil at location x?" The computer might then respond with "Based upon the physical characteristics of source x it is predicted that if you drill at this source then you should likely expect . . ." The predictive management system would include more analysis capability than the MIS did. This might require an intelligent data base query system, or perhaps just the simple use of some sort of spreadsheet or macroeconomic model. Thus we see that a *data base management (sub)system* is a fundamental requirement in a full *decision support system*. This discussion provides a conceptual illustration of how a management information system evolves into a decision support system. Not indicated in this discussion is the *dialog generation and management system* that is necessary to provide acceptable user interfaces to the computerized system. As will soon be indicated, this is a very important component of a decision support system.

To obtain a decision support system, we would need to add the capability of *model base management* to an MIS. But much more would be needed than just the simple addition of a set of decision trees and procedures to elicit decision maker utilities, as might be believed from examination of the paradigms of decision analysis. We would also need a system that would be flexible and adaptable to changing user requirements such as providing support for the evolving decision styles of the decision maker as these change with task, environment, and experiential familiarity of the support system users with task environment. Most decision situations are fragmented in that there are multiple decision makers and their staffs, rather than just a single decision maker. Also there are temporal and spatial separation elements involved. Learning is a fundamental requirement in a decision support system. This involves metalearning, or learning how to learn or how to decide how to decide. Further, as Mintzberg (1973) has indicated, managers have many more activities than decision making to occupy themselves with, and it will be necessary for appropriate DSS to support many of these other information-related functions as well. Thus the principal goal of a DSS, the improvement in the effectiveness of organizational knowledge users through use of information systems technology, is not a simple one to achieve.

FRAMEWORKS FOR DESIGNING DECISION SUPPORT SYSTEMS (DSS)

As discussed, there are three principal components of a decision support system:

- Data Base Management System (DBMS)
- Model Base Management System (MBMS)
- Dialog Generation and Management System (DGMS)

Also, there are three technology levels at which a DSS may be considered: the DSS tools, the DSS generator, and the decision makers' control mechanisms. The level of DSS tools themselves contains the hardware and software elements and those system science and operations research methods that would be needed to design a specific decision support sytem. The purpose of these DSS tools is to design a specific DSS that would be responsive to a particular task or issue.

Often the best designers of a decision support system are not the specialists familiar with the DSS tools. The principal reason for this is that it is difficult for one person to be very familiar with a great variety of tools as well as the requirements needed for a specific DSS. This suggests an intermediate level, that of the decision support generator, as being a very useful level for DSS system design. The DSS generator is a set of software, similar to a very high level programming language, that enables construction of a specific DSS without the need to formally use the DSS tools. A DSS generator would contain an integrated set of features, such as inquiry capabilities, modeling language capabilities, financial and statistical (and perhaps other) analysis capabilities, and graphic display and report preparation capabilities. A DSS generator may be structured such that its product contains more of one component of a DSS, such as a model based management system, than the other component. Often, the product of a decision support system generator is source code in a programming language, such as Pascal or Basic, that can be compiled to produce a specific decision support system. It will often be much less time consuming to design a decision support system using a DSS generator than to write code in a high-level programming language. The price paid for this is that the resulting DSS may be less flexible and tailored to the precise task at hand than the DSS that would result from appropriate design procedures in a high-level programming language. At an intermediate level between these two extremes are very high level programming languages specifically tailored to the requirements of typical decision support systems.

There are many actors that can become involved in the design and use of a decision support system. At a minimum, these include the DSS users and their staffs, the DSS designer, the technical support people who work with the DSS designer, and the specialists in computer and system science who develop the hardware, programming languages, and operations research methods that ultimately become the components of a specific DSS. The advantage to the DSS generator is that it is something that the DSS designer can use to directly interface the user group. This eliminates, or at least minimizes, the need for DSS user interaction with the content specialists in computer and system science. When it is recalled that users will seldom be able to specify the requirements for a DSS initially, then the great advantage to having a DSS generator for use by the DSS designer in interacting with the DSS user becomes apparent.

The design and development of a DSS can be patterned after the stages of the design process (Sage 1981). These stages include preliminary conceptual design, evaluation, and testing of the decision support system.

Since a decision support system is intended to be used by decision makers with varying experiential familiarity and expertise with respect to a particular task, it is especially important that a DSS design consider the variety of issue *representations* or frames that decision makers may use to describe issues, the *operations* that may be performed on these representations to enable formulation, analysis, and interpretation of the decision situation, the automated *memory aids* that support retention of the various results of operations on the representations, and the *control mechanisms* that assist decision makers in using these representations, operations, and memory aids. A very useful control mechanism results in the construction of heuristic procedures, perhaps in the form of a set of production rules, to enable development of efficient and effective standard operating policies to be issued as staff directives. Other control mechanisms are intended to help the decision maker direct use of the DSS and also acquire new skills and rules based on the formal reasoning-based knowledge that is called forth through use of a decision support system. This process-independent approach toward identification, design, and development of the necessary capabilities of a specific decision support system is due to Sprague and Carlson (1982) and is known as the ROMC approach. It also serves to specify the capabilities that a useful DSS generator, or the specific DSS tools, must have in order to build an effective decision support system.

Data Base Management Systems (DBMS)

A data base management system is one of the three fundamental components of a decision support system. An appropriate data base management system must be able to work with data that is internal to the organization and data that is external to it. In almost every instance in which there are multiple decision-makers, there is the need for personal data bases, local data bases, and systemwide data bases. One of the desirable characteristics of a DBMS is the ability to cope with a variety of data structures that allow for probabilistic, incomplete, and imprecise data, and for data that is unofficial and personal, as contrasted with official and organizational. The DBMS should also be capable of informing the support system user of the types of data that are available and how to gain access to them.

In order to construct a data base, we must first identify a data model. A *data model* is a collection of data structures, operations that may be applied on the data structures, and integrity rules that are used to constrain or otherwise define permissible values of the data. There are at least five models that may be used to represent data. The most elementary of these is the *individual record model*. The *relational model* is a powerful generalization of the record model. A relation is the fundamental data structure in the relational model, and there may be a number of fields in any given relation. The relational model enables mathematical set operations on records in terms of insertion of new records, updating fields within existing records, deleting existing records, creating relations that may be contained in records, deleting relations that may be contained in records, joining or combining two or more relations based on their containing common fields, selecting records by virtue of their containing certain specified relations, and projection such as to enable selection of a subset of the fields that exist in a relation.

The *hierarchical* or *tree data model* results in a relatively efficient representation of data. In a hierarchical model, the structure represents the information that is contained in the fields of a relational model. In a hierarchical model, there will be certain records that must exist before other records can exist since every data structure must have a root record. Because of this structured aspect of the model, it will be necessary to repeat some of the data that need to be stored only once for a relational model. The *network model* is a generalization of the hierarchical model in that there are links between records which enable a given record to participate in several relationships. There are often major problems associated with insertions, deletions, and updating in both the hierarchical and network data models due to the need to maintain a consistent data base. These do not exist in the relational model since the same data is never entered more than once. Also there is additional search complexity since a search can start anywhere in the network structure. Searches are, however, generally more efficient than they are in a relational model.

Due to the potential need to accommodate expert system type capabilities in a decision support system, it is desirable to consider a *production rule model* as a fifth data model. This will enable inferences to be made. This is a particularly desirable form of data model when one wants to use many predictive management information system capabilities. The "if then" type response to "what if" queries is especially natural in this representation. This may provide a very useful linkage to the natural language generation and management system element that is an essential ingredient of an effective user oriented DSS. Much additional discussion of DBMS design approaches can be found in Sprague and Carlson (1982), and Date (1977, 1983).

Model Base Management Systems (MBMS)

The desire to provide recommendation capability in a decision support system leads us to a discussion of model base management systems (MBMS). It is through the use of model base management systems that we are able to provide for sophisticated analysis and interpretation capability in a decision support system. The single most important characteristic of a model base management system is that it should enable the decision maker to explore the decision situation through use of the data base by a model base of algorithmic procedures and management protocols. This can occur through the use of modeling statements in some procedural or nonprocedural language, through the use of model subroutines, such as mathematical programming packages that are called by a management function, and through the use of data abstraction models. This latter approach is close to the expert system approach in that there will exist element, equation, and solution procedures that will together comprise an inference engine. Advantages to this approach include ease of updating and use of the model for explanatory purposes.

Typically, it will be desirable to allow for the use of multiple models in order to accomodate the decision maker's need for flexibility. Thus a mixed scanning approach might be incorporated in which a conjunctive or disjunctive scanning mechanism is used to allow for an initial scan to eliminate grossly unacceptable alternatives. After this is accomplished, further evaluation of alternatives might be accomplished by a compensatory tradeoff evaluation, or one based on a dominance search procedure (Sage and White 1984). The following discussion will expand upon these decision analytic notions of model base management systems design.

To allow flexibility, the MBMS should provide, upon system user request, a variety of prewritten models that have been found useful in the past, such as linear programming and multiattribute decision analysis which will be considered as ad hoc models. It should also be possible to perform sensitivity tests of model outputs, and to run models with a range of data to obtain the response to a varety of "what if" type questions. The MBMS component of a DSS will generally require some aspects of a decision analytic approach to judgement and choice.

In the decision analysis paradigm, it is assumed that a set of feasible alternatives $A = (a_1, \ldots, a_m)$ and a set $(X_1, \ldots, X_n)$ of attributes or evaluators of the alternatives can be identified. Associated with each alternative course of action a in A, there is a corresponding consequence $X_1(a), X_2(a), \ldots X_n(a)$ in the n-dimensional consequence space $X = X_1 X_2 \ldots X_n$.

The decision maker's problem is to choose an alternative a in A so that the maximum pleasure with the payoff or consequence, $(X_1(a), \ldots, X_n(a))$, results. It is always possible to compare the values of each $X_i(a)$ for different alternatives, but in most situations, the magnitudes of $X_i(a)$ and $X_j(a)$ for i not equal j cannot be meaningfully compared since they may be measured in totally different units. Thus, a scalar-valued function defined on the attributes $(X_1, \ldots, X_n)$ is sought that will allow comparison of the alternatives across the attributes. The existence of the value function as a mechanism for representation and selection of alternatives in a utility space is based on the fundamental representation theorem of simple preferences which states that under certain conditions of rational behavior there exists a real-valued utility function U such that alternative a_1 is preferred to alternative a_2 if, and only if, the utility of a_1, denoted by $U(a_1)$, is greater than $U(a_2)$, the utility of a_2.

A primary interest in multiattribute utility theory (MAUT) is to structure and assess a utility function of the form

$$U[X_1(a), \ldots, X_n(a)] = f\{U_1[X_1(a)], \ldots, U_n[X_n(a)]\}$$

where U_i is a utility function over the single attribute X_i and f aggregates the values of the single attribute utility functions such as to enable one to compute the scalar utility of the alternatives. The utility functions U and U_i are assumed to be continuous, monotonic, and bounded. Usually, they are scaled by $U(x^*) = 1$, $U(x^o) = 0$, $U_i(x^*_i) = 1$, and $U_i(x^o_i) = 0$ for all i. Here $x^* = (x^*_1, x^*_2, \ldots, x^*_n)$ designates the most desirable consequence and the expression $x^o = (x^o_1, x^o_2, \ldots, x^o_n)$ denotes the least desirable consequence. The symbols x^*_i and x^o_i refer to the best and worst consequence, respectively for each attribute X_i, i.e., $x^*_i = X_i(a^*)$ where a^* is the best alternative for attribute i, and $x^o_i = X_i(a^o)$ where a^o is the worst alternative for attribute i. In the simplest situation, additive independence of attributes (Keeney and Raiffa 1976) exists such that the MAUT function may be written as

$$U(A_i) = w_1 U_1(A_i) + w_2 U_2(A_i) + \ldots + w_n U_n(A_i)$$

Here the w_j are the weights of the various attributes of the decision alternative A_i and the U_j are the attribute scores for the alternative.

We have just described very briefly the case of certainty in a decision-making framework. Associated with each alternative there is a known consequence that follows with certainty from implementation of the alternative. The foundations for decision making under risk are provided by the classical work of von Neumann and Morgenstern and described in most textbook accounts of decision analysis. The implications of this work are that probabilities and utilities can be used to calculate the expected utility of each alternative and that alternatives with higher expected utilities should be preferred over alternatives with lower ones.

Multiattribute utility theory provides representation theorems, based on some forms of independence across the attributes, that describe the functional form of the multiattribute utility U as an additive, multiplicative, or multilinear function of the conditional single attribute utility functions U_i. The books by Keeney and Raiffa (1976), and Fishburn (1964, 1970) are perhaps the most comprehensive works that deal with these representations.

The methodology of decision analysis, using multiattribute utility theory, is generally decomposed into four major steps as shown in Figure 1.1:

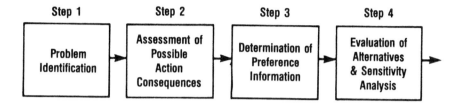

Step 1.   *Identification of the decision problem.* This includes the generation of alternatives and the specification of objectives and hence, attributes to be used in the evaluation of alternatives.

Step 2.   *Assessment of the possible consequences for each alternative.* In the case of certainty, this consists only of specifying the unique known consequence that follows from implementation of each alternative. When various possible consequences may occur, a probability distribution function over the set of attributes for each alternative must be determined.

Step 3.   *Determination of preferential information.* The structure of the model is determined and quantification of its parameters is made. This step requires relevant, precise, and consistent information about value assessment, value tradeoffs, and risk attitude.

Step 4.   *Evaluation of alternatives and sensitivity analysis.* The information gathered is aggregated by use of the expected utility criterion. The alternative with the highest expected utility is the most desired. Finally, the sensitivity of the decision to a variety of changes is explored in order to gain some confidence concerning the recommended decision.

Figure 1.1   Decision Analysis Paradigm

Even though the theory and procedures of decision analysis are conceptually straightforward, there are other circumstances that make its implementation very complex. Each of the foregoing four steps requires substantial interaction between the analyst and the decision maker. A very stressful thinking process is demanded of the decision maker while the analyst is in charge of coordinating a series of activities in order to facilitate this process. The analyst must obtain the minimum amount of relevant information about the decision problem to determine the various utility functions. Often redundant information should also be obtained in order to check for consistency. It is rather interesting that in most of the literature on decision analysis, there is little or no mention of the information system functions that need to be accomplished in order to evolve a recommended decision. In effect, it is assumed that the decision maker is an expert with respect to knowledge of relevant information but unable to aggregate this information in a proper fashion as needed for an effective judgement or decision.

In the exercise of an effective decision aiding process, much is required of the analyst. The analyst must be sensitive to biases and flawed heuristics that the decision maker may utilize; must be able to structure the decision problem regardless of the degree of complexity; and must, above all, retain the confidence of the decision maker in the belief that a formal analysis of the problem will result in a more intelligent and informed decision.

The large amount and complexity of information required for complete specification of multiattribute utility functions and probabilities leads, especially in practice, to the use of simplified heuristics. Often, these are flawed (Sage 1981). Even in prescriptive situations, screening procedures will often be needed to reduce the time, stress, and effort demanded from decision makers. Screening methods are intended to identify and reduce the size of the nondominated set of alternatives, that is to say those that are not bettered by at least one other alternative on each and every one of the attributes of importance, through use of behaviorally relevant and easily available information. One of the first to develop a screening method for decision making with incomplete knowledge of probabilities was Fishburn (1965). He was concerned with the use of incomplete information on probabilities in comparing alternative strategies in a typical formulation of decision making under risk. The criterion of choice or strategy that should normatively be used is the principle of maximum expected utility, so that the decision maker seeks a strategy a^* which is the maximum over i of the expected utility of alternatives a_i. The utility function $U_j(a_i)$ is a precisely assessed multiattribute utility function defined on the set of possible strategies $\{a_i\}$, and $p_j(\bullet)$ is a measure of the likelihood of the possible state of nature j given that a particular strategy was selected. The imprecise forms of the measure of probability that Fishburn considered are:

1. No information about $p_j(\bullet)$

2. Ordinal measure: an ordering of p_j (e.g. $p_1 \geq p_2 > p_3$)

3. Linear inequalities: an ordering of sums of p_j (e.g. $p_1 + p_2 \geq p_3$)

4. Bounded interval measure (e.g. $c_i \leq p_i \leq c_i + d_i$)

The search for the best alternative is performed in this approach by pairwise comparisons of expected utility among candidate strategies. Because of the restricted form of the available information on the p_j, the search for the best alternative can be put into a straightforward linear programming problem.

Sarin (1977) proposed a screening procedure similar to that of Fishburn with the additional assumption of additive independence on the set of attributes. This assumption simplifies the search for dominance structures and results in a procedure that can be formulated as a mathematical programming problem. The parameters of the mathematical programming formulation include probabilities, importance weights, and single attribute utility functions. A simple procedure is then developed for the case when the probabilities and the importance weights are precisely known and utilities are stated in the form of linear inequalities, thereby resulting in simple linear programming formulations. Extensions to this research have been reported by Sage and White (1984) who developed an Alternative Ranking Interactive Aid based on Dominance Structural Elicitation (ARIADNE) concept. The general mathematical programming formulation of the search for dominance results in interactive solution of a large number of relatively simple linear programs. Several cases have been considered:

1. The probabilities (p_j) are known precisely, and the importance weights (w_i) and utilities (U_i) are described by linear inequalities.

2. The importance weights (w_i) are known precisely, and the utilities (u_i) and probabilities (p_j) are described by linear inequalities.

3. The importance weights (w_i) and utilities (u_i) are known precisely, and the probabilities (p_j) are described by linear inequalities.

In cases 1 and 2 the solution results in a set of hierarchically organized linear programming problems. The simplest formulation is that of case 3, which is equivalent to the problems solved by Sarin and Fishburn, resulting in a set of simple linear programming problems.

Decision-making problems in which there are several conflicting objectives have been formulated in terms of multiobjective programming problems. The mathematical programming formulation of the multiple objective decision problem is

$$\max \ U[u_1(a), \ u_2(a), \ \ldots , u_n(a)]$$

where the u_i are the real-valued utility functions of the n objectives. The single attribute utility functions u_i are assumed known; the overall utility function U is unknown. Generally, the solution to this problem is not a unique alternative but a set of nondominated alternatives. Multiobjective programming techniques operate under the notion of dominance for generating the set of nondominated alternatives. Interactive algorithms to gradually gain knowledge about U and solve the above problem uniquely have been proposed by many researchers. The books by Cohon (1978), Chankong and Haimes (1984), and Zeleny (1982) present a number of these.

Screening procedures can be made to be interactive. Interactive approaches of this type assume that the decision maker can provide preference information on simple, often hyopthetical, alternatives. Initially, a reduction of the nondominated set is made with the available information. If the decision maker can select an alternative from the nondominated set, then the process is stopped. Otherwise, further information is requested. Often, but not always, very little guidance is provided by these procedures about the information needed. The decision maker is asked to provide further information when a single nondominated alternative is not present. This information may be redundant, in that the decision model could have inferred it from previous information. In this case it could serve only as a check for consistency. The new information may be inconsistent with the existing information. Alternately, the decision maker may never recognize and provide information needed to reduce the nondominated set. All this may make decision support processes that are based on interactive multiple objective procedures ineffective and inefficient. The flexibility that the interactive screening, or scanning, procedures provide, potentially result in a more effective support process. However, this flexibility complicates, to a considerable extent, the task of the decision analyst as a facilitator.

In order to make efficient use of these new screening procedures, it seems very necessary to provide the analyst with a suitable dialog generation and management system. Such a system must be designed with full knowledge of the particular data base and model base management system used to allow for the interactive dominance-based scanning. At the very least, it is necessary to provide assistance to the analyst in determining what information is most needed, in terms of relevancy to the task at hand and with due consideration being given to information that is both important and cognitively easy to assess. The analyst should be aided in the evaluation of acquired information for consistency and in ways that avoid and resolve inconsistencies that do result. Finally, the information that is acquired must be represented and used within a model base management system that is valid and appropriate for decision making.

The foundations of multiattribute expected utility theory provide useful models of normative behavior for decision making under risk. The assessment of precise utility functions in these models is mathematically justified by the existence of a real-valued utility function. Whether it is behaviorally justified is yet another question. In addition to the several practical difficulties encountered in assessing precise utilities, there are a number of semantic issues involved with the precise representations of preference judgements. One of the aims of contemporary research is to seek representations that incorporate incomplete measurements of preference and risk attitude and to provide a behaviorally meaningful as well as rationally correct approach for decision support. Instead of assessing a real-valued utility function, various "fuzzy" kinds of imprecise representation of utilities and probabilities are allowed.

Dialog Generation and Management System (DGMS)

The dialog generation and management system portion of a decision support system is designed to satisfy knowledge representation, and to control and interface requirements of the DSS. It is the DGMS that is responsible for presentation of the outputs of the DSS to the decision makers and for acquiring and transmitting their inputs to the DMBS and the MBMS. Thus the DGMS is responsible for producing DSS output representations, for obtaining the decision-maker inputs that result in the operations on the representations, for interfacing to the memory aids, and for explicit provision of the control mechanisms that enable the dialog between user input and output and the DBMS and MBMS. Thus the dialog generation and management system is strongly involved in each step of the ROMC approach to systems analytic design of decision support systems.

There are a number of possible dialogues. These are inherently linked to the representational forms that are used for the DBMS and MBMS. Menus, spreadsheets, tradeoff graphs, and production rules are some of the formats that may be used as a basis for dialog system design. Generally several of these should be used, as the support system user may wish to shift among these formats as the nature of issues and experiential familiarity with the system changes. The DGMS should be sufficiently flexible to allow review and sensitivity analysis of past judgments, and to be able to provide partial judgments based upon incomplete information. Of course the DGMS should be "user friendly" through provision of various HELP facilities, prompting the decision maker, and other abilities that support the knowledge of the support system user. It is especially important to avoid a system that destroys perspectives and to encourage development of a system that enhances them.

EVALUATION OF DECISION SUPPORT SYSTEM DESIGNS

It is very important to obtain an evaluation of decision support system designs. Chapter 11 by Rouse, on design and evaluation, provides a discussion of typical evaluation procedures. There are a number of behavioral implications to decision support system introduction that are very important. User involvement in the design process, management support for the DSS design effort, and the availability of user-training activities are but a few of the many requisites for successful DSS implementation. It is especially important that potential system users not regard it as too difficult to learn to use, too hard or too time consuming to actually use, or as producing inaccurate, incomplete, or out-of-date results or recommendations. Perhaps the most damning charges of all that affect potential user willingness to use the system are the feelings that it significantly interferes with the "normal" way of thinking about problems, or that it cannot adapt to changes in problem specifications, or that it does not produce intermediate results of value, or that it does not really address the actual problems that exist.

Implementation of a decision support system can fail if it introduces significant conflict between the form of economic and technical rationality of the recommendations of the DSS and the political-social behavior of the organization and users of the system. The way in which groups interact in the decision-making process is also of importance. Hakathorn and Keen (1981) have identified three types of group decision activities. In an independent group activity, the decisions of the individual decision makers do not interact. But often there are interactions and dialog among the decision makers such that pooled interdependencies exist. There also exist situations when there are sequential interdependencies such that the decisions of one decision maker are passed as inputs to the efforts of other decision makers. These and other characteristics of organizational and group decision making need to be considered at all of the design phases for a decision support system. The design requirements for a DSS and the implementation concerns will depend considerably upon these organizational variables. All of this will influence operational tests and evaluation of the effects of DSS introduction as well.

SOFTWARE FOR MICROCOMPUTER DECISION SUPPORT

There is a variety of software potentially useful for decision support. Relatively little of it is extraordinarily useful now for the integrated purposes of data base management, model base management, and dialogue generation and management. Instead, existing software generally emphasizes one of the first two purposes at the expense of the others. Doubtlessly this is due to the newness of both the microcomputer software industry and the newness of decision support concepts as well. With the expanded random access memory capabilities brought about by 16-bit microprocessors, and the expanded storage capabilities made possible by inexpensive hard disk units, the stage is set for rapid development of very useful and complete DSS software packages. This is, in fact, possible today with some of the newest software products available and through tailored design and use of two or more existing software packages in an integrated fashion.

In conformity with the organization in the earlier parts of the chapter, software packages for data base management will be discussed first. Next, available software for model base management will be examined. To the extent that dialog generation and management features support the various software packages, these will be discussed also. Finally, a comment is made upon the very limited amount of contemporary software available for integrated data base management and model base management.

Software for Data Base Management

Available software for data base management varies from elementary data base programs, to program generators, to very high level languages for data base construction, to software that combines features from these categories. Elementary data base software, which are more in the nature of electronic file cabinets than data base management systems, are not especially useful for decision support systems despite their potential value for purposes such as mailing list managers. The MicroPro products DataStar and InfoStar, and the Eagle Enterprises product Citation are representative of software in this category. There are also products that allow accomplishment of very specialized functions associated with data base management, such as report generation. FRIEND, the Report Generator, a product from Friends Software Corporation, is an example of a very well designed product in this category. This chapter will not provide commentary concerning products of this sort, despite their considerable potential usefulness.

Due to their simplicity and versatility, most of the available microcomputer data base management systems are relational in nature. One of the oldest, and surely the best known of these is an Ashton Tate product, dBaseII. Due to its age and considerable success, it has almost become a de facto standard against which other DBMSs are compared.

dBaseII—The relational data base management system dBaseII was initially available for CPM-based systems although the program has now been converted to enable it to run under MSDOS. dBaseII is both a relational data base management system and a very high level programming language. It is possible to design very simple data bases and those of considerable sophistication. Of particular value in dBaseII is the reasonably sophisticated calculations that can be performed through use of the very high level programming language. There is a considerable amount of support available for the product as its availability over time and its popularity have led to the cottage industry growth of books concerning the package, program generators that produce dBaseII source code for a restricted class of applications, and training courses and software that ease the burden of learning how to operate the software. On the other hand each record is limited to a maximum of 1,024 characters in no more than thirty-two fields, and a maximum of two records may remain open at one time. It is restricted to 65,535 records but this is no limitation at all except for users with a rather large storage capacity hard disk. Many of the relational commands are executed very slowly. The product was designed for 8-bit machines, and has not truly been upgraded into a 16-bit environment. While this makes the transition to using the product on a 16-bit machine trivial, it does suggest that the product could be improved in a number of ways. Ashton Tate's dBaseIII, (a new version of the very satisfactory dBaseII), takes advantage of the enhanced capabilities possible in a 16-bit environment.

Sensible Solution—The next product is promoted as a sensible solution to the problems of dBaseII. Sensible Solution is not only a relational data base management system, but contains provision for use of some 40 natural language procedural commands. Although the product is available in CPM and MSDOS, only the CPM version was examined for this chapter. The product is a bit easier to use than dBaseII with respect to design of data entry forms. The maximum record size is a slightly larger 1,536 bytes. Theoretically 1,000,000 records can be contained in a given data base, but this would severely tax the storage requirements of any contemporary microcomputer. The maximum number of fields per record is 384 but it would be very difficult to use anywhere near this number within the 1,536 byte maximum record size unless the data entry is almost exclusively numeric, in which case the number of fields an order of magnitude larger than dBaseII could be significant. The speed of operation of the product is comparable to that of dBaseII for most functions. The Sensible Solution software company, O'Hanlon Computer Systems, certainly has a product that is, in most respects, comparable to dBaseII. It would be impossible to indicate a preference for one or the other, as this will be highly application dependent. It would be easy to state a problem for which Sensible Solution would be functional, whereas dBaseII would find the required number of fields, or the record length, excessive. On the other hand, the large cottage industry surrounding dBaseII will make it easier to become proficient in use of the software.

MAG/base—MAG/base, distributed by MAG (Micro Applications Group) Software Inc., is a generalized set of data management tools that enables relatively easy and straightforward construction of a data base management system. It can be obtained in any of three configurations. MAG/base1 is a simple electronic file drawer only, useful for mailing list construction and the like. MAG/base 2 adds to this the capacity for relatively sophisticated report generation. MAG/base 3 adds to all of this, various menu and programming features which enables processing of files and complete accounting functions. A comprehensive data management language is available and, after an appropriate learning time, is capable of intricate interactions with data files. It combines many of the features available in a relational DBMS with some of the features of a very high level programming language, such as dBaseII, together with some of the features to be found in program generators, which we soon will discuss. Generally though, the software is menu driven and consequently easier to begin to use than the more programming-oriented DBMSs, such as dBaseII and Sensible Solution. Form definition is considerably easier than in dBaseII. Only the CPM version of the program was tested, and this seems to be approximately equivalent to dBaseII in speed and ease of setup. The software is available in MSDOS and CPM86, although these versions were not evaluated.

SUPER—SUPER is a menu-driven data base management system available from the Institute for Scientific Analysis (ISA). Up to forty fields and a maximum record length of 255 bytes per record, and 32,767 records, are possible. The program is supplied in Microsoft BASIC source code. No effort was made to compile the program. Generation of a data base management system seems slower than with many of the other packages. While the software does not have true relational data base features, it is somewhat more than an electronic filing system by virtue of the submenu-driven data manipulations that are possible. The software is among the least expensive of the software packages evaluated here. In most ways, it is the least sophisticated. Probably the most advantageous feature of the software is the fact that it could be much more easily user customized than the other packages such as to enable integration of the software into a decision support system. While SUPER retails for $295, most of the other DBMSs retail for around $700. Considerable discount from the prices is the rule and this may reduce the price spread considerably.

FMS-80—File Management System 80 is a very comprehensive menu-driven relational data base system from DJR Associates. It contains very extensive documentation and requires four double-sided floppy disks to hold all of the program material and sample applications. It is priced accordingly at $995. It is not an extraordinarily easy program to use, but must be considered as one of the best in terms of a complexity/ease-of-learning-to-use ratio. It contains an internal very high level programming language which is more powerful than the dBaseII language, and somewhat more difficult to learn how to use. There are a very large number of overlay, help, and other files called by the menu program as it operates. While this enables a very sophisticated program to run in the CPM80 environment, it does slow down operations and, especially when a large data base is involved, could require a good bit of disk swapping. It is possible to have a maximum of 255 characters per field and 255 fields per record. This is a theoretical limit; the practical limits are much less as there would be no way to store such a record in 64K bytes of RAM, and only a few such records could possibly be contained in a floppy disk. This is software that, primarily because of its size and complexity, really belongs only on a hard disk system. There exists an extensive set of error messages, and the error handling capability of the software is very good. On a hard disk system and for applications where considerable sophistication is required, software such as this clearly has a place. A potential difficulty with such a large amoung of code as is present here, is that it is not easy for other than an expert to determine what is the minimum set of files necessary to accomplish a particular subset of the many possible activities. Configuration of a minimally acceptable set of software for a particular task is not easy.

FORMULAII—The unique software package FORMULAII from Dynamic Microprocessor Associates combines many of the features of a relational data base management system with those of a program generator. It also has some modest word processing features and is available for a wide variety of CPM80 systems. Installation for a variety of terminals is a relatively simple procedure. The software does not contain a program generator in the conventional sense since there is no source code generated that is then executed by a high-level programming language. Rather, FORMULAII configures a set of preexisting program modules and then combines them into a specific data base management system. The result of this is data base management software that is similar to software that would be obtained through custom design or use of a program generator. These custom applications are obtained in much less time than it would take to write the specific source code. Doubtlessly the equivalent code is larger in size and slower in operation than the code that results from truly customized programming by an appropriately skilled person. There exist program generators for dBaseII, such as the Quickcode software by Fox and Geller. The result of using FORMULAII is, in many ways, not unlike the result of using a program generator like Quickcode to generate dBaseII source code, and viewing the Quickcode input as the software input, and the dBaseII output as the output of the software. FORMULAII is extensively menu driven, and generally easy to use. It does not result in a relational data base but rather a file management system that can be made to have many of the properties of a relational data base. Thus the software is extraordinarily versatile within the constraints of not requiring programming on the part of the user. For the occasional user or designer of a DBMS, the time required to obtain an operational system should generally be less than with a more programming-oriented package, such as dBaseII.

Sci-Mate—The Institute for Scientific Information has produced a two-part software package, the Online Searcher and the Personal Data Manager, that together constitute the product Sci-Mate. The Sci-Mate Personal Data Manager can search text material to create a data base. The "free-search" capability allows a user to search a text that has been entered into the system for any specified combinations of characters, key words, or phrases. A variety of bibliographic uses suggest themselves. The permitted relational searches form a powerful set, and are controlled by a set of menu-driven commands. Formatted reports can be generated based on information searches. The Universal Online Searcher is a companion product that, in conjunction with a communications modem, enables a user to search any of a restricted set of data bases for information. The software is nicely menu driven and very ably endowed with help files so there is infrequent need to refer to the large, well-organized, printed user's manual. Clearly, this is a very special purpose data management system. It is an extraordinarily useful product for the very special purpose for which it is intended. It should be of major assistance to those who need to do extensive bibliographic searches through data bases. The extent to which the $880 retail price is justified will be highly user dependent.

R:Base—R:Base is a potentially very powerful relational DBMS. Like dBaseII, it evolved from NASA data base technology and has a mainframe heritage. Unlike many otherwise similar software products, this one was first introduced into the microcomputer world with the 16-bit microprocessor in mind. The theoretical limits of forty open files at a time, 400 fields per record, and over a billion records surely exceeds the capabilities of microcomputers. The system has stand-alone query and data base fields definition capability. It is remarkably easy to learn how to use. This is due, in large part, to the extensive help prompts, the well-thought-out tutorial, and the nicely organized user's manual. The data base produced with R:Base is relatively easily integrated with that from other software packages, such as spreadsheets and graphics software. There are a number of supplemental support packages available. One of the most useful of these appears to be CLOUT, Conversational Language Option, which is a natural language interface to simplify human-computer interaction. This option was not evaluated, nor was the extended report generator, which augments the considerable number of features present in the routinely included report generator, nor the interface program, which enables one to interface R:Base data from a variety of application programs. An extended service contract is available for an annual fee. This will provide product updates and a "hotline" for resolution of difficulties in use of the product. The total cost of the product, and several of the options, easily exceeds $1,000. For the serious user with a significant application, this is an outstanding product. The relative ease with which data in R:Base can be converted for use by other programs makes this a very serious contender for use in an integrated DSS consisting of this DBMS together with an appropriate MBMS. This software, while functionally improved over dBaseII with respect to relational data base management does not contain nearly as significant a set of mathematical operations as dBaseII. Thus it would not be as useful a stand-alone product for applications in which other than the simplest mathematical operations are required. When used in conjunction with a model base management system that has these capabilities, this disadvantage may not be noticed.

The several software products discussed in the foregoing are protypical products for information management. To be sure their capabilities vary. Nevertheless, it is not possible to pick one as the "winner" or best, for this is so very critically dependent upon a specific application and the requirements of that application. It is also very dependent upon the people who will design and those who will operate the DBMS and their familiarity with computers and information systems. This discussion applies primarily to the situation in which use as a stand-alone software product is intended. For use with a model base management system, R:Base seems to have the edge, for many uses and for many people, over the others discussed as it is designed as a 16-bit product, has very natural syntax and English language queries, has good error checking, and seems to cope more easily with "foreign" format data entries than the other products do.

But the story does not end here. A data base management system can be constructed using a program generator, or by writing the DBMS directly in high-level source code, or even assembly code. Two program generators were studied and evaluated as part of this effort and now will be discussed.

Pearl System of Development—Pearl System of Development is an interactive menu-driven program generator developed by Computer Pathways Unlimited and marketed through PEARLSOFT, a division of Relational Systems International Corporation. An application is defined in accordance with a predefined set of structural restrictions and the software ultimately generates source code suitable for CBASIC2, a run-time interpretive interpreter from Digital Research. With (generally) minor changes, CBASIC2 programs are compilable using the Digital Research CBASIC Compiler. At this time, Pearl System of Development appears to exist in the CPM80 environment only. Again with minor changes, the produced source code should operate with CBASIC86 operating under CPM86. Pearl level 3, the software evaluated, is intended primarily for professional programmers who wish to evolve significant applications with this software intended to produce Error-free Automatic Rapid Logic. The produced basic source code, which is re-

stricted by the assumed structural assumptions to correspond to file management and associated report generation
with a minimum of mathematical sophistication, can be
modified to fine tune it for uses not fully compatible with
the structure assumed by the developers of the software.
The code produced by Pearl appears relatively efficient in
size and, considering the slowness of the interpreted
CBASIC2 language, in speed as well. Pearl has existed for
approximately six years. It was perhaps the first program
generator for microcomputers, and remains a very significant product. It is not nearly as easy to use as some of the
other software discussed earlier, and the manual is a relatively sophisticated 300-page single-space typed document.
Software of this sort is clearly the wave of the future, and
an upgraded version of this software that would result in a
program generator of comparable quality that would produce truly compilable code in a 16-bit environment would
be a very welcome and useful product.

Next Step—Next Step is another program generator written to
generate Microsoft BASIC source code for 16-bit MSDOS
machines. It is essentially restricted to data base file management and associated report generation. Form design is
possible and screens can contain up to 510 characters in as
many as ninety different fields, fifteen of which can be key
fields that can be indexed to enable rapid search for information. The report, and the entire file management system for
that matter, can only accomodate simple mathematics. In
most ways, the software will do what the Pearl software
will do. It appears somewhat more limited with respect to
mathematical operations, but this is not a highlight of Pearl
either. The manual is well organized and generally easy to
read. The source code that is produced is, with possibly
minor changes, compilable under Microsoft BASIC. The size
of the source code that is produced, at least for modest applications, is overwhelming. Doubtlessly this is due to the
highly structured design philosophy behind Next Step which
pulls in and modifies, for the described application, several
existing prototypical BASIC source codes. Often these will

simply be larger than they might be, to accomplish a given task. The person who is willing to spend the several hours required to use this software package very effectively is in a position to generate a great quantity of source code that would take considerably more time to write by conventional methods. The ease with which it is possible to modify or tailor the resulting source code in order to reduce its size and enhance efficiency of execution is an important concern not investigated here. The real question concerns how this approach compares with that of using one of the relational DBMSs. The question as to which is best is clearly application dependent. For the majority of the DBMSs discussed, altering the format or content of reports that are produced is a relatively simple programming task. Even adding to or deleting a field is typically straightforward. Modifying an already established data base to accomodate a deleted field, and often even an added field, is relatively straightforward. To do this with these program generators will generally require going back to the program generator and producing all new source code. Because of the particular way these software products are structured, modification of an existing data base to accomodate the changes may not easily be possible. If requirements such as this are not present, then these program generators may be used to produce quite useful specific model base management systems. The developer of this software, EXECUWARE, has produced perhaps not the final answer to important concerns in DBMS design, but surely a very useful intermediate product.

Software for Model Base Management

There are a number of prototypical models that can be used for model base management, and a corresponding variety of software for this purpose. Most of the available software assumes a spreadsheet type model. But there are important exceptions, including several very high level programming languages specifically useful for the construction of MBMS. Most of the following discussions will concern these two categories, but we will also take note of some of the other MBMS software packages that are available.

SuperCalc2—SuperCalc2 is one of a number of second generation spreadsheet products. Its publisher, Sorcim (micros
spelled backwards), is one of the developers of a very useful
first generation product, SuperCalc. A major advantage to
the SuperCalc products is the extensive use of help overlay
files. While these overlays provide much assistance to those
who need it, they are unobtrusive to the experienced user
who is very familiar with the product. Both versions of
SuperCalc are available for CPM80, CPM86, and MSDOS
operating systems. There exists an even newer version of
the software, SuperCalc3, which incorporates the ability to
produce very useful business graphics on 16-bit machines.
A special feature of all SuperCalc products is the upward
compatibility of the various versions of the software. Previously designed spreadsheets will work, without modification, on the new software, and the user of an earlier version
will find that precisely the same commands and command
structures will work. Of course, the newer versions of the
software are more powerful, and so the user will certainly
find it rewarding to learn and use the various enhancements. A very extensive set of mathematical operations is
possible on the various entries in cells of the spreadsheet.
By considering columns of the spreadsheet as representing
successive time increments, it becomes possible to model
even time-varying systems using a spreadsheet. Thus, formulation of problems using decision analysis and dynamic
programming concepts are possible. Of course, this is true
for any spreadsheet program. A major advantage to Super-
Calc is the ease of learning how to use the software, and
the later advantage that its rather powerful mathematical
operations, together with excellent error handling, provide
for the serious user. The addition of the graphics facility in
SuperCalc3, which was not evaluated, should further enhance the usefulness of this important product. It is especially useful for integration with other software as a Super-

Data interchange facility allowing production of DIF (Data Interchange Format) files that are readable by many other programs.

Multiplan—Multiplan is also a second generation spreadsheet. It is produced by Microsoft who also markets several expert system packages for the software. These are tailored to specific applications, such as finance, accounting, and budgeting. Like SuperCalc, Multiplan is a very powerful spreadsheet and is available for the MSDOS operating system. The comprehensive manual is a bit overwhelming at times, especially for a first-time user. There are many advanced mathematical operations possible and, like SuperCalc, Multiplan is a superior product. The data files produced by Multiplan are accessible by a number of other programs such that integration with other software is relatively easily accomplished. While the software is probably more difficult for the novice to get used to than SuperCalc2, the availability of the expert system supplements and demonstration disks do ease the learning burden considerably and provide a very useful support tool as well. These packages are expert systems in the sense that they request the spreadsheet designer to answer a series of questions and then create customized worksheets for a specific application. Formulas and the like for the operations are inserted by the expert system software. Following creation of the specific spreadsheet, all the user need do is enter the appropriate information. For the experienced user, the product is extraordinarily high in overall effectiveness and overall quality. SuperCalc3 has the advantage of the direct graphics support, whereas Multiplan has the advantage of the well-thought-out expert system packages.

The aforementioned two software products are basically and fundamentally spreadsheets. They generally lack a very high level programming language ability, except that specifically restricted to the structured format of the spreadsheet. Fortunately, a large number of problems can be modeled in the form of a spreadsheet. For some applications though, this representation may not be appropriate or convenient. There are several products available for model base management that allow more general representations, and three of them will be discussed here.

PLAN80—Business Planning Systems' PLAN80 is another very useful MBMS program in the form of a very high level financial planning language. Generally the results of this language are displayed in the structured form of a spreadsheet. But with a spreadsheet, usually only one spreadsheet at a time is possible. Consolidation of spreadsheets is often difficult. With a very high level programming language type design, there may be several spreadsheets called for from one set of code. This is accomplished in a straightforward way using a programming language type approach. It is more difficult with a spreadsheet, and analysis is sometimes more cumbersome, although surely always possible. Unlike SuperCalc and Multiplan, the user of PLAN80 must employ a word processor capable of producing ASCII text to enter the specifications for the code that ultimately results in the reduction of one or more spreadsheets. These specifications take the form of a set of very general inputs such as TITLES, ROWS, COLUMNS, DATA, RULES, DISPLAY, PRINT, OPTIONS. Under each subheading is listed the specific entries, such as the titles and code names to use for the various rows of the resulting spreadsheets. The mathematical functions that can be entered under RULES are quite extensive for software primarily aimed at financial planning and analysis. All of this should make it somewhat easier for many users to specify problems than in the standard spreadsheet approach in which entries are made on a small command line located below the spreadsheet that is being designed. The ability to construct a spreadsheet in terms of modular subtasks should be a significant advantage for many users. The natural language syntax and lack of special command symbols also make learning how to use the system remarkably easy. The CPM version of the software evaluated was very easy to install and quite user friendly to operate. The report generator is an especially good one. Very simple bar and line graphs may be generated. The user's manual is very simple, brief, and easy to read. Some topics are omitted. For example, there is no discussion of the type of output produced and how to integrate the PLAN80 output to other programs. Fortunately, ASCII data is produced and stored so that this should generally not be a difficult task. Like SuperCalc and Multiplan, this is a quality product. Unlike these two however, PLAN80 is not produced and marketed by a major force in microcomputers. As a result, PLAN80 is surely not a household word. Consequently there is not the cottage industry support for the product that could result in "how to use" paperbacks and sample spreadsheets, many on floppy disks, for a myriad of possible applications, primarily finance and business. The impact of this will vary, of course, from user to user.

Financial Planner—Financial Planner is a very high level financial programming language software product available from Ashton Tate for CPM operating systems. The supplied code is compiled Microsoft BASIC. Like dBaseII, the very high level language in unlike any other language; this one is even quite unlike the language of dBaseII. It is quite powerful and compact; after the initial effort to learn a new language, rather significant models can be constructed with very modest effort. The type of input entry for model construction is not unlike that of PLAN80, although not as simple to operate and more flexible. The user's manual is large and terse, and not at all easy to follow the first time through. It appears relatively complete and, for the experienced user, quite a well-done document. Ashton Tate supplies a demonstration disk and useful sample programs that should simplify the learning process considerably. The software is nicely menu driven and has good help facilities. Due to the 64K byte RAM limitation of 8-bit machines, there are a number of subprograms that are called from the master menu. Consequently, the overall speed of operation suffers when compared to what would be possible with the same software operating in a 16-bit environment with a much larger RAM. There is a separate editor with help, list, and add commands that make it easy to use. The rules, or arithmetic functions are comprehensive in nature; they contain a number of functions useful for engineering and financial applications. There is an extensive report generator and an extremely useful "what if" processor that enables the user to make changes in the input data and rapidly see the results of so doing. As with the PLAN80 software, there is virtually no information in the user's manual concerning how one might use data and reports generated by this software in other programs or with other software. It would be very useful, for example, to be able easily to interface this product with dBaseII, another Ashton Tate product. This product should be extremely useful in supporting financial analysis and planning, especially with respect to the construction of simple economic models. It probably would not be easy to interface it with a data base management system.

IFPS Personal—IFPS Personal is a MSDOS version of the Execucomp Interactive Financial Planning System that has been available for some time on mainframe computers. In many respects, IFPS Personal is similar in intent to Financial Planner and to PLAN80. It is a more comprehensive undertaking in that the software contains, at the executive command level, five subsystems; modeling, data file, command file, report generation, and universal consolidation. The modeling subsystem is the heart of IFPS Personal. It is in this subsystem that the user is able to create and modify models, and to run "what if" type analyses. IFPS Personal contains an editor that is generally helpful. The very high level programming language has been well thought out and contains natural language mnemonics that assist in programming. It is not necessary to have and use a separate data file subsystem, as data can be contained in the model equations. However, to maintain data in a separate file adds considerable flexibility to a decision support system, as we have previously discussed. Thus use of the data file subsystem, which is not nearly as sophisticated as that of the relational data bases discussed earlier, is highly recommended. The command and universal consolidation subsystems enable the creation of sequences of commands callable from a single command and the production of consolidated reports of a hierarchical organization. The report generator is a very good one, and takes advantage of the graphics capabilities of PC compatible machines. The software is capable of interactive operation and is very nicely menu driven. It requires a large RAM, 512K bytes of it, to operate. The software is compatible with the mainframe version of IFPS although the Monte Carlo simulation features of the mainframe version are not presently available. It is considerably easier to operate than the mainframe version however, due to the more interactive nature and extensive menu-driven commands. The graphics support is especially well done in the MSDOS version of the software. The user has the option of letting the software choose appropriate scales, or of doing it personally. The graphics displays are produced very rapidly, and are very nicely scaled, such that there seems little need for the user to attempt this, except for rather special purposes.

The aforementioned five software products are general in nature in that there is no absolutely fixed structures or computation process assumed for the model base management subsystem. The spreadsheet form is, after all, extraordinarily ubiquitous. There are MBMS packages available that assume very specific forms. We discuss four of these here.

Decision-Analyst—Like PLAN80, Decision-Analyst is available from Executive Software, Inc. It is described as an executive tool for analyzing complex decisions involving many alternatives. And so it is. Fundamentally, it is based on multiattribute utility theory for decision making where outcomes follow from decisions with certainty. Use of the software assumes that a multilevel hierarchical tree of attributes of the outcomes of a decision has been structured. Through appropriate assignment of attribute weights to reflect probabilities, it is possible to use the support system for decisions under risk. Since the documentation does not mention this, and since the procedure would be tricky to implement for one not familiar with decision analysis, we will not consider this aspect of the software further. Rather than describe the attributes (or criteria as they are called in the user's manual) in the form of a tree, the user is asked appropriate questions that enable a tabular representation of the criteria structured into attribute levels. The user is first asked to identify weights across levels in the hierarchy, and then for alternative scores on lowest level attributes. There is no concern expressed in the software manual for the problem that this procedure poses with respect to anchoring of the attribute weights, or for concerns relative to attribute independence. The brief user's manual is very easy to read, and the CPM software product is easily installed on any of a number of microcomputers. There is no provision for sensitivity analysis in any quantitative sense although the user is asked to assess the possible adverse consequences of each alternative in a qualitative "Murphy's Law" type fashion. Generally the software is very easy to use and considerable care has been placed into a design that encourages user documentation of the rationale behind decisions.

Harvard Project Manager—Harvard Project Manager is a relatively powerful and generally easy to use project planning and management software package from Harvard Software, Inc. The user's guide is very brief and easy to read. It contains a useful tutorial and a reference guide. Those familiar with PERT (Program Evaualtion and Review Technique) and CPM (Critical Path Method) will feel very much at home with this product. Project tasks and milestones are the "nodes" of the roadmap that will ultimately be constructed. Critical paths are determined and these form the basic ingredient that is used to support the project manager in evaluating various alternative courses of action. The software contains a very useful report generator that enables display of roadmaps, schedules, bar charts, and detail and status reports of information concerning a project. The software manual contains no discussion of the management science algorithms used, and there are alternate approaches to determination of project schedules. Doubtlessly, many users would not be concerned at all with this knowledge; but there are others who would be. If nothing else, it would more easily enable evaluation of this product in light of the other available packages for project scheduling and management. This highly specialized piece of software rates very high on the quality scale, especially in terms of ease of use and understanding of the results of using the product.

TK!Solver—TK!Solver is a very useful and innovative "equation processor" or "equation solver" from Software Arts, Inc. The usual process of problem solving in science and engineering generally involves steps such as problem recognition, model formulation, algorithm design, software program construction, and results. It is the intent of the designers of TK!Solver that the user not have to go through the algorithm design and software writing phases of problem solution. The present version of TK!Solver accepts mathematical models that have been formulated in terms of algebraic (i.e. nondynamic) equations, and data for the variables in these models. There are eight sheets and three subsheets that, together, constitute the heart of TK!Solver. The rule sheet is used for entering and displaying equations or rulers. The variable sheet is used for displaying variable names, for assigning input values, and for displaying results. Other sheets are used for various informational and support purposes. The documentation is very extensive, contrasting dramatically with that provided with Harvard Project Manager. Of course, this is a much more general problem-solving package and can be used for a great many more purposes. The basic idea behind TK!Solver is that it is possible conceptually to solve for the one unknown quantity in $a + b = c + d$ if *any* three of the four quantities are known. In the usual programming approach, the identity of the unknown quantity must be known prior to writing the software. This is not the case in TK!Solver. Thus the name Tool Kit Solver is very appropriate. A direct solver approach is used whenever an explicit solution for the unknown variable(s) is possible, and an interative solver is used when it is not. At least two support software packages are available that have been predesigned for typical elementary problems occurring in classical engineering areas. There are many potential uses for this software product. These involve almost all application areas, such as finance, science, and engineering, in which solution of a system of algebraic equations is a requirement. While this is a very useful software product in its own right at this time, it is possibly even more valuable as a prototype concept for the much more powerful products that could result from extrapolations of these concepts.

COPE—COPE is a very useful model base management system that assists individuals and groups in structuring knowledge in the form of "cognitive maps" relative to some issue. The software, available from Bath Software Research in England, assists in representing and structuring knowledge. It contains a useful natural language query system, in the form of various CHAT commands, that enables a user to express elements of importance to a particular issue and to enter three-level logic contextual relations among these elements. This can include enhancing, inhibiting, or making no impact among elements in a structure. The software does not make transitive, or negatively transitive, inferences among elements. It depends upon user input to determine relations among elements in a structure. At times this can become tedious. However the redundancy can serve as a check upon user input, and may encourage thought about the issue that would not occur if the software took full advantage of transitivity. A major use of COPE could be to assist decision makers to utilize specialized expertise relevant to some issue. It could also be used as a learning tool to assist in transferring expertise to novices. The two primary support features of COPE are assistance in identification of critical concepts relative to some issue, and concept grouping. A sampling of the principal commands indicates the potential versatility of the product. The ADD command enables one to add one model to another. The CHAT command enables one to enter the interactive natural dialog model-building sector of the software. There is an E command that causes the software to explain various concepts to the user (in terms, of course, of the information that has been entered into the computer). The LR command causes the computer to list all relationships that have been entered concerning the issue under consideration. The MAP command causes the computer to produce a cognitive map, or structural model, of the knowledge that has been entered. The C command causes the computer to list consequences of concepts, and the L command creates a listing of all concepts. The X command explores concepts in terms of additional implications, the M command enables merger of concepts believed to be similar, the PATH command results in a path analysis, and the CONFLICT command results in an analysis of possible conflicts in reasoning that have been entered into the model. The result of several hours of working with the software indicate that it could be of much potential use in the hands of a trained analyst. The CPM version of the software evaluated is, unfortunately, rather slow in executing. There are very useful help facilities associated with the software, and the user's manual is genuinely appropriate. The latter would be an even more useful document if there were some limited descriptions of the algorithmic theory of cognitive maps, as many users do not like to rely on software and computer output when they do not understand the algorithmic constructs behind the operation of the software.

For many applications, there will exist the need for an integrated data base management system and model base management system, and for the dialog generation and management system necessary for effective communication between the two and the human user. There have been several recent software developments that have resulted in at least limited integration among the DBMS and MBMS portions of a decision support system.

Software for Integrated DBMS and MBMS Support

Lotus 1-2-3—Lotus 1-2-3 is certainly the most heavily advertised of the integrated DBMS and MBMS products. While it is a useful product for many applications, it does not contain the very high level programming language features of dBaseII, Financial Planner, or IFPS. Nor does it contain the high quality graphics output capabilities of SuperCalc3 or IFPS. As a data base management system, it is certainly not as powerful as the R:Base 4000 or dBaseII relational data bases. But Lotus 1-2-3 does combine data base management (or really electronic file drawer capabilities since the DBMS facilities of the product are limited) with excellent spreadsheet capabilities, and good graphics support. It is very rapid in command execution and generally quite user friendly. It has commanded excellent cottage industry support in the form of books illustrating how to use the product, software containing a number of potentially useful application models, and training courses.

KnowledgeMan—KnowledgeMan is another integrated software product. Like Lotus 1-2-3, it operates on 16-bit machines only. Unlike Lotus 1-2-3, it is available for generic MSDOS machines, as well as for IBM PC compatible computers. A major operational difference is that Knowledge-Man contains a relatively sophisticated relational data base management system, as well as a most useful spreadsheet for model base management. The graphics support feature is excellent and allows production of high quality business graphics using information contained in either the data base management system or the spreadsheet. Thus Knowledge-Man provides the true DBMS suport that Lotus 1-2-3 does not have. It also contains much more of a very high level programming language, but not nearly as extensive a language as is available in IFPS or Financial Planner. Despite this, the product is a very flexible one. The price that must be paid for this sophisticated and high quality support system is a rather extensive learning time that is made all the more difficult by a very terse manual. The producer of Know-ledgeMan, Micro Data Base Systems, has extensive experience in DBMS software development for mainframe and minicomputers. Doubtlessly the developers of the software were influenced strongly by their experiences on these larger machines in the development of the present product.

Software developments in this area continue at a very rapid rate. Any attempt to discuss available products will surely be somewhat outdated when the discussion is published. For example, Symphony from Lotus Development Corporation and Framework from Ashton Tate are contemporary products that augment spreadsheet, file management, and graphics capabilities with word processing and communications. There will be many others. It can only remain an interesting conjecture whether the ultimate microcomputer decision support systems will consist of integrated products such as these, or design procedures that will enable the rapid integration of disparate software products into a package that has all the appearances of functionality and usefulness from the perspective of the user. This latter approach would allow the incorporation of distinctly different software products, such as COPE, TK!Solver, or Harvard Product Manager, which may be extraordinarily relevent to a specific intended application, but not sufficient in overall applicability to be included in an integrated software product intended for general decision support system use. This latter approach gives an expanded meaning to the decision support system generator concept in that it encompasses the generation of software support that will allow the integration of complete specialized software packages into a functioning system. Surely both approaches are viable. All of this activity based upon the considerable need for decision support productivity packages indicates that the future looks very bright indeed for developments in microcomputer decision support systems.

REFERENCES

Alter, S. L. 1982. *Decision Support Systems: Current Practice and Continuing Challenges*. Reading, Mass.: Addison-Wesley.

Anthony, R. N. 1965. *Planning and Control Systems: A Framework for Analysis*. Cambridge: Harvard University Press.

Bennett, J. L. ed. 1983. *Building Decision Support Systems*. Reading, Mass.: Addison-Wesley.

Bonczek, R. H., C. W. Holsapple, and A. B. Whinston. 1981. *Foundations of Decision Support Systems*. New York: Academic Press.

Chanking, V., and Y. Y. Haimes. 1984. *Multiobjective Decision Making: Theory and Methodology*. New York: North-Holland.

Cohon, J. L. 1978. *Multiobjective Programming and Planning*. New York: Academic Press.

Date, C. J. 1977. *An Introduction to Data Base Systems*. Reading, Mass.: Addison-Wesley.

—— 1983. *Database: A Primer*. Reading, Mass.: Addison-Wesley.

Fishburn, P. C. 1964. *Decision and Value Theory*. New York: Wiley.

—— 1965. Analysis of Decisions with Incomplete Knowledge of Probabilities. *Operations Research* 13(2):217–37(March–April).

—— 1970. *Utility Theory for Decision Making*. New York: Wiley.

Hakathorn, R., and P. Keen. 1981. Organizational Strategies for Personal Computing in Decision Support Systems. *MIS Quarterly* 5(3). pp. 178–189.

Hammond, K. R., G. H. McClelland and J. Mumpower. 1980. *Human Judgment and Decision Making: Theories, Methods, and Procedures*.New York: Hemisphere/Praeger.

Keen, P. G. W., and M. S. Scott Morton. 1978. *Decision Support Systems: An Organizational Perspective*. Reading, Mass.: Addison-Wesley.

Keeney, R. L. 1982. Decision Analysis: An Overview. *Operations Research*. 30(5):803–38 (SeptOct).

Keeney, R. L., and H. Raiffa. 1976. *Decisions with Multiple Objectives: Preferences and Value Tradeoffs*. New York: Wiley.

Martin, J. 1983. *Managing the Data Base Environment*. Englewood Cliffs, N.J.: Prentice-Hall.

Mintzberg, H. 1973. *The Nature of Managerial Work*. New York: Harper and Row.

Rescher, N., and R. Manor. 1970. On Inference from Inconsistent Premises. *Theory and Decision*. 1:179–217.

Sage, A. P. 1977. *Methodology for Large Scale Systems*. New York: McGraw-Hill.

—— 1981. Behavioral and Organizational Considerations in the Design of Information Systems and Processes for Planning and Decision Support. *IEEE Transactions on Systems, Man, and Cybernetics* 11(9):640–78 (September).

Sage, A. P., and C. C. White. 1984. ARIADNE: A Knowledge Based Interactive System for Decision Support. *IEEE Transactions on Systems, Man, and Cybernetics* 14(1) pp. 279–296 (Jan/Feb).

Sarin, R. K. 1977. Screening of Multiattribute Alternatives. *OMEGA* 5(4):481–89.

Simon, H. A. 1960. *The New Science of Mangement Decisions*. New York: Harper and Row.

Sol, H. G. 1983 *Processes and Tools for Decision Support*. Amsterdam: Elsevier North-Holland.

Sprague, R. H., Jr., and E. D. Carlson. 1982. *Building Effective Decision Support Systems*. Englewood Cliffs, N.J.: Prentice-Hall.

Zeleny, M. 1982. *Multiple Criteria Decision Making*. New York: McGraw-Hill.

Zmud, R. W. 1983. *Information Systems in Organizations.* Glenview, Ill.: Scott, Foresman, and Co.

2

The Use of Computers in Decision Making

Janice Fain

STEPS IN DECISION MAKING

Decision making is one of the oldest and most frequently executed human activities. Every person on earth makes literally hundreds of decisions each day deciding what to wear, what to eat and where to go. The majority of these decisions are so simple and made so rapidly that one is hardly aware that one has been engaged in decision making. However, when it is suggested that computers might aid in this activity, a rather more complex operation is envisioned.

In considering the question of decision making, the first fact to be noted is that there are wide variations in the areas in which decisions are required, in the types of people involved in the process (both as producers and users), and in the constraints (physical, legal, economic, political, etc.) imposed on the decisions. In spite of these great differences, the abstract activity, decision making, is usually considered to consist of the following steps.

Detection and Formulation of the Problem

First, there must be a recognition that decisions are going to be required in a given area.

This requirement may arise in one of several ways. The most dramatic is the sudden crisis in which demands are unexpectedly placed on a system without previous warning or time for preparation. A less dramatic problem recognition may come about more slowly as a result of studying long-term trend projections. The need for a decision in the future is recognized, but there is no accompanying sense of urgency.

However, problem recognition probably comes most commonly from the routine monitoring of a given system. Figure 2.1 shows an abstract monitoring system that could represent the steps in keeping track, say, of household budgets, steam plant operations, or approaching enemy missiles.

Normal operations generally loop around the box "Check Indicator" and the "Yes" exit from "Is Indicator Green?" A preliminary indication of potential trouble comes when the indicator turns "Yellow." Depending on the nature of the system and the potential consequences of a problem, the indicator may be designed to show continuous system degradation or it may have only two states: "OK" and "Not OK".

The point at which the system is declared to be in trouble, or "Not OK", is generally determined by physical, economic, political, or other factors exogenous to the system itself, although, in rare cases, choosing it could be considered a "decision" requiring the steps discussed here. To avoid getting mired in an endless "decision loop," a distinction will be drawn in this discussion between major decisions requiring the steps listed here and simple choices made in the course of decision making. (A common tactic of groups attempting to delay the process of decision making is to turn every simple procedural choice into a major decision requiring long discussion. While, as will be pointed out later, there will be some backtracking and repetition of steps, it is

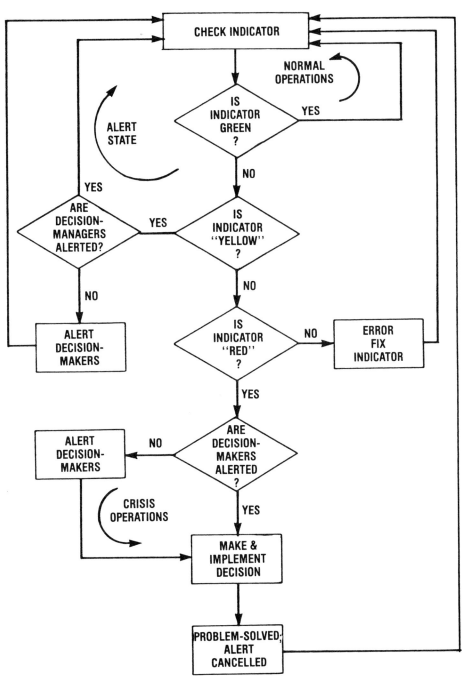

Figure 2.1   General Situation—Monitoring System

assumed here that the decision makers remain firmly focused on the decision at hand.)

Once its existence is recognized, the problem must be carefully defined, those responsible for fixing it identified, and any constraints on its solution noted.

Thus, the detection and formulation of a problem require answers to the following questions:

Is there a problem?

What part of the "real" world is invovled?

Who is responsible for solving it?

What are the constraints on the solution?

What are the goals of the decision makers?

Creation of Feasible Solutions

Having determined that there is a problem and having defined it and established goals, the decision maker must now create as many feasible solutions to it as possible. (Some problems may be so complex or the decision time so short that the decision makers are satisfied to create even a single solution. Once it is found, no further analysis is thought necessary. Such problems are not considered in this discussion.)

The concept of *feasible* is interpreted broadly at this initial stage so that new and innovative solutions are not ruled out of further consideration. In very complex systems it may not be readily apparent which solutions would be impossible to implement. In fact, solutions thought to be impossible by one criterion (say, economic or politcal conditions), may turn out to be so clearly superior from other aspects that the decision makers are impelled to find ways of removing the obstacles.

The number of solutions that can be considered is clearly a function of the time allotted to the decision-making process and of the method of evaluating the options. This leads to the next critical step.

Development of a Model

Here, the *model* is any device that assists in providing estimates of the likely outcome of each problem solution. It may, thus, be as simple as the rapid judgment of an expert or as complex as a long set of differential equations or a large computer program. Whatever form this evaluative tool takes, its usefulness is strongly related to the quantity of information (data, "hard facts," human experience, and judgment) incorporated into it.

Production of Outcomes

Now, the model is called on to estimate expected outcomes for the solutions under consideration. At this point it should be clear that real decision making will not proceed neatly through these steps in order, but that there will be a great deal of backtracking and repetition. For example, the production of outcomes and the creation of solutions are clearly related and both strongly dependent on the model. Operation of the model and a study of the outcomes of the first solutions will probably be the most fruitful source of new solutions. In some cases, this relation between creation and evaluation may be so close that it will almost appear that the model is creating solutions.

Selection of a Value System

The implementation of a problem solution will lead to a new state of the system. The decision makers must identify attributes which describe the world state, and, on the basis of the goals identified in the problem formulation stage, choose one or more attribute values to serve as criteria of desirability. The alternative outcomes belonging to the set of solutions under consideration can be evaluated on the basis of these criteria and ranked according to desirability.

Making the Decision

If all relevant factors have been considered in producing the outcomes, then making the decision can be as simple as choosing the top-ranked solution. Unfortunately, there are generally factors impossible to incorporate into the model so that the ranked solution set merely provides a starting point for the discussions and negotiations that are commonly considered to constitute decision making.

The purpose of this section is to consider how and where in these steps computers may prove useful to the decision makers. That is, the operational system to be discussed consists of computers plus their human users.

The extraordinary complexity of the computer-plus-human combination can, fortunately, be reduced for this discussion by abstracting from "real" computers and "real" humans those characteristics and activities actually involved in the single operation: decision making. Computer "activities" will be reduced to four classes of operations. Humans will be reduced to two "pure" abstract types distinguished by their knowledge of computers and of the subject area within which a decision is required.

THE DECISION-MAKING ELEMENTS: COMPUTERS AND HUMANS

Computer Operations for Decision Making

Many volumes have been written on what computers do and how they do it. For the purpose of this discussion, it will be asserted that computer operations of interest here belong to the four general classes that follow.

Information Retrieval—the selection, according to criteria set by the user, of specific items out of the larger information sets available.

The retrieved information may be re-stored within the computer system for later use, sent to a printer to produce hard copy for the user, or displayed on a screen as tables, graphs, bar charts, etc.

Calculation—the manipulation of information according to prestored rules to produce information not in the stored set.

This definition is probably too broad; *calculation* generally refers to the execution of one or more arithmetic operations on numeral data. The sequence of operations in a given set, or *program*, may be predetermined and carried out in the same order each time the program is executed, or there may be points within the program at which the next operation to be performed depends on values computed previously or on the user's choice made on the basis of such computed values or other exogenous factors.

Translation—the production of a different, but related, concept out of a user's concept statement.

A common example is the production of material in language *B* from text originally written in language *A*. This process, like calculation, consists of the manipulation of information according to a set of rules, which are either preset or chosen by the user during the program execution.

Learning—the modification of stored computer instructions during program execution.

Work is now underway in that field called *Artificial Intelligence* (or AI) to produce programs that teach the computer to carry out specific tasks. These AI programs have the goal of "teaching" the computer by interaction with humans, so that the "rules" by which new concepts are produced are modified by each program execution. It is intended that intensive interaction between the computer and its human user should gradually transfer some of the knowledge, wisdom, and experience of the human to the computer.

Of course, knowledge transfers between humans via computers is not new. Computer-aided instruction programs have for many years served all levels from prekindergarten toddlers through students in graduate and professional schools. However, in terms of what the computer is being asked to do, the differences between these instruction packages and the new AI programs are profound. The teaching programs depended primarily on the retrieval of stored information. Although the sequence in which the information was presented to the user was made to depend on his demonstrated mastery of the subject matter, the programs were essentially sophisticated information retrieval packages plus their data bases. The role of humans in executing these programs could be described as telling the computer *what* to do. That is, specifying the order in which its programmed actions should be carried out.

The new AI programs will be rather different. In executing the program, the user will tell the computer *how* to carry out a task. Not only can the stored data be changed, but also the stored computer instructions. As the computer interacts with its human user, its ability to perform its assigned tasks should improve.

An interesting speculation may be made at this point. The process of "teaching" the computer, as described above, envisions a possibly slow, but steady, improvement in the computer's progress until it approaches, but never exceeds, its human teacher. But, suppose that the biological world processes of genetic variation and natural selection come into play. These programs will, of necessity, be complex and it is very likely that the human "user/teacher" will make mistakes. Probably most of these "accidents" will produce nonsense, but it is possible that, in rare cases they may produce programs that go beyond their human creators. Should this happen, and the programs be permitted to survive, then the computer could "evolve" into an agency superior to its human creator in carrying out its assigned tasks. (A fifth class of operations, the reformatting of information, can be classed as *word-* or *text-processing*. While obviously helpful in assisting in communication, these operations are not themselves essential to decision making.)

Human Types Involved in Decision Making

As suggested above, the human participants will be defined on the basis of their relationship to the computer and to the subject matter of the required decision. There are basically two "pure" types:

The computer professional is thoroughly familiar with those aspects of computer operations required in the decision-making process, although he/she may not know much about the substantive subject areas involved. For example, he/she may know that, in a given data-file, the third column contains 5-digit integers, but he/she probably would not know whether the specific value "88926" is low, average, high, or clearly an error.

In practice, it may be rare that a single individual possesses sufficient knowledge alone, and the term *computer professional* may, in fact, refer to a computer center and its supporting staff. For this discussion, it is assumed that there are no purely technical computer problems; whatever computers can do will be available to the computer professional.

The analyst may never have used a computer, but he/she is knowledgeable in the substantive areas within which decisions are required. He/she may not know, for example, where the value "88926" is stored but he/she would know instantly that it must be an error, since values of that variable are never above "60000." For this discussion, it does not matter whether the analyst is one of the decision makers or a member of the decision makers' support staff.

Clearly, the computer professional and the analyst are hypothetical "pure" types, and it is possible for specific individuals to possess characteristics of both. When such an individual is referred to as a *computer professional*, he/she is to be considered as carrying out those activities assigned above to the computer professional. When he/she is referred to as an *analyst*, it is understood that he/she is engaged in an analyst's activities.

At today's stage of computer usage, it is most likely that, in any real organization, computer professionals and analysts will be found in separate groups. Indeed, one of the most troublesome problems in real decision making is likely to be the difficulty of communication between the two. Here, it is assumed that this problem is not present and that each is able to communicate clearly his/her needs and the results of his/her work to the other.

WHERE ARE COMPUTERS USEFUL?

With these four classes of computer operations and two human types in mind, consider again the steps in decision making.

Problem Detection and Formulation

Computers can play a major role in this step. Figure 2.1 suggests that some problems can be detected by situation-monitoring systems and that the procedure can be expressed as a series of predefined steps. When the situation indicators are measurable quantities and rules for the movement of the system into the "yellow" and "red" regions can be made explicit, then the monitoring may be automated. Examples are life-support systems in hospitals and devices in cars that warn their drivers of open doors, unfastened seat belts, malfunctioning generators, etc.

In systems with monitoring/warning devices, the possible problems are predefined and associated with their indicators. Knowledge of the status of the set of indicators provides knowledge of the state of the system. When the system operations are well understood, then the computer can take over the monitoring, problem detection, and in some cases, the decision making. The human stays around to monitor the computer and to intervene should unplanned-for events occur.

While these cases in which monitoring and problem solving can be automated are important in their own areas, they are not what generally comes to mind in discussions of decision making. The series of steps proposed above as constituting decision making is usually reserved for those situations in which the systems are less well known and the problems less easy to define.

There are two major types of situations in which problems requiring decisions arise:

- Short-term problems (or crises), and
- Long-term problems.

In the short-term, or crisis, situation, there is no doubt about the need for a decision. The initial task of the analyst is to determine the nature of the crisis, who is involved, and what, if any, are the constraints imposed on the decision makers.

The analyst's greatest need at this stage is for information. The computer will have two principal uses:

- Retrieving stored information, and

- Processing current information.

Depending on how much work has gone into anticipating the possibility of a crisis and in creating relevant data bases, the computer may provide instant answers to the question: "Has anything like this happened before?" Only straightforward data retrieval procedures need be involved here.

The processing of current information can take several forms:

- Comparison of new information with stored data to test its accuracy, or even, plausibility, and

- Provision of guidance on what information to collect.

Experienced decision makers may carry out this processing in their heads and operate, or appear to be operating, on intuition alone. That field of AI concerned with developing *expert systems* is attempting to endow computers with the ability to carry out some of these operations when experienced decision makers are not available. Programs that ask questions and make suggestions on the basis of the answers are being developed to assist in guiding inexperienced decision makers through crisis periods.

Whether computer handling at this stage is done by the analyst or by the computer professional depends entirely on how user friendly the available software has become. Clearly, it will be more efficient if the analyst works directly with the computer rather than through another person. However, the middle of a crisis is not a suitable time to take a course on computer operations, so if the analyst is not already familiar with the necessary programs, then he/she must employ the services of the computer professional.

For those problems identified through long-range forecasting, there may be some differences of opinion as to whether they really exist. For generally recognized problem areas—defense, the economy, social welfare, education, etc.—there is likely to be disagreement over the nature of the particular problems. Computers are useful in retrieving and analyzing data to provide support, but identifying potential problems and arguing the need for a decision is a task for humans.

As in the crisis situation, who handles the computer work depends on the software. There are two current trends—one toward developing software that is easier to use and one toward greater computer literacy for the analyst—that suggest that the analyst will soon take over the computer handling. The computer professional will be freed from spending time in a purely supporting role and may devote his/her energies to new program design. (In other words, low-level programmers and those providing simple computer-supporting services are going to find their jobs disappearing while creative program designers will have more work than they can handle.)

In addition to finding potential problems, data retrieval may be essential in identifying groups affected by proposed decisions. Retrieval from the census tapes, for example, may inform welfare planners of the percent of families in selected communities with four or more children and annual family income of less than $10,000.

It might be pointed out that computers may make this stage of decision making more, rather than less, difficult. Most decision making, at least in the public sector, involves the allocation of scarce resources. One of the most difficult choices will be the selection of those groups to be affected by the decision. When strong, articulate groups are involved, the decision making may be easier if it is not immediately clear just who will be affected. With computers, accessible data files, and powerful retrieval programs, the decision making group cannot plead ignorance, but must face the implications of their choices. Thus, although the choice at this stage may be more painful, the use of computer-provided information may prevent even more painful surprises later.

Creation of Solutions

This step requires the creativity and imagination of the human mind; at the current state of computer technology, it cannot be handled by computers alone. Some of the work in Artificial Intelligence is directed toward the goal of producing software to emulate the human mind in its more creative thought modes, but there is nothing as yet that will substitute for the innovative analyst.

Indeed, such efforts to reproduce human creativity face grave difficulties. First, the software will always be developed on the basis of old information. Even if it were possible for the programmer to have an understanding of all factors relevant to a given situation, the program development time is such that the information is already old by the time his program is operational.

I am speaking here of programs to emulate human creativity, an area in which the subtlest of signals—a glimpse, an odor, a remembered fragment—can trigger in the human a totally new line of thought in which he sees old elements in new patterns. This sudden response to stimuli is the essence of human creativity. Computers cannot do this. Of course, bits and pieces of concepts can be fed into a computer along with a random number generator which allows the computer to reconnect ideas in new and unexpected ways. What comes out will generally be nonsense for a specific situation. At its best, such a procedure could produce inserts for fortune cookies, phrases that are sufficiently abstract to allow some kind of interpretation by a human.

In answer to the problem of the timeliness of software, it could be pointed out that computer software itself is generally developed in abstract terms, and relationships to the "real" world are provided by data entered into the program by the user at the time the program is executed. To make use of the input data to provide to the computer a late, up-to-the-minute picture of the world requires that the "real" world be described by a small number of parameters, or that the user face the tedious task of providing large quantities of program input.

There has, of course, always been a tradeoff between the convenience of using prestored input files and having the latest facts entered by the user at execution time, but here the difficulties are greatly magnified. In either case, the user cannot, at execution time, enter the odd fact that has not been given a place in the software structure, but would suggest to an analyst a new set of decision alternatives.

A second, possibly more serious, reason for not turning this task over to a computer is that the software is developed by a single individual, or by a group of individuals having a single world view. (If they don't have the same world view, then integrating their work into a coherent whole would be difficult, if not impossible.)

The highly creative, oddball mind is left out, yet it may be that the most successful, innovative ideas will come from these sources that have not been involved in the software development. Attempting to locate such minds during program development so that their creativity can be incorporated into the software merely guarantees that the programs never will be finished.

A compromise might be reached in which the computer produces the mundane, obvious, easily-arrived-at solutions, which then serve as a starting point for the human thought processes. Such a compromise would guarantee that, at least, the obvious is not overlooked, an event that can occur even with, or some might say, especially with, highly creative minds.

Computer-generated solutions may then be, I think, properly used as "pump primers," or as ways of getting the decision makers started on their discussions. Even so, I think we are many years from having such programs available for more than one or two specific problem areas, and they will probably never be available for the majority of decisions that have to be made.

Development of a Model

Choosing a method of evaluating the solutions requires human direction. To some degree the computer can assist, but not take over, this task. All models are developed out of information. There are two basic forms in which information can exist. In one, the computer can be of a great deal of assistance; in the other, its help can be only marginal.

Judgment-based Models. When the information underlying a model consists of the knowledge, experience, and wisdom of humans who understand the operations of the systems involved, the computer can play no major role in the development process. However, it has been given small peripheral tasks in some cases. The following are examples:

- The Design and Develement Language (DDL) has been developed to record the progress of work on models (or any large computer-based project). It is basically a specialized word processor and data retrieval program that assists in communication among members of the development/programming team.

- Graphics programs have been used to aid in drawing flow diagrams.

- Programs have been developed to "analyze" other programs, listing variables, cross-indexing subroutine "calls," etc. These programs provide somewhat more information than that provided by compilers.

Thus, for very large and complex software developments, the computer can provide convenient ways of recording and communicating progress, but the model design itself is carried out primarily by the analyst. However, if the model is to have a companion computer program, it is well to have the computer professional involved in the design process. Some ways of structuring the world will be much harder to translate into computer instructions than others, and the computer professional may point out to the model development group the consequences, in computer terms, of their design decisions. Naturally such considerations should not dictate the design. If a particularly troublesome element, event, or interaction is, in the opinion of the analyst, essential to the valid evaluation of the solutions, then the computer professional must find a way to deal with it.

Once the model design is completed, it is given to the computer professional to turn into a computer program. At this point, the analyst may take on the role of consultant to supervise the myriad little choices required by a computer, but not foreseen in the model design.

Data-based Models. When the model development is to be based, not on the knowledge held by humans, but on stores of collected data, then the computer can be of very great assistance. In this case, the part of the world about which a decision is required is not understood in terms of "actors" and "operations," but is described by sets of numerical observations—economic data, demographic data, voting data, marketing data, etc.—and the relevant model must be "coaxed" out of them.

The model will consist of an equation (or sets of equations) relating the option outcomes to the relevant factors included in the decision. The role of the analyst is to select the variables to be employed, the form of the equation, and the methods of data analysis to be used.

In principle, the computation of the model parameters could be carried out by hand, but for complex equations and large data sets, a computer is a practical necessity. The computer and analyst roles may be seen in the following simple example. Consider the model:

number of widgets produced per month =
    .694 x number of machines + .589 x number of operators
    + .894 x investment dollars - .209 x number of gadgets produced

The analyst has selected the output variable, number of widgets produced per month, and the input variables, machines, operators, dollars, and gadgets, and has specified linear relationships. Computer analysis of the data has produced the specific parameters, .694, .589, .894, and -.209.

It is clear that the computer operation, *calculation*, is involved. Data retrieval may be employed in those cases where separate equations are required for different states of the world. For example, if widget production is more strongly related to gadget production during the spring and summer when Christmas inventories are being readied, then data retrieval programs may select March—August and September—February data for separate computation of the parameters in the equation.

The computer operation, *translation*, is a major component of the new general purpose retrieval and analysis programs that allow the program user to address requests to the computer in terms closer to "natural language," or the language used to address human colleagues. One should be able to enter a question like: "What is the linear relationship between the dependent variable, U, and the independent variables X, Y and Z?" The retrieval/analysis program should be able to translate this question into a search for variables, U, X, Y, and Z in its data base and to call out a linear regression program to operate on the retrieved values.

At this point it is interesting to speculate on the possibility of applying the fourth computer operation, *learning*, to the problem of model development. Compared with the usual model development, this one is not overly complex. It is assumed that the "real" world is described adequately by data stored in the computer. *Model development* consists of the following steps:

1. A selection of those factors under the control of the decision makers (i.e., the "independent" variables),
2. A selection of those factors that change, as the independent variables change (i.e., the "dependent" variables),
3. A choice of the form of the relationship, and finally
4. Computation of the parameters linking the dependent variables to the independent ones.

With a high-speed computer, all combinations of variables and a wide range of functions linking them might be tried. In principle, this should eventually produce a usable model for evaluating the decision alternatives. If, however, there are many variables and a large data base, then such a procedure may be practically impossible, and another approach is needed. We may try to reach the computer to develop a model.

For the first time the process described above is carried out, human ingenuity and intuition will be needed. However, once a model has been developed, the computer should begin to "learn" how to proceed on future developments.

The goal of such computer "learning" is to be able to collect data and have the computer organize it into a usable structure. There are two feasible approaches:

- A purely technical approach based on numerical manipulation without regard to the substantive area involved or to any meaning attached to the numbers, or
- An analysis based on what the computer has been "taught" about the significance of the numbers and how they are related to the "real" world structure.

The differences in these two approaches is analogous to the differences between the stock market technical analyst's study of the fluctuations of stock prices and other market indicators, and the fundamentalist's study of company markets, balance sheets, and management personnel.

The first approach relies on mathematical principles and is likely to be more generally applicable. The second requires specialized knowledge of the systems involved and can be more accurate for those areas covered. The mathematically inclined computer professional could undertake the technical approach. The analyst, with his substantive knowledge of the systems involved, is needed for the second. A combination approach carried out by a team including both computer professionals and analysts could probably outperform either single approach.

Production of Outcomes

Either the computer professional or the analyst may be responsible for evaluating the alternatives. The choice will depend on the complexity of the computer program, the quantity of input required, the source of that input, and the working relationship between the two.

Ideally, the computer program will be very easy to use, the alternatives to be examined will be described by a small number of parameters that may be specified at execution time and the analyst will have easy access to the computer. Under these conditions, the analyst may examine a wide range of alternatives, including those formally derived at the second step as well as those that occur during program execution. Under these conditions, the interaction between analyst and computer will be so productive that it will almost seem that the computer is creating, as well as analyzing, the options.

On the other hand, if the program is difficult to use or if the analyst does not have access to the computer, then the list of alternatives may be presented to the computer professional with a formal request for the required number of runs.

This latter procedure will work, but the creative interaction between analyst and computer is not possible unless the program is under the analyst's control. Making this control possible is one of the goals of the work on "natural language" processing.

Selection of a Value System

The next task in decision making involves choosing values related to human goals and objectives. Since it requires sensitivity to human desires and needs, this task is left entirely in the hands of the analyst; no role for the computer in actually making these choices is ever foreseen.

However, if the analysis of alternatives is easy and fast, then the analyst may employ the computer to investigate the consequences of any particular choice of values. Logically, the choice of values should be entirely independent of the analysis of alternatives in terms of those values. However, in the real world, the value system will usually play a major role in "selling" the decision. Thus, it is important that the values selected satisfy the criterion of producing an alternative-ranking system on which the decision makers can eventually hope to agree. The computer can aid immensely in illuminating the relationship between the value system and the ranking of alternatives.

Making the Decision

Responsibility for choosing the alternative will always lie ultimately with the human decision maker. Even if it is agreed ahead of time that the alternative ranked first by the computer will be chosen, this is itself a human decision.

There are, however, circumstances in which the computer may perform a critical function in assisting the desicion makers. For example:

- The alternatives are judged by not one but several values and each value leads to a different ranking of the alternatives.

- Disagreement among several decision makers over the interpretation of the analysis of alternatives leads to different rankings.

A single computer may produce a single optimal ranking that comes closest to satisfying all values, or all decision makers. This computer-produced ranking may then serve as the basis for discussions that will lead to a final decision. For difficult and unpopular decisions, it might be expedient for the decision makers to disclaim responsibility by pointing to the computer as the ultimate decision maker, but this excuse is not likely to be credible.

The Distribution of Tasks Between Humans and Computers

The various intellectual tasks involved in the complex series of operations called *decision making* have been outlined. Each task is seen to be a combination of prespecified activities and ad hoc actions improvised on the basis of the state of the world at the time the decision is being contemplated. Some tasks are primarily activities that can be preplanned; others are almost entirely ad hoc, while still others are balanced between the two.

A simple principle may be stated: Preplanned tasks are candidates for computer handling; tasks requiring human judgment are not.

Thus, computers may retrieve selected information from a data base; they may not decide which data to store or to retrieve. Although work is underway to allow humans to communicate more easily with computers and to use less cryptic and more nearly "natural" language in making requests, the human clearly remains in control even in those programs that apparently endow the computer with some power of discrimination. Thus, instead of asking for the "July sales figures for St. Louis," the analyst may request the "July sales figures showing the greatest increase over June," leaving the computer to figure out that the St. Louis figures are wanted.

The selection criteria and the "if this, then that" type instructions may be combined almost without limit, but the final computer output is controlled by the human's initial request.

Tasks in which the computer can play no role are those requiring human experience and judgment. The recognition that a decision is, or is going to be, required, the identification of who is involved, and the choice of objectives and values are all human tasks.

In apparent violation of this principle is the current work in AI which has the goal of endowing the computer with a measure of human judgment. The "expert systems" are designed to carry out a course of action as a human might be expected to do. If the human's experience can be analyzed and codified as a series of "If the situation is A, then do B" statments, then the computer may emulate the human's thought patterns and behavior.

As yet there is no clear verdict as to the value of these programs. In some areas, they may prove successful; in others, of little value. I suspect that their ultimate usefulness will depend greatly on the attitude taken toward them and the goals underlying their development. If expert systems are perceived as replacements for human experience and knowledge to be used instead of humans, then I would expect them to fail. If, however, the programs are regarded as mechanisms whereby human experience and judgment may be preserved for use when the humans on whose wisdom they are based are no longer available, then they may prove very valuable.

The decision aids designed to lead inexperienced decision makers through crises have been mentioned earlier. As long as these programs are considered to operate in a supporting role, offering information and suggestions, but leaving their human user to judge the value and relevancy of those suggestions, then they may play a vital role in decision making in the future.

SUMMARY

The making of a decision involves creative thinking and careful analysis. Humans are best at creative tasks and at constructing logical patterns of analysis. Computers are best at repetitive computational tasks and data-searching. Thus, the ideal human-computer decision-making teams uses each in the role it carries out best, with the human asking "What if we do . . . . .?" and the computer, chugging through its preprogrammed operations to answer "The result will be . . . . .." The human is freed from tedious tasks so that he might explore the outer limits of his imagination. The computer is employed to evaluate each idea, store its outcome, and finally, produce a list of alternatives ordered according to its value in human terms.

II

DECISION SUPPORT SYSTEMS TECHNOLOGY

INTRODUCTION

How does one build a decision support system? If you want to invest in one off-the-shelf how do you make the selection?

This part of the book introduces some of the tools and techniques of decision support systems design and development. The first article by Barth and Lehner looks at the ever-visible field of artificial intelligence (AI) and how it can be used to "drive" decision support systems and, perhaps more importantly, how it can be implemented on microcomputers. They address the most popular AI languages—LISP and PROLOG—as well as several of the expert systems building tools now on the market.

Significantly, while extremely current, the article has already been overtaken by some events. The time between when the article was submitted to this book and when this Introduction was written has been barraged with AI tools, systems, and gagdets. Teknowledge, Inc. of Palo Alto, California has released a microcomputer-based expert system generating package called *M1*. Texas Instruments has released its Personal Consultant software, and Donald Michie of the University of Edinburgh has released Expert-Ease, just to name a few of the many *in addition to the ones discussed so well by Barth and Lehner*. This rush toward commercialization suggests that a lot of investors think that (a) decision support is here to stay, and the (b) AI will figure prominently in its evolution. Is decision support here to stay? And will AI figure very prominently in its evolution? The first question deserves a qualified "yes," while the second a "maybe." The major challenge to the AI community will come from within as it learns (or fails to learn) how to temper its rhetoric about the power of its systems. If the community can focus on requirements, and much less so on the business of rising expectations, then AI may indeed make some major contributions to decision support technology.

Barth and Lehner also look at some AI-driven decision support systems, systems that will provide you with a solid feel for the potential of "intelligent" decision support.

MacLean's article, "User-System Interface Requirements for Decision Support Systems," is practical and timely, given how unfriendly many systems are today. It is probably safe to say that first generation decision support systems were designed with reference primarily to function, not friendliness. While later generations were much friendlier, there still remains much to do in the general areas of "man-machine relations."

Human factors specialists have for years harped upon the importance of friendly interfaces, though it took the wide distribution of computing systems to raise everyone's consciousness about the leverage that might be gained via the transplating of a hostile interface with a genuinely friendly one. The new buzz words and phrases include *ergonomics, user friendly,* and *intelligent interfaces*, among others. MacLean's (*user-system interface*) phrase is just right.

He also spends some time discussing *how* to design an effective user-system interface, offering a number of recommendations about how to conduct a systems specification, how to design displays and controls, how to design user-system dialog, how to build in consistency, how to develop effective error routines, and how to build in report capabilities, a particularly important part of many decision support systems.

John Sutherland and Bennett Teates move into an area known in the military as command and control, or "C2," though Sutherland's focus is much less on military applications than Teates'.

Sutherland is concerned with distributed knowledge, though not necessarily from an AI point of view. He is also concerned with network reconstitution and the means by which interruptions in distributed processing can be converted into information processing "feedforward" opportunities. The concept is in reality a network architecture designed to overcome the disadvantages of conventional distributed data base systems and managers. The significance of the architecture lies principally in the recognition of events and conditions that disrupt information networks and the preplanned development of mechanisms to deal effectively with such disruptions. In effect, Sutherland has developed a typology of command/control situations that acknowledge the disruptive influence of certain events, the inability of conventional feedback systems to cope, and the conceptual "feedforward" means to deal with disruptive events.

Teates carves out a practical role for decision support systems to play in command and control. But he begins cautiously, noting that many past systems have failed to engender any real enthusiasm. He identifies several scenarios for profitably applying decision support systems technology; he also identifies some key decision support system characteristics.

Finally, Andriole looks at how some specific decision analytic methodology has been used to develop some aids with applied corporate problem-solving potential.

3

Artificial Intelligence on Microcomputers

Stephen W. Barth and Paul E. Lehner

Artificial Intelligence (AI) is a branch of computer science concerned with the development of computer systems that exhibit intelligent behavior. This chapter is a survey of some systems and software from this field that have been developed for, or can operate within, microcomputer environments. In particular microcomputer software systems from the key AI sub-areas of knowledge-based expert systems, natural language interpretation, and machine learning are reviewed. Languages available for the development and implementation of AI software on microcomputers are also described. In addition, some of the advantages and disadvantages of using microcomputers for AI applications, and some projected future trends in the area are briefly discussed.

LANGUAGES AND ENVIRONMENTS

Until recently, efficient implementations of programming languages traditionally associated with AI work, in particular LISP and PROLOG, have not been available for microcomputers. Consequently, most microcomputer-based AI systems have been implemented in more standard languages, primarily Pascal. However, with the development of larger memories for microcomputer systems, this historical limitation is disappearing. Several versions of LISP, the most common language for AI systems implementation, are now available for many microcomputers, while PROLOG has been implemented for microcomputer systems with as little as 64K bytes of memory. The principal characteristics of these two languages are briefly summarized below.

LISP

LISP, invented in 1968 by John McCarthy, has been the computer language of choice for most research and development in AI (Barr and Feigenbaum 1982). Several important ideas behind the design of LISP have made it a useful tool for AI applications. LISP is a language designed for symbolic computation with the linked list as the basic data structure. It has a control structure based on function composition and recursion. An essential feature of LISP is that it allows representation of "code as data"; i.e., the ability to interpret a LISP program as data and vice versa. The essential core of LISP can be defined by about ten primitive functions, and the rest of the language can be defined in terms of them. A LISP interpreter can thus be written in LISP itself and serve to define the language. It should be noted, however, that most practical LISP implementations include many built-in functions, and, as a result, several dialects of LISP exist and have significant differences in features. The extendibility of LISP, the elegance and simplicity of its representation and control structures, and, as a result, the powerful interactive debugging capabilities that are usually included in LISP implementations, make it an ideal language for testing ideas rapidly and developing prototype systems. This approach of using a flexible and extendible language for quick experimentation and cyclic development has been characteristic of AI research and systems development.

Recent articles in the microcomputer literature have reviewed several LISP implementations for microcomputers that offer reasonable performance characteristics (Levitan and Bonar 1981; McClellan 1983; *Microsystems* 1983).

PROLOG

PROLOG is a programming language based on mathematical first order logic, that has been used for a number of AI applications and research (Clocksin and Mellish 1981; Clark and McCabe 1982). It has been very popular with researchers in the European AI community, and, in addition, has been selected to play a major role in the development of the well-known Japanese Fifth Generation Machine project (Feigenbaum and McCorduck 1983). It has built-in mechanisms for deductive inference, and has a uniform representation for the facts and rules that make up a knowledge base. New facts can be derived from existing facts and the rules, via the built-in backtracking and efficient theorem-proving mechanisms. Like LISP, the simplicity and elegance of the underlying mechanisms, (although they are completely different than those of LISP), and the extendibility and flexibility of PROLOG, make it a powerful tool for describing and developing solutions for the problems of a programmer or system developer, using the approach of iterative refinement.

Micro-PROLOG is an implementation of PROLOG developed at Imperial College, London, under the direction of Professor Keith Clark (McCabe 1981). Micro-PROLOG differs from the verson of PROLOG developed for the DEC–10 in some aspects of syntax and semantics. Work is presently underway to extend it to define a more flexible and robust language. Micro-PROLOG is available for nearly any microprocessor-based system with 64K bytes, or more, of memory.

The APES system for building expert systems, described below, has been implemented in PROLOG and Micro-PROLOG.

KNOWLEDGE-BASED SOFTWARE

One popular area within Artificial Intelligence today involves the development of knowledge-based expert systems. Expert systems are designed to assist users with domain-specific problem-solving expertise, by encoding the same problem-solving heuristics that are used by human experts. Expert systems have been developed for a wide spectrum of problem areas including chemical spectogram analysis (Buchanan and Feigenbaum 1978), medical diagnosis (Shortliffe, et al. 1979), mineral exploration (Duda, et al., 1979) genetic engineering (Stefik 1980), and computer system configuration (McDermott 1980). Many other applications of this technology have been developed or are currently in progress. Most of these systems were or are being developed using versions of the LISP programming language on large mainframe computers (e.g., the DEC–10), or, in recent years, machines with specialized LISP processors.

While LISP and PROLOG environments have recently become available for microcomputers, most of the microcomputer-based expert systems have not been implemented in these languages. As a result, these efforts have demonstrated that certain knowledge-based programming techniques can be taken out of the LISP environment in which they were originally developed and moved into the more standardized and structured programming environment currently needed to make efficient use of the limited capabilities of microcomputers.

Several different software systems have been designed for implementing expert systems on microprocessor-based computer systems. All are problem-independent tools for building expert systems. They utilize a variety of inference mechanisms and knowledge representation schemes. All are currently being used for a wide variety of expert system applications, and are undergoing enhancements or improvements for future releases. They run on a variety of microcomputer-based computer systems, including the more popular personal computers with mini-floppy or Winchester disk storage capabilities. Most of the systems can run in as little as 64K bytes of memory with small knowledge bases, but with more memory larger knowledge bases are possible. The systems to be described, and their developers are listed in Table 3.1. Some of the specific application areas of the systems are described in Table 3.2. AL/X and APES are commercially available as software packages for microcomputers or larger mainframes. AL/X, in fact, was the first expert system building tool to be commercially licensed.

System	Acronym	Developer
Advice Language/X	AL/X	Intelligent Terminals Ltd. Oxford, UK
A PROLOG Expert System	APES	Imperial College London, UK
Embedded Rule-based System	ERS	PAR Technology Corp. New Hartford, NY
Diesel Electric Locomotive Troubleshooting Aid	DELTA	General Electric Research and Development Center Schnectady, NY
Generic Expert System	GEN-X	General Electric Research and Development Center Schenectady, NY

Table 3.1   Microcomputer-based Expert System Tools

System	Applications
AL/X	Oil production platform fault diagnosis
APES	Determining eligibility for social security benefits, pipe corrosion diagnosis, suitability of sites for dam construction, care for terminally ill patients (under development)
ERS	Interpreting military sensor information, aircraft design for maintainability evaluation
DELTA	Troubleshooting for diesel locomotives and plastic injection molding equipment, process controller design
GEN-X	Troubleshooting for jet engines, industrial process control

Table 3.2.   Microcomputer-based Expert System Applications

AL/X

The first significant effort in the implementation of expert system capabilities on microcomputers was AL/X (Advice Language/X) (Reiter 1981; Paterson, 1981). It was developed by Intelligent Terminals Ltd., under the direction of Professor Donald Michie and sponsorship of British Petroleum Development Ltd., at the Machine Intelligence Research Unit of the University of Edinburgh, Edinburgh, Scotland. AL/X , which operates on computer configurations as small as an Apple II + with 64K bytes of memory, provides an inference engine, rule description language and consultation system capability that is modeled after PROSPECTOR (Duda, et al. 1979) and EMYCIN (van Melle 1980). The original application was for fault diagnosis on North Sea oil production platforms. AL/X is similar to EMYCIN in that it is designed to be used with any set of rules supplied to it in the format of the AL/X rule description language. It can be applied to a particular problem domain by simply creating a file with domain specific rules that represent the relevant problem-solving expertise.

For comparison purposes, AL/X will be described in some detail. Its design illustrates the microcomputer implementation of some techniques, drawn from early successful work in expert systems, that are also incorporated in several of the other microcomputer-based systems described below.

With AL/X, as with PROSPECTOR, rules are represented in the form of an inference network. As illustrated in Figure 3.1, an inference network contains top level hypotheses, called goal hypotheses, which are decomposed into various levels of subhypotheses that are further broken down into specific items of evidence that can support those hypotheses. With each node, there is an associated prior degree of belief and the rule for combining subnode degree-of-belief values into an updated degree of belief for the node. Available combination rules, using the example in Figure 3.1, are illustrated in Figure 3.2.

In a consultation session, AL/X attempts to evaluate the degree of belief of a goal hypothesis by chaining down the inference net, identifying the evidence items that affect the goal

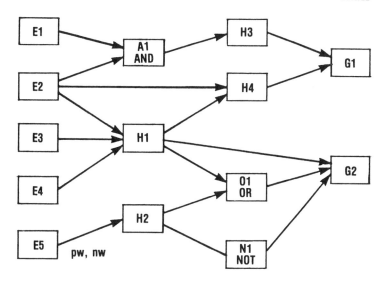

Figure 3.1.   Sample Form of an Inference Network

Type of Rule	Degree of Belief Calculation
AND	$Deg(A1) = min(Deg(E1), Deg(E2))$
OR	$Deg(O1) = max(Deg(H1), Deg(H2))$
NOT	$Deg(N1) = -Deg(H2)$
Bayesian	$Degree(H2) = W + Deg(H2)$, where W is calculated by a linear interpolation on $Deg(E5)$ between the positive and negative weights, pw and nw, linking E5 to H2.

Figure 3.2   AL/X Degree-of-belief Propagation Rules

hypothesis, and querying the user about each relevant item of evidence. Consequently, user interactions with AL/X during a consultation session consist primarily of answering system questions, and occasionally requesting an explanation of the inference process. For example, for the simple inference net in Figure 3.3a, from a rule base for diagnosing automobile engine problems, a consultation session such as in Figure 3.3b is representative.

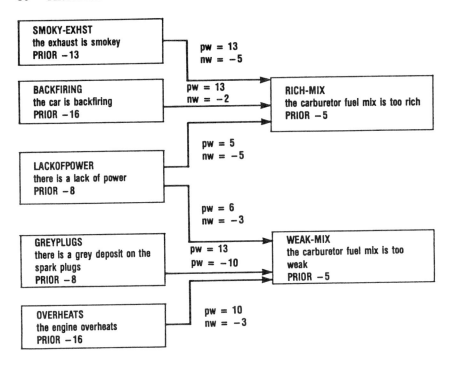

Figure 3.3a.   A Sample Inference Network

The current goal is whether or not
the carburetor fuel mix is too rich (rich-mix)
Current degree is -5.0.

How certain are you that the exhaust is smoky?
>5

How certain are you that the car is backfiring?
>c

The car is backfiring (backfiring)
with degree -16.0
     is evidence for (pw = 13.0 nw = -2.0)
The carburetor fuel mix is too rich (rich-mix)
with degree 8.0

How certain are you that the car is backfiring?
>-5

...that there is a lack of power?
>3

After considering all significant questions,
the degree that the carb fuel mix is too rich (rich-mix)
initially was -5.0. It is now 11.0.

There are no more significant questions for the current goal
****
Investigated goals with degree of belief >= 0.0 are:

The carb fuel mix is too rich (rich-mix)
Prior degree was -5.0. Current degree is 11.0.

Other goals with degree >= 0.0 are:

The carburetor fuel mix is too weak (weak-mix)
Prior degree was -5.0. Current degree is 1.0.
****
(at this point, AL/X would begin to consider yet unanswered
evidence for the weak-mix goal).

Figure 3.3b   Excerpt from a Sample AL/X Consultation Session

AL/X was originally developed on a PDP 11/34 under the
UNIX operating system. It was written in standard Pascal, as
defined in Jensen and Wirth (1974). AL/X has been installed on
an Apple II+ and an LSI-11/02 under UCSD Pascal, a Cromemco
Superbrain under Pascal/M, all with 64K bytes of memory, and
on an IBM PC, which can have in excess of 512K bytes of memory.
AL/X has also been installed on a number of larger mainframe
computers under various operating systems and Pascal language
implementations. Since Pascal is available for most microcomputers, transferring AL/X to other microcprocessor environments
does not present any difficulties.

With 64K bytes of memory, AL/X can process about one hundred rules in a single consultation session. It is possible, however, to process a much larger rule base by decomposing it into smaller rule sets and storing each rule set in a separate file. AL/X would then proceed through several consultation sessions, one for each rule set. In this way AL/X could, for instance, process a rule base of the same size and structure as PROSPECTOR's.

ERS

A second system that supports expert system implementation on microcomputers is ERS (Embedded Rule-based System) (Barth 1984). ERS is like AL/X in that both systems implement inference engines similar to the one found in PROSPECTOR, and both systems can be used to implement expert systems in multiple problem domains. However, unlike AL/X, ERS is not simply a consultation system, but is also designed to support development of expert systems that function as "intelligent interfaces." Specifically, instead of asking the user questions to ascertain basic pieces of evidence ERS can call up any set of application-specific primitive functions which, in turn, can consult (get input from) various data bases for factual information.

An example of an expert system that operates as an intelligent interface is the Duplex Army Radio/Radar Targeting (DART) system (Barth, et al. 1984). DART provides expert advice to a military analyst on identifying certain types of activity nodes. Identifications are based on data reported from various sources. The DART system uses expert rules to interpret this data as it is presented to the analyst, and delivers a recommendation on the possible activity nodes that the data may represent. The analyst may reject this advice or accept it and make the appropriate modifications to a data base of known or probable activity nodes.

At the heart of the DART system, which operates on a VAX 11/780, is the same application-independent inference engine component found in ERS. As with PROSPECTOR and AL/X, probabilities or weights of evidence are propagated through an inference network of hypotheses and evidence via Bayesian or fuzzy logic techniques. Unlike those systems, however, DART uses a set of application-specific primitive functions to evaluate the degree of belief of evidence nodes in the inference network. The Evidence Manager, which contains these primitive functions, consults data bases containing information on known activity node locations and activity node characteristics, as well as incoming reports. An Advice Interpreter component presents the conclusions and their explanations to the user. Consequently the user not only receives expert system advice, but also a summary of information, obtained from several data bases, that is relevant to that advice. A Display Manager component allows the results of analysis to be displayed graphically.

One of the interesting aspects of the process of developing the DART rule base is that this process began by working with the essential system operating in a consultation mode. This allowed the system developers to begin the process of knowledge engineering without consideration of data base interfaces. Primitive functions for the evidence nodes encoded in the inference network were gradually incorporated as they became well defined. This two phase process for implementing intelligent interface systems is precisely what ERS is designed to support. Namely, first using ERS in a consultation mode to support knowledge base engineering, and then incorporating primitive functions to tie the system into an existing data base or decision support system.

Like AL/X, ERS is written in Pascal, and has been implemented on an IBM PC/XT under UCSD Pascal, with 256K bytes of memory.

A second prototype application of ERS is in the area of design for maintainability, where ERS is used in a consultation mode to assist an engineer in evaluating the maintainability aspects of the designs for a large complex system, such as an aircraft (Lehner and Donnell 1984).

DELTA

DELTA (Diesel Electric Locomotive Troubleshooting Aid) is an expert system to assist maintenance personnel in isolating and repairing diesel train engine problems (Bonissone and

Johnson 1983). It has been developed by General Electric Corp. at their Research and Development Center in Schenectady, NY. While it was developed with a particular application in mind, the architecture and software of DELTA is flexible and general purpose and can be applied to a variety of fault diagnosis or troubleshooting problems. In fact, DELTA is also being applied to troubleshooting for plastic injection molding equipment and, in a SACON-like system (Bennet et al. 1978) to provide expert assistance for using computer software for process controller design.

Like AL/X, DELTA is a consultation system and incorporates a software architecture consisting of a domain-independent inference engine with a domain-specific knowledge base. DELTA, however, uses a hybrid inference mechanism that allows both forward reasoning, from facts to conclusions, and backward reasoning, to confirm or disprove hypotheses. The overall reasoning of the system is based on a troubleshooting paradigm that involves finding a fault, repairing it, and checking to see that no problems remain, repeating the cycle if necessary. Troubleshooting knowledge is represented as AND/OR rules that describe the conditions for detecting faults. A sample diagnostic rule in simplified form for the diesel locomotive application is:

IF:
        engine-set-idle
        AND
        fuel-pressure-below-normal
        AND
        fuel-pressure-gauge-ok

THEN:
        fuel-system-faulty.

Rules may contain necessary or sufficient conditions for detecting faults, and are partitioned into knowledge spaces of possible problem areas, such as the mechanical system or electrical system of a diesel engine. Metarules provide a smart index to the knowledge spaces for retrieving the relevant rule sets given an initial set of user-specified fault symptoms. When a fault is isolated a treatment or repair prescription is provided. When the user has completed the prescribed repairs the system asks questions to confirm that the problem has been fixed, and continues on to check for other faults if problems remain.

DELTA uses over five hundred rules to assist a technician in locating and repairing problems with diesel engines. Diagnostic and repair knowledge is contained in approximately three hundred rules, and the other rules provide a help system to answer user queries and provide additional information. A unique feature of the DELTA system is an optional interface provided for a video disk. The video disk system provides visual and audio segments of training firms to assist the technician in carrying out repair instructions and collecting the information to answer system queries. Also, DELTA can use CAD files, stored in TEKTRONIX standard format for providing help to the user; for example, schematics of the diesel engine system or its parts that are being analyzed.

The DELTA system was originally implemented in LISP but was translated into the FORTH language for installation on microcomputers. The diesel locomotive troubleshooting application uses a PDP-11/23 microcomputer with a 10M byte Winchester disk, a portable video disk player and a graphics display terminal. Field testing of DELTA has begun at General Electric's locomotive repair facilities.

GEN-X

GEN-X (Generic Expert System) is designed to assist a user with the knowledge engineering task for building an expert system, and produce an efficient compilation of the system for downloading to a variety of microcomputer environments (Lewis 1983). It also was developed at General Electric's Research and Development Center. Like DELTA, GEN-X is designed to be applied to troubleshooting or fault diagnosis problems. Applications of GEN-X are currently underway for troubleshooting in jet engines and industrial process control.

GEN-X provides a different approach to expert systems implementation than systems like AL/X. The GEN-X system consists of a knowledge manager, interpreters, and code generators. The *knowledge manager* provides an interactive graphics facility for knowledge base creation and editing. The user can choose among AND/OR networks, an inheritance network, or decision tables as a knowledge representation scheme. *Interpreters* use the knowledge base and user-interface specifications to drive a consultation session. During the knowledge engineering phase, GEN-X is used to provide consultation sessions, and maintains separate knowledge base and inference engine components, like the architecture used in AL/X. When knowledge base development has reached a satisfactory level, the GEN-X *code generators* allow the knowledge base and appropriate interpreters to be translated into compact C, ADA, Pascal, and FORTRAN programs for execution in more constrained environments.

GEN-X is implemented in C using the portable C library and can itself be run on an IBM PC with a color graphic display terminal. Ideally, however, it would be used in a mainframe environment to generate code for downloading to target microcomputer-based systems. It is estimated that a knowledge base as large as 1000 AND/OR rules could be compiled by GEN-X for implementation on systems with 256K bytes of memory, and that nontrivial rule bases could be loaded into systems with as little as 322K bytes. Current applications contain approximately 100 rules and have been generated for IBM PCs and LSI-11s.

APES

APES (A PROLOG Expert System) is an expert system user interface, or shell, for the Micro-PROLOG logic programming language (Hammond 1982; Sergot 1983; McCabe 1981). Along with Micro-PROLOG it was developed at Imperial College, London, under the direction of Professor Keith Clark. APES has been designed to provide explanation capabilities and other user-interface features for PROLOG to facilitate expert consultation system development.

Like AL/X, APES has separate inference engine and knowledge base components, but allows the user to define the way that uncertain reasoning is handled. The user can select an inference mechanism like that used in EMYCIN, or a Bayesian one (like AL/X). Other inference techniques are currently being incorporated into APES. The mechanisms for uncertain reasoning can be combined with the logical deductive reasoning capability that the system derives from PROLOG. An APES knowledge base is a collection of PROLOG statements, or clauses as they are called, representing the expert rules and facts of the problem domain.

The first Micro-PROLOG release of APES does not contain modules for uncertain reasoning, because 64K bytes is too small for the full APES implementation, but the basic system has been implemented in Micro-PROLOG systems on North Star Horizons, IBM PCs and IBM PC look-alike machines, all with minifloppy disk drives.

Applications with APES so far have used up to four hundred Micro-PROLOG clauses (facts and rules). Some of the applications have been expert consultation systems for determining Social Security benefits, suitability of sites for dam construction, assisting with the care of terminally ill patients, and pipe corrosion diagnosis. The terminal care application is being carried out by the Imperial Cancer Research Fund where an initial EMYCIN knowledge base is being translated for use with APES.

NATURAL LANGUAGE INTERPRETATION

Within AI, a major research and development area is that of natural language processing. Broadly stated, the goal of work in this area is to develop computing systems that can converse with people in languages that they already know, such as English. Although natural language processing is a broad and diverse field, one particular class of systems are Natural Language Interfaces (NLIs) that are designed to provide users with a flexible and easy-to-use information access and retrieval capability from one or more data bases.

Although various NLI systems for data base access have been developed (see Harris 1977; Hendrix, et al. 1978; Kaplan 1979; Templeton 1979; and Waltz 1975), all of these systems have in common some type of ability to automatically create a data base access program to answer a variety of questions that can be input by the user in a natural language format. Generally, these systems operate by iterating through a sequence of intermediate representations of the natural langauge query, resulting, in the final iteration, in a well-defined data retrieval command or program. Usually at least three stages are involved. The first applies grammatical parsing rules to determine the function of the input sentences' words, thereby creating an internal structure that consists of relations between individual words (e.g., ". . . this adjective modifies that noun which is the subject of . . ."). This parsing activity, in the simpler systems, is based on expected key words and restrained to limited phrase structures. The second stage then translates the structured query resulting from the first stage into an internal language description of a target data base access sequence that defines the specific steps required to search for and retrieve the requested data. The third stage then translates the target data base access sequence into the data retrieval procedures specific to each of the target data bases. Since most NLIs are designed to provide a user with access to multiple data bases, similar-looking access sequences after the second stage may result in very different data retrieval procedures for different data bases.

From the perspective of microcomputer-based systems NLI work has been very limited. The reason for this is probably not, as might at first have been imagined, that microcomputers do not have the computational power necessary for this type of natural language processing. Rather it is that the utility of developing such capabilities has in the past appeared somewhat limited. Since the goal of an NLI is generally to provide easy access to one or more data bases, then implementing an NLI on a stand-alone microcomputer that does not contain any important data bases has little value. However, the increasing power of microcomputers and the corresponding increase in the use of microcomputers for serious decision support applications (as evidenced by this book) is likely to result in proliferation of important microcomputer resident data bases. This in turn may very well result in the development of a number of natural language systems for microcomputers.

Three software systems that do have the *potential* of providing significant NLI capabilities for microcomputers are AQF, (Mah 1980) which is a FORTRAN implementation of NLI capabilities; a self-contained microcomputer data base system under development at Symantec Corporation (Haas 1984) that will have a natural query language, and a microcomputer version of the popular INTELLECT system being developed by Artificial Intelligence Corporation (Eisenberg and Hill 1984).

AQF

AQF (Advanced Query Facility) is an NLI system designed to provide users with a single means of transparent access to multiple existing formatted data bases. It was originally designed to assist users in accessing the many large data bases resident at various DOD installations. The heart of the AQF approach is an extension of the relational data base model (Codd 1975) to include hierarchical relations among the data elements. Essentially, this means that hierarchies of relations can exist within the data base. These hierarchies closely correspond to the structure of relationships in English, permitting a relatively simple mapping from the user's query into the intermediate AQF representation. Other AQF facilities translate this intermediate representation into the specialized language required by each target data base, retrieve the appropriate data, and format a response to the user's initial query. The user query may include pronoun references, ellipsis, and other familiar natural language features. A short example of a dialog with AQF exhibiting features standard to any NLI is shown in Figure 3.4.

AQF was designed to be portable. It was originally developed in FORTRAN to run on PDP–11 16-bit architecture. It is designed to operate in 64K byte address spaces using segmented overlays. With some modifications to the I/O procedures AQF could be transported to many of the 16-bit architecture microcomputers that have become available in the last few years, such as the IBM PC. Once again, however, the need to transfer an NLI facility such as AQF to a microcomputer environment is somewhat limited until the environment has some resident difficult-to-access data bases.

The Symantec System

The system under development at Symantec Corporation is a microcomputer data base system that has embedded within it a natural query language. That is, the Symantec system not

"A Q F DEMONSTRATION'
" VERSION 08-06-00 "

QRT > TELL ME ABOUT AIRCRAFT.

THIS IS A SOVIET FIGHTER AIRCRAFT DATA BASE,
DERIVED FROM UNCLASSIFIED PUBLICATIONS. IT
DESCRIBES CREWS, FUSELAGES, WINGS, ENGINES,
ARMAMENTS, AND PERFORMANCE.

QRT > LIST FIGHTERS ORDERED BY NATO NAME.

ROLE	/NATO/ NAME	
F/B	FARMER	MIG-19
F/B	FARMER-C	MIG-19SF
F/B	FARMER-D	MIG-19PF
F/B	FARMER-D	MIG-19PM
FGA/T	FISHBED	MIG-21
FGA/T	FISHBED-C	MIG-21F
FGA/T	FISHBED-D	MIG-21PF
FGA/T	FISHBED-F	MIG-21PFK
FGA/T	FISHBED-J	MIG-21PFMA
FGA/T	FISHBED-J	MIG-21MF
FGA/T	FISHBED-K	MIG-21MF
FGA/T	FISHBED-L	MIG-21MF
AWF	FISHPOT	SU-9
FS/A	FLOGGER	MIG-23
FS/A	FLOGGER-B	MIG-23B
FS/A	FLOGGER-C	MIG-23U
F/B	FRESCO	MIG-1T

QRT > WHAT ARE THE DIMENSIONS OF THE FARM-
ER?

```
----------------------------------FT------------FT-------------FT
MIG-19 FARMER LH= 48.83  HT= 13.19  WS= 29.54
```

QRT > HOW MUCH DOES IT WEIGH?

```
                          WEIGHT
-------------------------------------------LB
MIG-19     FARMER     19180
```

QRT > PRINT THE ARMAMENT OF THE FARMER.

```
-------------------------------------------------------------------
MIG-19  FARMER "CFGN"   1 AA MISSILE ALKALI
                        3    CANNON
             "CFGN"     4 AS ROCKET
                        2    BOMB
                        3    CANNON
             "CFGN"     1 AS ROCKET
                        2    BOMB
                        3    CANNON
```

QRT > HOW FAST CAN IT FLY?

		MACH	SPEED FT
MIG-19	FARMER	0.50	80000
		0.60	70000
		0.75	60000
		0.97	50000
		1.24	40000
		1.32	30000
		1.09	20000
		.084	10000
		0.66	0

QRT > THE FRESCO

		MACH	SPEED FT
MIG-17	FRESCO	0-39	40000
		0-48	30000
		0-62	20000
		0-80	10000
		0-92	0

Figure 3.4   Sample AQF Session.

only allows users to retrieve data from the data base, but also to specify the contents of the data base. The system's vocabulary of nouns and adjectives is totally expandable, thereby providing users with a flexible ability to define new types of data items and to enter/update the value of any given data item.

The Symantec system, which should be on the market by the publication of this book, operates on an IBM PC with a 10 megabyte Winchester disk. Its implementation is in Pascal, operating under a specially modified version of the UCSD P-system. It is anticipated that the primary consumers of the Symantec system would be users in need of large personnel data bases, such as middle-level managers in large corporations or small business managers maintaining vendor lists.

INTELLECT Systems for Microcomputers

Artificial Intelligence Corporation (AIC) also is developing a microcomputer implementation of NLI capabilities that will provide users with a stand-alone data base system with natural langauge features. Specifically, they are in the process of developing microcomputer versions of the commercially available INTELLECT system that provides NLI capabilities for IBM mainframes. Unlike Symantec, which is developing a complete system with natural language capabilities embedded, the AIC approach is to develop natural language software that interfaces with existing, commercially available, microcomputer software. As noted in Eisenberg and Hill (1984), the AIC approach involves interfacing on the input side with popular personal computer data base systems such as dBase II, while on the output side, the NLI would call existing graphics packages to format displays.

The microcomputer version of INTELLECT is being implemented in PL/I. The initial minimum hardware configuration for which it is being developed will be an IBM PC with 512K bytes of memory and a hard disk drive.

Overall it would appear that as microcomputers become increasingly popular for use in data management and decision support problems, the desire for significant natural language capabilities on microcomputers will substantially increase. The Symantec and AIC systems may simply be at the forefront of this potential trend.

One final note: natural language systems for data base interface have been available for approximately a decade. Early prototypes for such systems have been available since the early seventies. Consequently, the microcomputer-based natural language capabilities discussed above reflect implementations of known techniques, and are not representative of ongoing natural language research activities which deal in domains of discourse for more complex and dynamic than data bases with well-defined structures. (See Hendrix and Sacerdotti 1981 for a review.)

MACHINE LEARNING

Machine learning is a critical area of research in the field of Artificial Intelligence. The main bottleneck to expert systems development is the massive amount of time required for knowledge engineering, or translation of a domain specialist's expertise into some knowledge representation scheme. If machines could learn from experience, or in some way automatically aggregate the massive amounts of data that they are capable of collecting, dramatic reductions in the manpower required for expert systems development could be realized. The problem from the AI point of view is that this aggregation should result in human understandable knowledge for solving a problem. Thus the AI approach differs from that of classical pattern recognition, which provides for the statistical categorization of data.

One system has been developed for a microcomputer-based environment that takes a step toward addressing the problem of machine learning. ACLS (Analog Concept Learning System), was developed at the Machine Intelligence Research Unit at the University fo Edinburgh under the direction of Professor Donald Michie [Paterson 1982].

ACLS allows a user to generate classification rules from examples or cases of a rules application. The algorithm it uses is based upon earlier work in inductive learning (Hunt, et al. 1966; Quinlan 1979). Essentially ACLS involves the automatic induction of IF-THEN rules. It provides a capability for describing the basic features or attributes of a classification problem, using them to describe a set of examples that illustrate the application of an as yet unknown classification rule, and from the examples, generating a rule that accomodates them. In expert systems like AL/X, described above, knowledge engineering involves obtaining the rules for problem solving directly from the domain specialists; in ACLS the expert descriptions of the important features of a problem are used to derive the rules for solving it.

Using ACLS involves first defining a set of primitive attributes and the set of classes upon which the classification problem depends. These are obtained from the expert and need not be complete or entirely relevant to the problem in the early iterations of the system. Next, a training set of examples is composed by the expert in the form of records with the values for the attributes of the example and the resulting class that the expert would assign to them. These are fed to ACLS and the system induces a rule in the form of a decision tree that accounts for the set of examples. Attributes that turn out not to be relevant are not used in the classification rule. ACLS can produce executable Pascal code, embodying the logic of the induced decision tree in the form of nested if-then-else expressions, that can then be used for classification of other data described by the set of attributes.

ACLS can be used interactively or in a batch mode to analyze the training set of examples. Interactively, the system allows the user to review the decision rules as it is revised by each new example that is provided. The role of the expert, aside from supplying the necessary attributes and training examples, is to evaluate whether the ACLS-induced rule expresses his classification expertise accurately. ACLS essentially uses the list of examples to "observe" the expert's behavior as a classifier and construct the simplest rule it can to describe that behavior. If initial attempts fail to derive a satisfactory rule, new examples or new sets of attributes can be added to the system.

The ACLS program has been written in UCSD Pascal, and has been implemented on the APPLE II+ and IBM PC.

An improved version of ACLS, called Expert-Ease, with a graphics and menu-oriented user interface is being marketed by Export Software Internation (ESI 1983; Taylor 1984). Expert-Ease is available for microcomputers under the UCSD Pascal

Operating System. Expert-Ease, or the underlying ACLS system, has been applied to derive rules for classifying chess end-game positions as won, lost, or drawn. They have also been applied to determining a decision tree for diagnosis of lymphatic cancers.

CONCLUSION

Although the systems described above represent only a subset of the work on microcomputer-based AI, it is clear from the variety and success of these systems that using microcomputers is becoming a serious option for potential users of AI technology. Furthermore, as the trend toward more and more powerful microcomputers continues, the number and diversity of AI systems available for these computers will significantly increase. In this regard, two near-term trends should be noted. First, because of the recent availability of efficient implementations of the traditional AI languages (LISP and PROLOG) on microcomputers, it's likely that many of the future microcomputer-based AI systems will be developed in these languages, rather than the more standard languages, such as Pascal, that previous systems were implemented in. Second, some of the newer microcomputers are designed to emulate the capabilities of certain mainframes. For instance, the new MicroVax computer will provide users with all of the capabilities of the rest of the VAX line. Consequently, AI software implemented for the VAX environment, of which there is a great deal, should be immediately transferable to the MicroVax.

The issue to be addressed, then, is that of determining the contexts under which it is desirable, or even feasible, to utilize microcomputers for AI applications. Clearly, the primary motivations for using a microcomputer for an AI application involve the same factors that make microcomputers popular for other types of applications. Among them are their low cost, availability, and transportability. The low cost and availability of microcomputer systems makes it possible to cost-effectively distribute multiple copies of the same system. This, for instance, makes it possible for General Electric to distribute multiple copies of the DELTA expert system for use at different centers.

With regard to transportability, both hardware and software aspects of this characteristic are relevant. The small size and robust design of microcomputer systems make them appropriate for applications where physical space is limited and harsh environments may be encountered, such as the North Sea oil platforms that AL/X was intended for. For expert systems applications, the physical convenience of a small microcomputer system also makes interactive, online knowledge engineering with experts who may be on remote sites more feasible. At the same time the fact that much of the work in microcomputer-based expert systems is done in standardized, portable languages, such as Pascal, makes it relatively easy to transfer these systems to new hardware configurations. Note, for instance, the variety of different computers that AL/X and APES have been installed on. In addition, in the case of ERS, the software portability of Pascal facilitates the process of embedding expert systems into a larger data base or decision support systems.

With regard to determining the feasibility of a microcomputer-based AI application, an important characteristic to note about the systems described above is that all of them implement capabilities and techniques that were previously developed and tested by the AI research community. Consequently, implementing some AI application on a microcomputer currently appears to be most feasible where a good prototype of the proposed system already exists in the AI research domain. This makes it possible to generate precise specifications for reimplementing the system on microcomputers with memory and storage space limitations.

Overall, it appears that a primary advantage of AI applications on microcomputers is that these computers provide potential users with a low-risk opportunity to bring AI capabilities inhouse, and, as a result, determine the probable value of this technology for their applications.

REFERENCES

Barr, A., and E. A. Feigenbaum. 1982. *The Handbook of Artificial Intelligence*. Vol. 2. Los Altos, Calif.: William Kaufman Inc.

Barth, S. W. 1984. ERS User Manual. PAR Technology Corp., Seneca Plaza, Rt. 5, New Hartford, N.Y. 13413.

Barth, S. W., H. Coyle, and D. Sobik. 1984. User Guide for the Duplex Army Radio/Radar Targeting Aid (DART). PAR Technology Corp. *See* Barth 1984.

Bennet, J., L. Creary, R. S. Engelmore, and R. Melosh. 1978. *SACON: A Knowledge-Based Consultant in Structural Analysis.* Heuristic Programming Project Report No. HPP-78-28, also Report No. STAN-CS-78-699. Computer Science Department, Stanford University.

Bonissone, P. P., and H. E. Johnson. 1983. An Expert System for Fault Diagnosis in Diesel Electric Locomotives. General Electric Corporate Research and Development Center, Schenectady, N.Y. 12345.

Buchanan, B. G., and E. A. Feigenbaum. 1978. DENDRAL and Meta-DENDRAL: Their Applications Dimension. *Journal of Artificial Intelligence* 11:5–24.

Clark, K. L., and F. G. McCabe. 1982. Prolog: A language for implementing expert systems. In *Machine Intelligence 10*, ed. J. E. Hayes, D. Michie, and Y-H. Pao, 455–75. New York: John Wiley and Sons, Halsted Press.

Clocksin, W. F. and C. S. Mellish. 1981. *Programming in Prolog.* New York: Springer-Verlag.

Codd, E. 1975. A Relational Model of Data for Large Shared Data Banks. *Communications of the ACM* (November 18): 377–87.

Duda, R. O., P. E. Hart, and J. Gaschnig. 1979. Model Design in the PROSPECTOR Consultant System for Mineral Exploration. In *Expert Systems in the Micro-electronic Age*, ed. D. Michie. Edinburgh University Press.

Eisenberg, J., and J. Hill. 1984. Using Natural Language Systems on Personal Computers. *BYTE* (January): 226–38.

Export Software International. 1983. *An Introduction to Expert-Ease.* ESI, 4 Canongate Venture, New St., Royal Mile, Edinburgh, UK EH8 8BH.

Feigenbaum, E. A., and P. McCorduck. 1983. *The 5th Generation.* Reading, Mass.: Addison-Wesley.

Haas, N. 1984. Personal communication.

Hammond, P. 1982. *APES: A Detailed Description.* Research Report 82/10. Department of Computing, Imperial College of Science and Technology, University of London, 180 Queens Gate, London UK SW7 2BZ.

Harris, L. R. 1977. User Oriented Data Base Query with the ROBOT Natural Language Query System. In *Proceedings of the Third International Conference on Very Large Data Bases*, Tokyo, October.

Hendrix, G., and E. Sacerdotti. 1981. Natural Language Processing: The Field in Perspective. *BYTE* (September):304–52.

Hendrix, G., E. Sacerdotti, D. Sagalowicz, and J. Slocum. 1978. Developing a Natural Language Interface to Complex Data. *ACM Transactions on Database Systems* 3 (June): 105–47.

Hunt, E. B., J. Marin, and P. Stone. 1966. *Experiments in Inductive Learning*. New York: Academic Press.

Jensen, K., and N. Wirth. 1974. *Pascal User Manual and Report*. New York: Springer-Verlag.

Kaplan, S. 1979. Cooperative Responses from a Portable Natural Language Data Base Query System. Ph.D. diss., University of Pennsylvania.

Lehner, P. E., and M. L. Donnell. 1983. Maintainability Design Expert System. PAR Technology Corporation Report. *See* Barth 1984.

Levitan, S. P., and J. G. Bonar. 1981. Three MicroComputer LISPs. *BYTE* 6 (9) pp. 172–181 (September).

Lewis, John W. 1983. Personal communication. General Electric Corporate Research and Development Center, Schenectady, N.Y. 12345.

McCabe, F. G. 1981 *Micro-Prolog Reference Manual*. Logic Programming Associates, 10 Burntwood Close, London, UK SW18 3JU.

McClellan, D. P. 1983. LISPing with Your PC. *PC Magazine* 2(7) (December).

McDermott, J. 1980. *R1: A Rule-Based Configurer of Computer Systems*. Report CMU-CS-80-119. Department of Computer Science, Carnegie-Mellon University.

Mah, C. P. 1980. *Advanced Query Facility*. PAR Report No. 80-53. PAR Technology Corp. *See* Barth 1984.

Microsystems, the CP/M User's Journal. August 1983.

Paterson, A. 1981. *AL/X User Manual*. Intelligent Terminals, 15 Canal St. Oxford, UK OX2 68H.

——— 1982. *ACLS User Manual*. Intelligent Terminals, 15 Canal St. Oxford, UK 0X2 68H.

Quinlan, J. R. 1979. Discovering Rules by Induction from Large Collections of Examples. In *Expert Systems in the Micro-electronic Age*, ed. D. Michie. Edinburgh University Press.

Reiter, J. E. 1981. AL/X: An Inference System for Probabilistic Reasoning. M.S. thesis, Department of Computer Science, University of Illinois, Urbana.

Sergot, M. 1983. A Query-the-user facility for Logic Programming. In *Integrated Interactive Computing Systems*, ed. P. Degano, and E. Sandwell. New York: North-Holland.

Shortliffe, E. H., B. G. Buchanan, and E. A. Feigenbaum. 1979. Knowledge Engineering for Medical Decision Making: A Review of Computer-Based Clinical Decision Aids. *Proceedings of the IEEE* 67: 1207–24.

Stefik, M. J. 1980. *Planning with Constraints*. Ph.D. diss., Report No. STAN-CS-80-784, HPP-80-2, Computer Science Department, Stanford University.

Taylor, J. 1984. Putting a Ph.D. in Your PC. *PC Magazine*, 21 February, 167–74.

Templeton, M. 1979. EUFID: A Friendly and Flexible Frontend for Data Management Systems. In *Proceedings, 1979 National Conference of the Association for Computational Linguistics*, San Diego, Calif.: August.

van Melle, W. 1980. A Domain-Independent System that Aids in Constructing Knowledge-Based Consultation Programs. Ph.D. diss., Report No. STAN-CS-80-820, Computer Science Department, Stanford University.

Waltz, D. 1975. Natural Language Access to a Large Data Base: An Engineering Approach. In *Proceedings, 4th International Joint Conference on Artificial Intelligence, Tibilisi, Georgia, USSR*, 868–72. Los Altos, Calif.: William Kaufman.

4

User-System Interface Requirements for Decision Support Systems

Robert F. MacLean

There are two distinct types of decision support systems:

1. Real-time systems such as those required in air traffic control or military command and control; and
2. Non real-time applications such as financial planning and project management applications.

This distinction is made at the onset, since user-system interface (USI) requirements differ significantly depending on the real-time requirement. Foley (1983) makes the distinction between the two underlying requirements as "lives and dollars." Real-time decision support systems generally monitor and control life-critical situations in which delay or error on the part of the operator can be disastrous. An inefficient user-system interface in a life-critical real-time system would be intolerable. Because of the critical nature of most real-time decision support systems, years of study and development have been spent improving real-time user-system interfaces, and this process will no doubt continue.

Although most real-time decision support systems are part of large communication and sensor networks supported by mainframe computers, the application of microcomputers in support of communications networks and user workstations promises to provide substantial technical improvements in these systems in the near future. Eventually, all real-time systems will employ hundreds of microcomputer devices. However, because of the continuing interest in the user-system interface in real-time systems, improvements will be evolutionary when compared with the dramatic changes that are occurring in non real-time systems.

Non real-time decision support systems historically have not been as directly accessible to the decision maker as have real-time systems. For this reason the user-system interface has not recieved the attention paid to real-time systems. Until recently, the user-system interface of non real-time decision support systems such as financial modeling systems or project management systems has consisted of coding sheets and large computer printouts. The recent availability of the microcomputer has spurred the develoment of various types of non real-time decision support systems.

Because the subject of real-time systems has been covered extensively elsewhere, this discussion will focus on developments in non real-time decision support systems. The intent is to examine the trends and the user requirements for non real-time, microprocessor-based decision support systems. Because of the dramatic changes seen in direct user involvement with microcomputer-based systems, their impact on the quality of user-system interfaces will be examined. Some ergonomic and user-system dialog considerations will be discussed in an attempt to provide insight to those who may be developing requirements, preparing specifications, or just considering the selection of an off-the-shelf decision support system.

THE INFLUENCE
OF THE MICROCOMPUTER REVOLUTION

The introduction of the personal microcomputer in the late 1970s initiated one of the most exciting technological and sociological periods since the beginning of the industrial revolution. For the first time the computer industry was marketing a product within the economic grasp of a large segment of our society.

Today, less than ten years later, most people who have followed the advances in microcomputers will agree on the profound impact they are having on our society. Advances are occurring so rapidly that computer industry professionals are simply not able to keep up with developments. Traditional solutions to many system design problems have been overcome by the tide of new approaches.

The advent of the personal microcomputer has focused a great deal of interest on direct user-system interaction and the quality of the user-system interface. The availability of microcomputer-based systems at a low cost has greatly expanded the interest for direct user involvement with many applications, including decision support systems. The introduction of commercial microcomputer software systems such as VisiCalc, Lotus 1-2-3, and Knowledgeman, among others, has generated a great deal of excitement among many business planners and financial analysts. The packages have given managers and financial planners a taste of what can be provided with more sophisticated decision support systems.

One of the most exciting aspects in the rapid development of the microcomputer industry has been observing the unbounded creativity of software and hardware developers in search of the pot of gold that comes with a "million seller." Because of the fierce competition among the hundreds of software and hardware development "cottages," as well as the more established computer corporations, we have seen a great contribution to the development of user-friendly systems. A multitude of new devices and techniques have been created for interfacing the user with the application. As illustrated in Figure 4.1, the popularity of the personal microcomputer has caused an explosion of new

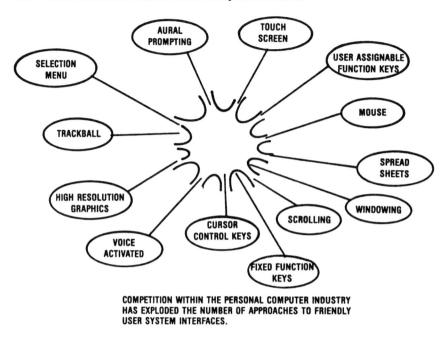

COMPETITION WITHIN THE PERSONAL COMPUTER INDUSTRY
HAS EXPLODED THE NUMBER OF APPROACHES TO FRIENDLY
USER SYSTEM INTERFACES.

Figure 4.1   The User-System Interface Explosion

techniques in the user-system interface field. Pull-down selection menus, light pens, windows, bit-mapped high-resolution graphics, user-assignable function keys, touch screens, voice recognition/synthesis, various forms of digitizer tablets, and the friendly "mouse" are a few of the more notable contributions.

As a result of this technological explosion, we have greatly expanded the repertoire of user-system interfaces available to the system designer. This does not mean that we have succeeded in developing truly user-friendly systems. Actually the proliferation of possible techniques and devices has made the job of designing a user-system interface more difficult, since there are so many more choices. Much experimentation with the new hardware and techniques is ongoing, but so many alternatives exist there are no pat answers for designing a quality user-system interface. The explosion in USI technology has actually created a gap in understanding the best ways of applying the new

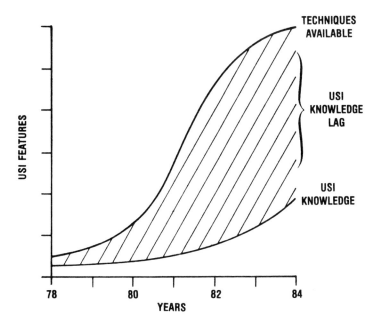

Figure 4.2   Growth of USI Techniques and Knowledge

techniques and hardware that will take years of experimentation and study to close. Figure 4.2 illustrates this knowledge lag.

In summary, the microcomputer revolution has created a situation in which:

1. The lower cost of decision support systems is making them very attractive to consumers who are not computer experts.
2. Potential users of decision support systems expect and are demanding user-friendly systems.
3. So many new techniques and hardware devices are becoming available for USI designers to work with that no standard answers exist for good user-system interface designs.

THE DECISION SUPPORT SYSTEM REQUIREMENT

What is a decision support system and, more specifically, what are its user-system interface requirements? Unfortunately, the term *decision support system* means different things to different people. For some it may be a data base management system, while for others it may be an artificial intelligence expert system with a natural language processor front end. Logically, a decision support system may be any of a wide range of systems as long as it meets the requirement of supporting the user.

This discussion will focus on the key elements that affect the user-system interface. Let us assume that the purpose of a decision support system, from the viewpoint of a human factors engineer, is to provide decision makers with tools that will *help* sort out and digest relevant information and evaluate the potential effects of various alternative actions. Remember, the term *support* as used here implies that the decision maker will be interacting with the system; the system is not a "black box" that provides answers. The primary difference between one decision support system and another is the type and amount of support each provides to the user. This, in turn, determines the type of user-system interface that is required.

This direct involvement of the decision maker with the support system is the reason that the user-system interface is so important. Thus, the better the user-system interface, the better the design of the decision support system.

Computers have traditionally played a role in the support of decision making because they can so quickly reduce large amounts of data to summary information. However, the interface between the system and the decision maker in non real-time systems has often been limited to the use of coding forms and computer-generated printouts. With the availability of microcomputer-based systems and user-friendly interfaces, decision makers can now become more involved in the direct use of new systems. With the availability of data communications, systems can now be designed that link microprocessor-based workstations with each other and with mainframe computers. The microprocessor workstations can be used for data preparation, analysis, and reporting, while the large computers can be used to pool data and do the large-number crunching and data base manipulations for which they are best suited.

REQUIREMENTS OF THE DECISION MAKER

The role of the decision maker is key to the design of a user-system interface for decision support systems. The design of every system must start with an examination of the user, the job he or she has to do, and how the system is going to help. This careful and disciplined analysis of the requirements and expectations of the user is the key to establishing clear design objectives.

While it is not good practice to generalize about a system or its users without prior analysis, in this case we shall assume that the primary users of most decision support systems will not be computer experts. They will typically fall into the category of discretionary users who make use of the system when they have questions they cannot easily answer with normal means. We can characterize the decision maker as one who wants to review trends, make projections, and verify hypotheses about a particular phenomenon. Typically this person is an expert in the field in question and knows the appropriate line of reasoning to follow in coming to a decision. The system should allow the deicision maker to manipulate and summarize the data, look for trends and relationships, and have the system project trends forward, given certain assumptions. In short, the design of the system should not contrain the user in the decision-making process.

The question for the human factors designer is, what is the best way for this user to communicate with the machine? Although a wide variety of techniques are available, the answer depends on many factors including the cost of the system, the type of information-processing models it has, and the range and type of answers the user expects. The ultimate Star Wars style decision support system, for example, would possess an artificial intelligence model, a natural language processor, a bit-mapped color graphics display, and a voice synthesizer to support verbal and graphic dialog between the decision maker and the support system. Clearly, this type of system is beyond the state of the art in 1985 and would be cost-prohibitive for most organizations.

The user-system interface is also dependent on the type of computer model, the required inputs, the amount of information in the data base, and the type of output desired. Some decision models are very data dependent. Others use algorithms, and still others use Monte Carlo sampling techniques. If a model is data dependent, it must have access to a data base or it will require the user to enter a significant amount of data. This type of model is subject to the inaccuracies of data entry errors. Monte Carlo and algorithmic models require that users provide only parametric data and are not as subject to data entry errors. Most decision support systems are set up to allow the user to play "what if" games with the system. In this case, the user-system interface must allow the user to easily change only the data and/or parameters relevant to the question, holding the other paremeters constant. For repetitive trials, the user should be able to have the results saved for later comparisons, done graphically if possible.

This leads to the other side of the decision support system requirements, the output generated by the system. The value of the system depends largely on the quality of the system products. These should be designed to meet the user's expectations and requirements, and should be immediately useful to the decision maker. Voluminous outputs are generally unacceptable because of the time necessary to study them to find the answer. Reports should be structured to provide what the decision maker needs to know. Information on turning points, inflections, or intersections in trend lines are generally of vital interest to the decision maker. Exception reports can focus the decision maker's attention, often by charting the output on a plotter or by generating graphs that support the printed output.

Many of the USI requirements depend on the type of system and type of information needed by the user. Although similarities may exist, no two systems are alike. System designers should rely on disciplined front-end analysis to define the requirement for the user-system interface, and to be certain that all user expectations are accounted for in a system specification early in the design process.

USER-SYSTEM INTERFACE

From all indications in the microcomputer revolution, it appears that decision makers are going to be more directly involved with the user-system interface in the new breed of decision support system. Therefore this chapter will examine in more detail the definition of the user-system interface.

The user-system interface has two primary dimensions:

1. *Ergonomics*—Those aspects of human engineering that deal with physical parameters, e.g., lighting, glare, size, positioning, audible sound, etc.; and
2. *Computer-user dialog*—The communications between the computer and the computer user.

As the computer field has developed, the focus on the physical configuration of computer terminal devices and their keyboards, displays, and other ancillary devices has increased in order to reduce operator fatigue and increase efficiency. The work of researchers in Europe and the United Kingdom has led to the adoption of the European DIN (Deutsche Industrie Normandy) ergonomic standards. Their influence can be seen in the detached, low-profile, tiltable keyboards with muted pastel color-coded keys and adjustable matte surface displays now appearing in many computer terminals and personal computers.

For the most part, many of the ergonomic considerations of the standard user-system interface have been answered in the "human engineered" computer workstations because of the influence of the European DIN standards. However, a wave of new hardware devices growing out of the personal computer revolution in the United States is causing human factors engineers to reconsider their designs. Touch screen response systems, trackballs, various types of digitizing tablets, voice synthesis and response systems, as well as the "mouse" have recently made their appearance. What will be the impact of these new devices and how can they best be used in decision support systems? Not enough data is available on the performance of these new interface devices to establish their effectiveness. Clearly, they have potential for providing very user friendly systems, but their contribution to the user-system interface has yet to be proven.

Now let us look at the user-computer dialog dimension of the user-system interface. For many years, a computer-user dialog was entirely the realm of experts in computer operations. They were experts at the special codes and procedures that made the computers run. They used keyboard sequences such as "control-x" or "/*" to make things happen. The computers responded in kind with printed symbols and messages such as " " and "syntax err".

For a number of years the trend has been to make user dialog understandable by people other than computer operations personnel. Situations using real-time systems and data entry systems in which large numbers of people had to learn to work with a system led to the development of less cryptic user-system interaction. *Design of Man-Computer Dialogues* (Martin 1973) was a leader in the design of quality user-system dialog. Martin's text is still an excellent guideline. In 1975 Engel and Granda published guidelines for man/display interfaces. Smith (1982) tried to categorize all possible types of user-system interaction and to suggest guidelines for designers. However, the greatest impact on the user-system interface has been caused by the introduction of personal computers, which quickly showed that many computer-user dialogs were not suited to the wider population of noncomputer experts. The resulting improvements in user-computer dialogs within the competitive framework of the personal microcomputer revolution are having a profound effect on the entire computer industry.

THE USER-FRIENDLY SYSTEM

One of the most overused terms applied to computer systems in the past five years is *user friendly*. It is one of the claims that developers feel they must include when describing their system to convince the prospective buyer that all specialized operator codes and messages have been eliminated. Who would buy a system that is not user friendly and run the risks depicted in the cartoon?

What is a user-friendly system? At the risk of oversimplification, let us first attempt to understand what users typically

Reprinted with permission of author.

mean when using the term. Although people may have trouble describing a user-friendly system, they can usually tell when a system is not being very friendly. One of the problems is that not everyone has the same view of user-friendliness. Some typical reactions of a novice user to a system might be:

> The system didn't tell me what to do next.
> The system wouldn't let me go back and change my entry.
> I'm not sure if I made the correct entry or not.
> I don't understand what I did wrong.
> How do I change my response?
> I have too much trouble finding the right keys.
> I can't understand the error messages.
> I have to type so much.
> There are so many things to remember.

A more experienced user's reaction might be:

The system makes me go through too many procedures.
I don't need a dissertation every time I make an error.
The system keeps going back to the base menu.
I have to keep typing in the same things over and over again.
Why can't I go from *A* to *C* without doing *B* every time?
Why do I have to enter that information when I know it's in the data base?

Both users think that the system is not very friendly. This example shows that differences in the perception of user-friendliness exist among users with different levels of experience. The novice lacks understanding, finds it difficult to remember the correct procedures, and lives in fear of doing something wrong. If the novice user is discouraged by this apparent unfriendliness, he or she may choose not to use the system. On the other hand, the experienced user is bothered by repetitive entries and having to go through selection menus and other aids designed for the novice users. The experienced user does not want to be impeded or restrained by the system.

To complicate matters, somewhere between the novice and the experienced user is the occasional user who needs help only some of the time. The novice and occasional user typically need more support from the system in terms of help routines, prompts, and selection menus. Their options and their next moves must be obvious at all times. Dialogs must be designed to minimize errors, and when errors are made, these users must be told what they did wrong and how to correct the error. Since novice and occasional users do not know the system, they do not understand the many options that are available. System designers generally provide user aids such as selection menus and help functions to meet their needs.

Too much support of this type will get in the way of experienced users. They should be given a means of suppressing or bypassing user aids. One option is to provide experienced users with alternate methods of more direct entries such as user-definable function keys or macrocommands.

Some things are unfriendly to both novice and experienced user alike. When a user has to reenter data or when a user inadvertently loses a file, the system design is clearly in error and should be corrected.

DESIGNING A USER-SYSTEM INTERFACE

The process of designing a quality user-system interface is not unlike that of a good structured system design process. In fact, the design of the USI should go hand-in-hand with the system design process. The first step is a structured decomposition of the primary user functions into the specific *task requirements*. At the same time an analysis should be made of the data to be passed from the user to the system and vice versa. The *data flow* may be analyzed using data flow diagrams from the structured system design methodology.

These data flow diagrams will identify all the user-system *transactions* for each requirement. The transactions should be categorized by type, and estimates made of the frequency of each transaction. The estimates of user frequency will be helpful in determining the transactions that may require more attention in the design.

The process should include an analysis of the users and the *capabilities* they bring to the table. Some of the factors to be considered are the number of users, their level of education and experience, the amount of time available for training, the percentage of time they will be using the system in their job, the average number of years of experience in the job, and whether they will be dedicated or occasional users of the system. The answers to these questions will help determine the criticality of the user-system interface and the amount of support to be provided.

Although the ideal is to design the optimal user-friendly system, remember that the greater the amount of support the system provides to the user, the more sophisticated the design and the more programming necessary to achieve the design. Although more design and programming will drive the cost of the system development higher, a system that is not used because of a poor user interface provides no return on its investment.

Once the task requirements, the data flow, the transactions, and the user capabilities have been defined, the designers can begin to design the user-system interaction. Standards should be established early, including selection menus, function keys, prompting sequences, report formats, error routines, and help support. Standard terminology familiar to the users should be adopted for all system messages and prompts. These standards along with examples from the system design, should be reviewed with the prospective users. User involvement in this part of the design process will pay off later.

Once agreement is reached on the general philosophy for the USI, the design work can get down to specifics. A tree of selection menus can be laid out starting from a base menu of user options to each of the individual data entry or request procedures. Procedures for user prompting can be specified using flowcharts of user-system interaction. After all this design work is completed, another review should be held with the future user group.

Once the design of the USI is solidified, the designers must work with the programmers to ensure that it is implemented correctly. No matter how good the design, a number of unanticipated interactions will always have to be modified or added. It is essential that any changes follow the general guidelines for the design. If possible, in-process reviews should be held with the customer as the system is being built. Hands-on demonstrations early in the software development process can confirm the design or identify weaknesses before it becomes too difficult to make changes.

One promising technique used for developing and testing a user-system interface involves the use of a user-system interface prototyping system. Wong and Reid (1982) describe a USI prototyping language that allows much of the USI to be simulated on a separate prototyping system prior to any software development or hardware configuration. This system is used for the development of the USI and testing of the actual dialogs in hands-on tests with the future user or customer. By using a prototyping system, the design may easily be modified and different types of hardware devices substituted to determine the most effective design. Although prototyping systems are expensive and are typically used for multimillion-dollar real-time applications, the concept is useful for smaller systems using off-the-shelf software packages.

CONCLUSIONS/RECOMMENDATIONS

In the current state of affairs of the computer industry, hardly a day goes by that a new software or hardware package is not being introduced. The flood of new product announcements brings expanded capabilities, new ideas, and great promise for the future. It is truly an exciting period in which to live, but also an unsettling one. If you commit to a design today, you can expect it to be obsolete tomorrow. However, you cannot let the pace of progress intimidate your own progress. To get into a system, you must take the best of what is available at a given point, go with it, and make it work. With technology moving as fast as it does today, most systems will always be behind the latest advances.

The development of a user-friendly user-system interface is an important part of any system development. The user interface is the single most visible part of any new microcomputer system today. Its design cannot and should not be left to chance and must be approached carefully.

Fortunately, the last two years have given us some excellent examples of what can be done with a user-friendly interface. These examples should be reviewed and tried out as part of any new system specification. They contain many good ideas. In the area of decision support systems, some excellent off-the-shelf packages merit consideration. Although these packages may not be able to do all of the things that are necessary for your application, certainly some parts of the problem can be approached with existing commercial packages. The experience gained in working with the commercial packages will be well worth your while when you start to specify the system that you need. Working with the existing commercial packages will open your eyes to problems and vistas that you would not have thought of otherwise. By working with existing packages, you or your people will be much better prepared to write the specifications of a system that will meet all your needs.

System Specification

It makes no difference whether you are creating a specification for a new system or selecting an existing off-the-shelf package; a number of basic standards should be established for the user-system interface to ensure user acceptance and successful transition of operations from manual to automated methods.

Displays and Controls   First and most important is the need to keep all displays immediately understandable to the user. If a display is cluttered or confusing, it will be difficult for the user to understand and will therefore become an excuse to resist using the system. If the user cannot find what he or she expects on a display 95% of the time, use of the system will not be rewarding, and the user will find a reason not to use it. The best test of a display is to ask the question, "Is its purpose immediately obvious?" If you have to hesitate to answer, chances are that the display is not going to communicate its purpose to the user.

Second, the user must feel that he or she is in control when using the system. The user should never be in the situation of saying, "What do I do next?", or "Why did that happen?", or "How do I . . . ?" The user should, with a minimum of training, be able to navigate around the system without getting lost. This can generally be done with a system of selection menus such as are found in systems like Lotus 1-2-3 or Multiplan. Such systems give the user excellent prompts about menu selections and frequently have help routines linked directly to these menus. Figure 4.4 shows an exaple of a horizontally oriented selection menu and its prompts from Lotus 1-2-3. Assists of this type are very helpful to the new and the occasional user and do not get in the way of the experienced user.

User-System Dialog   All user-system dialogs should attempt to minimize the complexity of user entry tasks as well as the probability of creating entry errors. Laborious or tedious dialog will lead to user frustration and errors. Generally, dialog

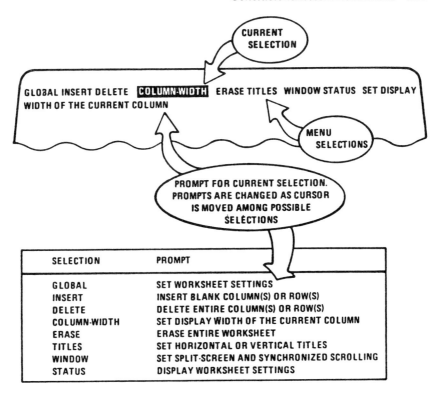

Figure 4.4 Lotus 1-2-3 Display with Selection Menu and Prompts

can be kept simple and efficient by minimizing the number of keystrokes and eliminating the requirement for touch-typing. It is best to assume that most decision support system users will not know the "qwerty" keyboard well enough to be efficient typists. Limiting interaction to the use of the space bar (to move the cursor) and the return key (to make entries) is desirable, since it minimizes the amount of time the user has to search for other keys.

Wherever possible, cursor position entry selection menus such as those in Multiplan and Lotus 1-2-3 should be used to minimze the need to type for menu selection. Figure 4.5 shows the difference between cursor selection menus and numeric entry selection menus. Although the numeric selection requires fewer

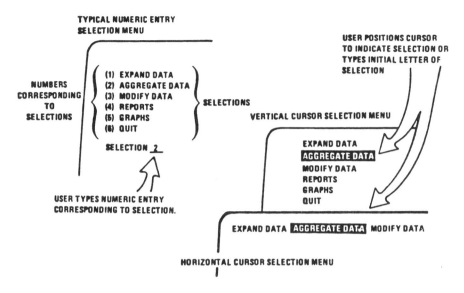

Figure 4.5   Comparison of Selection Menu Techniques

keystrokes, the entry task is more difficult since the user must translate the desired selection to a number and then find and enter the number on the keyboard. To minimize typed entries, prefills of default, logical, or computed entries should be used whenever possible.

Consistency   User displays and dialog with the system should be consistent across various applications. Users can be totally confused when the method of interaction changes from one application to another. Newer integrated software packages such as Lotus Symphony, MacIntosh, and Windows establish standard patterns for user-system dialog across all applications. The user is completely unaware of the change in application software from word processing, to spreadsheet, to graphing, because the style of dialog remains the same.

Reentrant Dialog   People who work at computer workstations are frequently interrupted—interruptions are simply a part of modern-day existence. User-system dialog must allow for various types of interruption and user-friendly *reentrance*. Users may also interrupt themselves by requesting additional information or a help routine, or the system may interrupt by displaying an error message. In real-time systems, users may receive an alert that requires immediate action. Whatever the nature of the interruption, the work in progress should be preserved, and the user should be able to return to the same status without repeating entries. Note that most spreadsheet systems such as Multiplan and Lotus position the cursor at spreadsheet load to the same cell at which it was located when the sheet was last saved.

Alternate Entry Methods   Decision support systems are typically used by occasional or discretionary users. Because these users do not become expert in the use of the system, they often need a help function, selection menus, and prompting. However, there are occasions when this type of user will use the system regularly and repeatedly for the same or similar query or analysis. In this type of application, the user becomes expert and does not want the bother of selection menus and prompts. What is needed in this case is the ability for users to define macrocommands that string together a series of menu selections and other entries into a single macrocommand. This allows the user to run his or her application by making a single entry of the macrocommand. The design should allow macrocommands to be assigned to function keys or a selection menu, thus reducing the entry of the macrocommand to a single key stroke. This capability also allows the user to define special purpose macros and allow less experienced clerical personnel to run the application on a regular basis.

Error Routines   Although possible sources of entry errors should be minimized by use of simple entries and selection menus, all systems will inevitably need some error messages. Error messages should be friendly and helpful, particularly to the new user who is not a computer buff. At the risk of alienating the experienced users, error messages should characterize the error that has been detected and, more important, provide directions for resolving the error condition. To satisfy users of varying experience, it may be desirable to have two tiers of error messages. For example, the novice could press the question mark key after receiving a brief error notification, to initiate a more complete explanation and directions for correction. The experienced user could bypass the error dissertation by pressing return and continuing.

Report Capabilities Two basic types of reporting capabilities are provided in most decision support systems: standardized or canned reports, and ad hoc reports. The standard reports should be available to the user through selections via a library of standard reports. As with any library, the selections should be categorized logically, for example, by a selection menu tree. Users may want to assign a report initiation request to a function key or allow a direct entry such as "report abc", where abc is the serial number of a standard report.

More mileage can be obtained with standard reports if users are allowed to enter qualifying parameters at the time of submission. This should be done with a series of user prompts that appear following the report request, before the submission of the request. The prompts may have default entries for the most common requests that will eliminate the need for frequent user entries. Also, wherever possible, the prompts for standard reports should be use selections rather than constructed (typed) entries. Use of selection entries whenever possible will reduce entry errors and the incidence of erroneous reports.

Online Report Display Most decision support system users expect to display reports at their workstations. Online review of reports serves several purposes. The user may want to make a rapid inspection of the data either in preparation for printing the report, or to ascertain that prior updates have been made properly. Or the user may wish to look at the report online as an alternative to printing the report.

To facilitate the rapid review of reports online, the workstation software must permit the user to scroll and page throughout the report contents. This requires up and down scrolling and paging as well as right and left scrolling of report data in a manner similar to automated spreadsheet systems. However, column and row heading information must be continuously displayed in the manner of spreadsheet windowing so that the user has a reference to the data being displayed. When a multiple-page report is displayed, the current page number should be included in the heading information. This information is necessary particularly if the system has a print screen option that provides the user with an option to print the whole report. Figure 4.6 illustrates the types of things that are helpful to the decision maker when reviewing a displayed report.

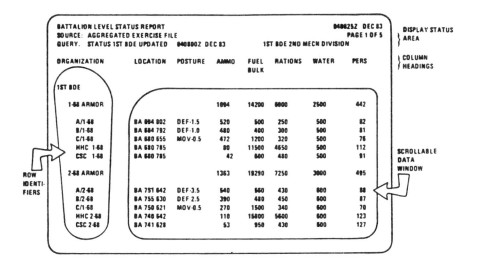

1. *Display Status Area*—Provides information on the current display contents including:

   Title of the report
   Date/time created
   Date/time of last update
   Source(s) of the data
   Report query if applicable
   Page number of total pages.

2. *Column Headings*—Labels for the data columns being displayed.

3. *Row Identifiers*—Identifiers for data being displayed in each row.

4. *Data Window*—Scrollable area in which data is displayed.

Figure 4.6   Decision Support System Report Display Requirements

Ad Hoc Query Language   Users of decision support systems will generally want to make interrogations of the data contained within a system. Many of the interrogations can be made through the standard reporting capabilities discussed above. However, what users typically expect from decision support systems is the capability to go beyond the confines of the standard interrogations and reports provided with the system. To meet this need, a user-friendly query language must be provided.

James Martin (1981) describes an easy-to-use IBM data base language called QUERY-BY-EXAMPLE. QUERY-BY-EXAMPLE contains many of the query capabilities expected in decision support systems. These include the ability to create files, relations, and tables, as well as to access data, perform manipulations such as sorting, and make computations including totals, maximum and minimum values, and averages. To prepare a query, a user calls up a logical record from a data base. The record appears as a form on the display. The user defines both the query and the format of the query report by making entries in the appropriate columns of the logical record. Figure 4.7 contains an example of a user query. The most important part of the QUERY-BY-EXAMPLE system is the ease with which the user can query the data and formulate the report format at the same time.

LOGICAL RECORD FOR EMPLOYEE

EMPLOYEE #	NAME	SALARY	DEPT.	YEAR OF HIRE	TRAINING
P	P	20000		1977	FORTRAN

This user query means: Print the employee number and name of all employees that have a salary greater than $20000 and have training in Fortran.

Figure 4.7   Example of QUERY-BY-EXAMPLE.

Online Report Help Facility   Most systems being created today have user help facilities that provide procedural help to the user. Additional help features with displayed data are desirable in decision support systems to help users understand the reports produced by the system. An *online report help* feature would allow the user to obtain an explanation of the type and/or source of data found in the reports. The user could also obtain information regarding specific headings in the report by placing the cursor on the heading and pressing the question mark key on the workstation. (Some systems have a HELP key, but the defacto standard of using the "?" key has developed within the personal computer field.) The help information displayed would be stored with the report format in the host computer and transmitted to the workstation with the report.

Graphics Display Capability   A picture is worth a thousand words. A decision suport system should be able to translate data into graphs and charts. Many fine business graphics packages are available today to provide excellent examples of what can be done in this area. As a minimum, the user should be able to specify the generation of line, bar, scatter, and pie charts based upon data from the decision support system. The user should be able to specify, through user prompts, the information identifying the graph. All graphs should be displayable on the workstation display and printable on the workstation dot matrix printer. For more extensive graphs, pen plotters of various sizes and features are available as output devices to most microcomputer systems.

Data Review and Modification   One of the primary reasons for online review of data is to identify data in need of modification. Some decision support system users, although not all, should have the ability to perform online data modifications. A cognizant user responsible for the integrity of the data base needs to have the ability to review and modify data in the system. Ideally, this user would be able to modify data appearing on the display by simply overtyping the displayed data. Because of the criticality of data updates in many systems, this action should initiate a user prompt containing the original data value, and the new data value, along with a request that the user confirm or cancel the change. This type of prompt allows the user to check the entry before it is entered into the data base.

Bulk Data Maintenance Tasks   At some time, most decision support systems will require the entry of substantial amounts of new data or the submission of a significant number of update transactions. Although data entry tasks are not normally the responsibility of the decision maker, to preserve the integrity of the data it is important that a decision support system provide means for accurate and efficient data base maintenance. Because of the amount of work required, these transactions have historically been created through use of coding forms, keypunching, verification, and bulk update transactions.

In a fully automated decision support system, provision should be made to capture bulk data base entries and updates in an online data entry session or through data transfer from an external system.

External Data Capture   Most microcomputers available today have provision for data communications. Data communications from an external system can be a valuable source of data for a decision support system, but before data can be transferred from one system to another, proper arrangements must be made. Although the concept of data communications is simple, the most difficult transaction is the first one. Making all the technical arrangements for this type of transaction is definitely not user friendly. Perhaps in the future this type of transaction will be easy, but at present, a number of specialists must be brought in to establish the necessary interaction.

Initially, data communication must be established through compatible data transmission devices (called modems) and communications lines. Then both the sending and the receiving systems must have appropriate software to support the transmission of data.

Once all the technical provisions are made, the user of the decision suport system should be able to initiate a request for data transmission from the external system without having to enter any "computerese." When the transaction is complete, the system should provide the user with direct confirmation.

Online Data Maintenance   Online bulk data entry can be done if the decision support system provides a *data entry form* capability. Data entry forms can be created that match coding forms or the source data. The user or data entry clerk makes the entries by typing the data in the online data form. The system automatically positions the cursor to each data field as the user makes the entries. Most systems will also provide a listing of transactions for verification.

Data entry forms generally provide a number of data entry assists to minimize data entry errors and speed the process. Some of these capabilities are:

1. *Prefilled fields*—Two types of prefilled data fields in which the data entry is automatically provided by the system are possible: (a) protected, in which the user is not able to change the entry, and (b) overtype, in which the user could elect to accept the prefilled entry or change it by overtyping the prefilled data.

   Several types of entries may use prefilled fields. These can be the data from the same field in the prior entry, the data from the prior entry incremented, the current data and/or time, the user identification, the current data base, the most common or expected entry for this field, or a computed value based upon one or several prior entries. Use of these types of prefills can simplify and speed the data entry process and provide greater accuracy.

2. *Must fill fields*—This type of field does not let the user advance the cursor to the next field without making an appropriate entry.

3. *Alpha only and numeric only fields*—This type of field automatically rejects either alphabetic or numeric data by prompting the user of the error.

4. *Range check fields*—This type of field automatically checks to see whether the entry was within a present range.

5. *Option selection entries*—Many data entries require the user to enter one of a finite set of entries. When this is the case and the number of possible entries is fairly small,

less than fifteen in most instances, a data entry system may reduce the number of errors by presenting this entry as a selection menu, as shown in Figure 4.8.

This assist would present the user with a list of possible options for a given field directly below the field. This capability would look and operate similarly to the "pull down" selection menus initiated by Apple Computer, Inc., on the Lisa user-system interface and now further implemented on the Macintosh. The user could select any of the options by repeatedly pressing the space bar to move the cursor down to the desired option. Upon reaching the desired option, the user would make the entry with the return key, at which time the option would appear in the entry area and the cursor would move to the next entry cell.

Although this type of entry capability is attractive to inexperienced users, many experienced data entry personnel would not find it helpful. For this reason, the capability of typing the entry should be permitted, with appropriate error checking.

SUMMARY

It is difficult to write about a quickly moving target, in this case, the rapidly developing field of microcomputers. We are living in a truly exciting technological period, with many creative minds developing highly innovative approaches to the uses of microcomputers. The future of microcomputer-based decision support systems holds great promise.

The development or selection of a decision support system should be done with an understanding and appreciation of the many developments now going on in the microprocessor world. Careful, disciplined analysis of the user requirements and capabilities at the front end is all-important to having a successful system and a quality user-system interface. Use of prototyping to develop a good user-system interface is valuable, but time-consuming and expensive. An examination of the commercially available products is a good place to start. Many excellent exam-

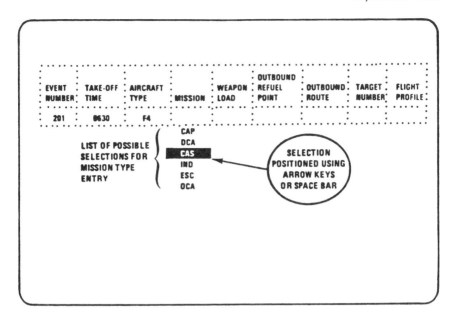

Figure 4.8 Spreadsheet Type Data Entry Form Utilizing "Pull-Down" Selection Menu (Example for BattleCalc Data Entry Form)

ples of user-system interfaces exist within the commercial personal computer arena, which can be helpful in matching the user-system interface with system requirements and with user experience and sophistication in computer use. Finally, when you have done all your work and developed or selected your system and have begun to use it, be positive and try not to think about the fact that surely its user-system interface is already out of date.

REFERENCES

Engel, Stephen E., and Richard E. Granda. 1975. *Guidelines for Man/Display Interfaces*. IBM Technical Report. Poughkeepsie, N.Y.: IBM.

Foley, James D. 1983. Managing the Design of User-Computer Interfaces. *Computer Graphics World*, December, 47–56.

Martin, James. 1973. *Design of Man-Computer Dialogues*. Englewood Cliffs, N.J.: Prentice-Hall.

——— 1981. *An End User's Guide to Data Bases.*Englewood Cliffs, N.J.: Prentice-Hall.

Smith, Sidney L. 1982. User-System Interface Design for Computer-Based Information Systems. Prepared for Deputy for Technical Operations and Product Assurance, Electronic Systems Division, Air Force Systems Command, United States Air Force. Hanscom Air Force Base, Mass.: April.

Wong, Peter C. S., and Eric R. Reid. 1982. FLAIR—User Inferface Dialog Design Tool. *Computer Graphics* 16(3): 87–98.

5

Enhancing the Role of Microcomputers in Command/Control Systems: An Inquiry into "Feedforward" Technology

John W. Sutherland

Increasingly, microcomputers are being employed as low-level links in the chain of information system facilities designed to effect distributed command/control configurations. Usually located at the lowest order, remote- or forward-echelon units of a geographically dispersed organization, micro-type computers will generally have two roles: they will be programmed to assist in the execution of the essentially well-bounded, tractable decision functions that tend to devolve on such units, but will also operate as intelligent terminals linking lower order units with the more powerful information-processing facilities owned by higher echelon command/control elements. Should the former be confronted by a problem that exceeds the resolution power of its local resources, the latter are expected to pass forward—in effective real-time—an appropriate set of decision premises or solution specifications. The key here, of course, is that the command/control facilities are embedded; should it fail for some reason or be deliberately interrupted as a result of a competitor initiative, overall organizational losses may be serious indeed. Where such interruptions are at all probable, organizations might consider augmenting traditional distributed system architectures with "feedforward" provisions. These have the effect of equipping lower order units with a capability for dealing with issues normally reserved for higher order elements, thus expanding the range of situations over which the former can be expected to successfully "stand alone." Of perhaps more general interest, these same provisions offer an attractive alternative to artificial intelligence technology as a basis for developing truly portable knowledge-based systems, and may also serve as a means for reducing the likelihood of distributed systems suffering "overload" when forced to operate under stress.

DEFAULT CONDITIONS IN DISTRIBUTED SYSTEM CONFIGURATIONS

The advent of distributed data processing architecture, coupled with recent advances in telecommunications capabilities, has authored something of a shift in basic managerial technology. Particularly, an increasing number or organizations (especially those resident in competitive environments) may now be said to be operating under what amounts to a *real-time command/control posture*. The distribution of information system facilities and decision prerogatives typical of such a configuration are shown in Figure 5.1.

In the command/control context, the much-touted extension of genuine decentralization (greater symmetry in the allocation of authority and decision support facilities among organizational units at various levels of the hierarchy) has not really been the most significant effect of the transition to distributed system configurations. More pertinent is the employment of technical innovations to actually intensify the extent to which higher echelon units are able to orchestrate the behavior of subordinate

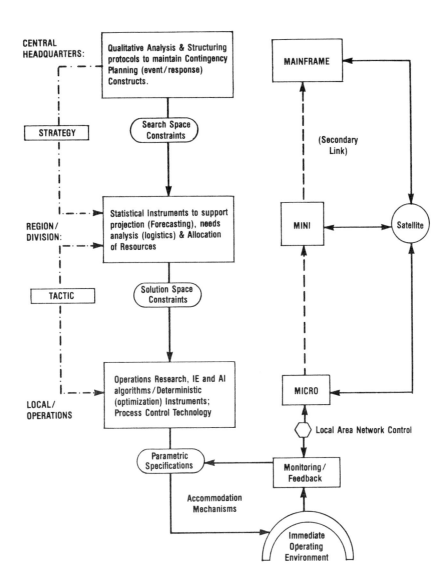

Figure 5.1 Prototypical Command/Control Configuration (by Level, Decision Support Facility, and Hardware)

organizational elements, and a consequent increase in the extent to which the functions performed by these lower order units depend upon inputs derived from their superiors—often via the channels that connect the microcomputers resident at local installations with the system instrumentation serving the latter. For the network structure in which modern distributed systems are embedded makes available real-time linkages among the different organizational levels, which may in turn be taken as a practical basis for constantly expanding the set of decision categories that demand a superior's advisement or release. Higher order functionaries are thus led toward a feeling of immediacy and intimacy with a situation from which they are in fact remote.

It is then critical to understand that when advocates of distributed configurations talk about their contribution to decentralization, what they have in mind (though this is seldom made explicit) is not decentralization of decision prerogatives, but rather decentralization of data processing functions, per se. As a consequence, a large number of empirical excursions into distributed system technology may have done very little to increase either the autonomy or raw problem-resolution capabilities of line units and can, in some instances, be posed to have actually increased the net vulnerability of the host organization. Consider, in this regard, the simple typology in Figure 5.2 setting out the several "states" in which a network-based command/control system might appear.

The focus of this typology is on some organizational unit existing at some lower level of the hierarchy, most particularly, a forward-echelon unit remote from its tactical and strategic superiors (a local branch of some geographically dispersed commercial organization; a military unit deployed in some forward areas of operations). The dimensions of the typology thus represent the primary qualifiers in the command/control environment: the condition of the linkages among the various levels of the organization, and the extent to which the organizational unit is confronted by a problem it is routinely equipped to handle. The top-left quadrant represents the best of all possible worlds: the unit has contact with some superior organizational unit, and is faced with problems for which its training and facilities are

	CONGRUENT EVENT:	EXCEPTIONAL EVENT:
Command/Control Links Intact	Primary processing methodology in force	Feedback data on local situation to higher order unit.
Command/Control Links Severed	Backup processing modality employed/manual or local alternative.	Feedforward facilities

Figure 5.2   Typology of Network-based Command Control System

adequate, i.e., the event to which the unit must respond is "congruent" with respect to its capabilities. In the top-right quadrant, the unit is confronted by some event that falls outside its usual repertoire, but is able, in real-time, to obtain appropriate advice and direction from some higher echelon authorities via the command/control link. Indeed, it is here that we find the basic rationale behind the contemporary interest in network-based, distributed systems.

It is, however, the remaining cases that most concern us here—the instances where a forward-echelon unit is forced to "stand alone" over some interval. The degree of dysfunction that will accompany the forced transition to a stand alone posture will first of all depend on the nature of the event—the degree to which it is well-precedented for the unit at hand, or extraordinary—and secondly on the extent to which even routine operational functions have come to depend on the receipt of inputs or decision premises passed down from above. To elaborate on these cases, we might focus briefly on their implications for that organization that, perhaps more than any other, is known for the intensity of its embrace of modern distributed and telecommunications technology, the United States Navy.

Consider the organizational unit of interest to be a naval vessel (or set of such) operating in the open ocean. Also assume that the unit(s) have, on board, a microcomputer facility of some kind, which is in effect the end-link in a command/control chain dependent, for the most part, on the real-time interchanges between ships and shore allowed by modern communication satellites. In the lower left-hand quadrant of the typology is the situation where the unit is engaging in operations with which it is familiar, but has for some reason been deprived of its link with other network members. In the most benign case, the unit will simply be forced to shift to some secondary methodology for performing necessary tasks. For example, it may be that the issue involves relatively normal navigational problems, and that the severed link had been providing the vessel with LORAN fixes, or some new equivalent. In their absence, the vessel would have to revert to some more primitive method of reckoning position and determining course parameters. The point is, that the navigational function is one for which feasible alternative methodologies exist should a normal command/control communications connection be violated, though as a rule, a price will have to be paid in terms of the precision of the locally derived solution, or in terms of the incremental time involved, in its generation. There are, however, certain functions that cannot be performed at all should the network be interrupted. A good example would be "over the horizon targeting," which almost invariably demands a remote platform (sensor) of some kind and more or less constant communications back to the warship or weapons platform; should the link between these two platforms be severed, the combat role for the asset in question will be sorely constrained. More seriously, should an adversary's remote targeting capabilities remain intact, then the friendly vessel is in real peril.

But of absolutely greatest concern is the situation that would occur in the remaining quadrant of the typology, which in the context of our naval scenario would mean:

1. There is a severing of the telecommunications link between ship and shore, either because of a concerted elimination of a major component by an adversary (e.g., a

satellite is destroyed) or because of some sort of inadvertent event such as extraordinary levels of radiational interference or a mechanical malfunction.

2. An operational unit is confronted by a situation that would normally be handled at a higher echelon, or is placed into the position of having action alternatives whose consequences are far more global and generally impactful than was anticipated and allowed for under the standing information system and managerial structure.

Such a situation is perhaps not as far-fetched as it might appear. In fact, recent naval history tells of several instances where a mismapping of events onto organizational units resulted in a simultaneous failure (or degradation) of the command/control links. There was, for example, the Pueblo incident, where a vessel commander was forced into a confrontation whose parameters and implications were entirely beyond those for which he had been trained. Or there was the case of the USS Liberty, which in 1967 was attacked by Israeli warplanes and ships, leaving 34 Americans dead and wounding 171 others. A situation where there is a simultaneous interruption of the communications network and a mismapping between event and echelon is not so far-fetched as to warrant neglect and, indeed, might very well be expected to occur by adversary design as a trigger to any large-scale conflict.[1]

Thus, when we move to the lower right-hand quadrant of the typology we depart from the realm of precedented or familiar system concepts, and enter full stride into what, to this point, remains largely uncharted ground. For here an organizational unit is not only challenged by an effectively unprecedented event, but required to deal with it largely without benefit of any timely advice or input from its tactical and/or strategic superiors. Moreover, because the event at hand is incongruent with respect to the repertoire of situations the unit is programmed to handle, there will be no ready-made secondary methodology that can be put into effect (as was the case in the lower left-hand quadrant). Thus we have two critical conditions: on the one hand, the break in the command/control communications link has put the forward-echelon unit into the position of having to *stand alone* over some interval; while the emergence of an incongruent event has, in effect, put that unit and the organization itself into positions of *stress*—into a situation where a decision error becomes both probable and potentially costly in terms of either real or opportunity losses. It is here that we find the rationale for a system protocol that we shall refer to as *feedforward*.

FEEDFORWARD: LOGICAL AND TECHNICAL PREMISES

The term *feedforward* shall be reserved here to define the following: a set of provisions instituted by an organization that results in lower order units being equipped with certain system facilities (hardware, data and model bases) that will provide some level of stand-alone capability should they be confronted by events that would in normal circumstances by handled by higher level organizational units. Such provisions should only interest organizations that have particularly critical missions (e.g., national or civil defense), and that are forced to operate in significantly complex environments—in highly competitive, rapidly changing, and "imperfect" markets, or in fields at which an intelligent adversary is at play. This restriction is necessary because positioning an organization towards a genuine feedforward posture will involve what may often be a rather radical restructuring of basic managerial and information system characteristics. For, again, feedforward in the context of these pages is designed to put microcomputers to work doing jobs that are targeted for larger, more powerful machines in normal distributed processing configurations.

The types of accomodations that will have to be made under the feedforward modality are:

1. Initially, organizations must abandon traditional contingency planning technology in favor of some scheme that will serve to maximize the amount of standing intelligence (a priori strategic discipline and tactical doctrine)

that can be supported at all levels of the organization—
including those levels where microcomputers are the primary decision support medium. One way to do this is to
invoke procedures that have elsewhere been defined
under the paradigm of *Structured System Design*[2], the
key to which is a radical shift in the level of abstraction
at which event/response alternatives are defined.

2. If microcomputers are to be employed to attack what are
   in effect nonoperational level problems (i.e., those of tactical or even strategic significance), then some way must
   be found to minimize the analytical and system resources
   required to handle exceptional problems and at the same
   time to maximize the "learning" efficiency of stand-alone
   units. One way to accomplish this is to displace traditional units of analysis—data base elements qua decision
   premises—with what are called *templates*. Their effect
   is to considerably compress both the time required to
   properly define some at least partially unprecedented
   problem, and the interval delay in the development of a
   treatment scheme.

3. As a complement to the above, there will have to be a
   recognition of the need to alter basic analytical procedures and processing methodologies in order to allow
   microcomputer configurations to deal with decision problems that would normally be thought to exceed their raw
   resolution power, to be too complex in terms of the
   number of variables involved or the transactions that
   would have to be performed in any interval. This then
   suggests the need for certain innovations that will serve
   to minimize average transaction time and system resource loadings at microcomputer sights. Three innovations are particularly important: (*a*) the employment of
   *graphic solution protocols as substitutes for traditional
   mathematical/numerical methods*; (*b*) a shift from the
   usual fixed-logic, single-state processing algorithms to
   the types of model-base components that would be defined under *simoptimization* methodology; and (*c*) certain
   applications of parallel processing protocols.[3]

Feedforward operations thus pose the need for certain non-trivial organizational accommodations, mainly in terms of requirements for greater analytical sophistication on the part of managers at all levels and also for system designers. Moreover, there will usually be some price paid in terms of the precision of the solutions generated under feedforward technology as opposed to those that would have been obtained under traditional decision-making protocols. Yet some loss of precision is perhaps a reasonable price to pay when the alternatives are considered: no genuine provisions for stand-alone operations, such that critical decisions may, by default, be predicated on little more than unaided, undisciplined intution; or, just as serious, that the lack of local rationalizing facilities will lead to a kind of paralysis, such that potentially dangerous events are allowed to run their course entirely unchallenged.

The remainder of these pages will show how the various feedforward provisions might actually be developed and put to work, following the general logic outlined in Figure 5.3. First, an equivocation is in order: interpolative programming and templating operations remain largely just speculative in significance; they have not really been attempted in any controlled way in real-world contexts. The following discussion will thus be directed at their elaboration and defense, yet the arguments raised must be considered merely suggestive of lines of development potential users might follow. With regard to the three process techniques just mentioned (graphic solution protocols, simoptimization models, and parallel processing), they can be dealt with quite briefly here, as ample references exist in other literature. Discussion will focus on those aspects unique to the feedforward context, which in the case of graphics and simoptimization are quite substantial. However, the capabilities under discussion are projective only, not facilities that can be picked up on the open market and put right to work in actual organizations.

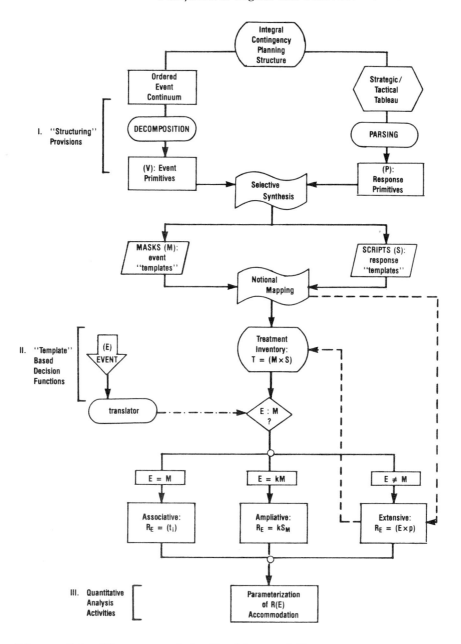

Figure 5.3   Elements of the Feedforward Process

STRUCTURED SYSTEM REFERENTS AS ALTERNATIVES TO INTEGRAL DECISION MODELS

Most organizations with critical missions, operating in competitive environments, may be said to share the following basic managerial philosophy: organizational *readiness* involves the development and maintenance of a contingency planning structure that serves to define a strategic/tactical response appropriate to each of the various event-alternatives that can be assigned some significant probability of occurrence.

Under this paradigm, the sine qua non of organizational survival is *preadaptation*, such that the organization has invested in a collection of resources sufficient to meet some subset of these alternatives, and has predefined the way in which these resources would be allocated and put to work given any of the predictable events. In the most basic sense, then, management by contingency planning ultimately resolves into a mapping of more or less elaborately specified resource/response alternatives onto a set of situational or event alternatives, with the key determinants of the process being the following:

- The number of different event alternatives to which significant probabilities of occurence must be assigned, and the degree of difference (heterogeneity or variance) among the members of the event set (this is a reflection of the complexity inherent in the environment in which the organization has elected or been assigned to operate.)
- The range over which the event-alternatives extend, which is an indicator of the scope of the organization's mission (or the breadth of the functions for which it is responsible)

As a general rule, then, the more complex an organization's environment and/or the more extensive its mission, the larger and more intricate will be the contingency planning structure it must maintain in order to be deemed "ready" in some sufficient degree. It should be clear that any addition to the event-set implies a geometric increase in the load on system resources under the normal managerial configuration graphed earlier in Figure 5.1. For in a hierarchical framework, any additional strategy implies the elaboration of one or perhaps more tactical response alternatives, which in turn implies perhaps many associated expansions of operations-level specifications, and so forth. The strain on system storage and processing equipments is thus truly awesome for sizable contingency planning structures, and the temptation to curtail them is thus both constant and compelling. But this is troublesome also, for there are basically only three ways in which structures can be constricted, all of which imply some penalty in terms of putative organizational readiness:

1. By collapsing the range over which contingencies are allowed to extend (that is, by reducing the spread of events that are assigned significant probabilities of occurrence, usually by increasing the probability threshold required for an event to become actively considered), there is a commensurate increase in the likelihood of an event occurring for which the organization has no appropriate predefined response, and no appropriate at-hand resources.

2. By reducing the number of alternative events that are defined *within* any set—that is, by recognizing fewer unique members of the bounded event-set—there is a corresponding increase in the probability that an event will occur and somehow or other fall between the gaps left among the defined contingencies. This, in turn, implies a general reduction in the expected response time of the organization, as again there will be no readily executable response alternative available that is significantly well-tailored to the exact event at hand.

3. By reducing the degree of elaboration within the contingency planning structure—that is, by reducing the level of specification at the tactical and operational levels associated with each strategic entry—the organization can reduce its aggregate system resource requirements, but at the same time would increase the average time to respond to any particular contingency because of the

necessity to fill in the lower order elements of any re-
source/response program only after the event has occurred and in part matured.

There is, then, a continuous tension between the maintenance of a contingency planning structure that is relevant with
regard to the richness of possibilities inherent in an organization's environment, yet feasible in terms of available system
resources, planning manpower, and overall manageability—both
physically and conceptually.[4] For a variety of reasons, this tension is most often resolved in favor of practical considerations
like the latter, such that most organizations will have contingency planning structures that are to some degree insuffi-
ciently elaborate in terms of the range or number of events
considered, and the degree of detail associated with the response
correlates.

Even more to the point, however, significant feedforward
cannot be obtained under such conditions, for the lower level
organizational units will not have the physical capacity in their
system facilities to replicate the full-blown contingency planning
structure maintained at the organization's central headquarters.
Rather, the former will generally be restricted to maintaining
only that limited subset of response specifications that is thought
to pertain directly to them, and only that collection of decision
support facilities appropriate to that subset. Indeed, it is precisely
such considerations that have gradually discouraged practical
interest in artificial intelligence technology (particularly of the
knowledge-based or "expert" system categories) as the basis for
enhancing the analytical capabilities of remote or forward-echelon units. For if the versatility of breadth-of-relevance of AI
constructs is to be maintained, then there must be an expansion
of the set of endogenous event referents and rules, which in turn
results in a geometric expansion of the "semantic memory" and
hence storage requirements (and a logarithmic increase in average response time). Such acceleration of hardware requirements
reduces the likelihood of their being well accomodated in outlying
operating contexts.[5] Hence, from yet another direction, there is
a lack of provisions for stand-alone operations associated with
distributed configurations such as that shown in Figure 5.1.

Hence, also the focus on "structured" decision referents as a method of *making as symmetrical as possible the distribution of standing intelligence among all organization levels,* such that all units will have some minimal likelihood of being able to generate a timely, functional response to any event falling somewhere within the boundaries within which the organization's mission is defined. One way of obtaining this versatility is to alter the level of abstraction at which an organization's event/response alternatives are defined, as expressed in the following proposition:

> . . . the key to the development of adaptive managerial decision support structures is the reduction of event and response alternatives to their most fundamental form—to "primitives," as it were— such that a theoretically infinite number of different events and response correlates can be formulated on a "roll your own" basis from a finite set of stored referents.

This proposition has certain practical precedents. Consider, for example, the referents and procedures of the police artist. He/she can create, in more or less real-time, a virtually unlimited number of unique portraits by selectively accessing his/her collection of primitives: files holding a set of basically different facial shapes, different eye configurations or hair styles, etc. By selecting different elements from these files, and ordering them in certain ways, the police artist can interactively generate a composite drawing of a suspect from one or more witness accounts. In the absence of such a facility, there would be no recourse to identification unless a suspect happened to have his integral portrait (i.e., a photograph) in the local "mug book". When the police artist's primitives are resident in a computer— and when the "mug shots" are properly ordered—the emergent composite portrait can be used to successively bound a witness's search through the integral portraits, gradually isolating that subset that correlates with the primitives that have been selected. The result is a considerable acceleration of the average search-time to effect a positive identification. Moreover, when law enforcement agencies in different locations are members of a network, composite portraits can be sent long-distance merely by forwarding the standard identification codes of those primitives that were employed by the local police artist (given that all members of the network possess the same set of component referents).

Another precedent is even more familiar. Consider, for example, that computers themselves are basically little more than collections of primitives, both at the level of microfunctions (add circuits; compare circuits; basic control gates, etc.) and in certain cases at the level of the "chips" from which contemporary machines are constructed. When programmed—which in effect merely suggests what subset of the primitives are to be exercised in what order—virtually an infinite variety of functions can be generated from a highly limited set of basic components.

Structuring merely extends these concepts into the arena of decision support systems. Its goal is to generate referent sets that are both elegant and robust. *Elegance*, in the current context, means the following: the ability to generate, in effective real-time, a more or less precise model of any event that might occur within the organization's domain of interest, from effectively minimal collections of stored model elements (qua primitives). Elegance is thus a leverage concept that concerns the richness of the unique situations that can be portrayed from any standing set of basic referents. Clearly, given the constricted storage capacity associated with microcomputer configurations (or, more generally, the inability to support or accomodate large-volume storage devices at forward-echelon locations), elegance is one of the critical determinants of an effective feedforward capability.

Robustness, on the other hand, refers to the ability to generate, in a timely fashion, an appropriate resource/response posture irrespective of the nature of the triggering event or contingency—the essential indicator of organizational readiness so far as decision-making functions are concerned. Structured design processes seek to instill robustness by treating response alternatives in much the same way as the event alternatives. In particular, the emphasis is on identifying that set of response-related primitives that is minimally sufficient for generating (on a "roll your own" basis) the full repertoire of action initiatives pertinent to an organization's mission and environment.

Thus, the major point of disparity between contingency planning and the structuring protocol is clear enough: the former maintains event-response alternatives as *discrete* referents (integral models); these command large volumes of storage and of necessity leave "gaps" between the predefined cases through which real-world events might fall. In contrast, structuring provisions allow for what amounts to a *continuous* distribution of event-response alternatives, and hence for a continuous mapping between situations and organizational reactions. Events and responses are treated somewhat differently, however, as will be made clear in the following discussion.

Decomposition of Events

In effect, *structuring* of event referents is basically an exercise in the successive reduction of data base components. The first task is to *define the extremes of the continuum of events* to which an organization might have to respond as a consequence of its mission and the nature of the environment in which it is resident. Depending on the context at hand, this could be done in any of several ways:

- By an examination of *the range of existing contingencies defined in specific*. For example, consider the naval scenario. Contingencies would generally appear in terms of probable threats as defined by standing intelligence sources (e.g., an invasion of South Korea by North Korea; an incursion across the West German border by elements of the Warsaw Pact forces; an attempt by the Soviets or some client to blockade the Hormuz Straights; deployment of Cuban warships off the coast of Nicaragua, and so forth).

- By considering *the set of generic contingencies* to which an organization is directed, usually ordered in some way so as to reflect their level of significance or threat. For example, fire departments within large metropolitan areas usually maintain a certain protocol whereby the number and types of units responding is determined by the category of an event, such as a one, two, or three alarm fire.

- By evoking some sort of *artificial scheme*, perhaps of the following sort. There are defined, for a particular organization, two fictional event-extrema,[6] such that events A and B represent logically opposite states of the world (i.e., the properties of A are the effective inverse of the properties of B).

The purpose here is to establish the boundaries of the integral event-set as a requisite for the second step in the decomposition process:

- *Reduce all events within the defined range to their lowest order definitional components,* much as one would decompose a mathematical function into its fundamental operators, or a sentence into those elements that are of basic structural significance (e.g., nouns and verbs) and those that are more superficial (e.g., the adjectives and adverbs).
- *Examine* the resultant decomposed models for any *isomorphisms* (underlying morphological or structural similarities), or for points where two or more events share common structural or dynamic properties, i.e., have *causal commonalities*.
- *Remove all redundant elements* from the set, such that each unique event-related property appears only once; the result should be the reduction of the entire spectrum of integral event models to a set of *exhaustive but mutually-exclusive primitives*.

As brief as this explanation was, it should be clear that any of the original integral events can be rapidly regenerated merely by the appropriate ordering of the relevant primitives; moreover, there is now the capacity to model any event that might fall somewhere within the extremes of the referent continuum, even if was not one of those discrete cases entered into the original contingency set. But the major effect of the above decomposition operations is this: a compression of the absolute amount of data required to comprehend the range of contingencies to which an organization might be subject. Hence we have some practical basis for *making more symmetrical the distribution of standing intelligence* among organizational units, including those forward-echelon or low-level components equipped only with small-scale information system facilities.

Parsing of Response Alternatives

It is possible to accomplish the same kind of compression on the response dimension. If the decomposition of event alternatives is aimed at making more symmetrical the distribution of standing intelligence, then the parsing operations we shall describe here are designed to make more symmetrical the distribution of *doctrinal discipline* among all organizational levels. The generalized parsing procedures are the following:

1. Generate a continuum of generic strategic responses the organization might adopt, given the continuum of generic events (contingencies) determined above.
2. Generate a simple one-for-one mapping between the various generic contingencies and generic strategic postures.
3. Isolate a continuum of tactical response options consistent with each of the categorical event/strategic posture pairings.
4. Subject each of the tactical response options to a detailed decomposition process, similar to that to which event alternatives were subject.
5. Eliminate redundancies to produce a set of *response primitives*—an exhaustive, yet mutually exclusive set of determinants from which virtually any tactical variant can be constructed on a "roll your own" basis.

As the parsing process is somewhat intricate and less algorithmic than the decomposition process directed at events, a simple illustration might help us here. Consider, again therefore, our Naval scenario, though in a deliberately artificial formulation. Assume that a generic continuum of contingencies to which the Navy might have to respond has been formulated as shown in Figure 5.4.

| 1. Harassment of a minor US client by an adversary's client | 2. Invasion of a US client by adversary forces | 3. Siezure of a vital US interest (e.g.: the Hormuz Straights) | 4. Threat of all-out attack on the US itself |

Figure 5.4.   Generic Event Continuum

Note that these events are generic in that they do not relate to specific contingencies, but rather to cases that might involve any number of different real-world parties and locations. They thus lead naturally to the formulation of generic strategic response postures, perhaps like the following:

- DETERRENCE: a generally passive posture that attempts to head off aggressive adversary ambitions by demonstrating a US presence ("showing the flag," as it were). In some instances, deterrence may also involve the projection of a US force at some other location, in an effort to distract the adversary from his present intentions.

- INTERJECTION: a posture of limited or constrained aggressive potential, consisting mainly of attempts to interfere with adversary's lines of supply (e.g., selective blockade; seizure of illegal arms shipments); selective jamming of adversary-based command/control communication links; or, more commonly, provision of certain types of material or procedural support to the US client (e.g., provision of arms and ammunition; employment of specialized assets such as the AWAKs platforms)

- INTERDICTION: selective engagement of adversary forces (client or third-party) that are in the act of actually attacking the US or the US' client's forces or assets; interdiction thus represents the use of force in what amounts to a defensive posture.

- PREEMPTION: the use of force on the initiative of the US or its client against adversary assets on a first-strike basis; preemption is thus aggressive (offensive) force projection.

Note that there is an implicit ordering of both the event and strategic response continua, with the least threatening event and hence least complex (and most innocent) strategic posture sitting at the origin of the two sets. We thus have a basis for arraying the various generic tactical response alternatives in a complementary tableau (see Table 5.1).

GENERIC STRATEGIC POSTURES

GENERIC EVENTS:	Deterrence	Interjection	Interdiction	Preemption
1. Harassment of a minor client.	$T(1,1)$	$t(1,2)$	$t(1,3)$	$t(1,4)$
2. Attack on a major client	$t(2,1)$	$T(2,2)$	$t(2,3)$	$t(2,4)$
3. Seizure of vital interest	$t(3,1)$	$t(3,2)$	$T(3,3)$	$t(3,4)$
4. Attack on US itself	$t(4,1)$	$t(4,2)$	$t(4,3)$	$T(4,4)$

Table 5.1 Generic Events and Corresponding Strategic Response Postures

The effect is to bound the full range of tactical response options of interest, and to distinguish those that are most major in significance (these being the tactical responses falling along the major diagonal, appearing as $T(i,j)$, whereas the secondary tactical alternatives are entered as $t(i,j)$). Thus, for example, $T(1,1)$ would be the means for executing a strategy of *deterrence*, which in turn is indicated as the preferred strategy for dealing with the first of the generic contingencies, harassment of a minor US client (as is the case currently in the limited aggressive activities that Nicaragua is directing towards Honduras). $T(2,2)$ would thus define the tactical response(s) appropriate to the case where an important US client has actually been the subject of an invasion, or overt military aggression (such as in the Syrians' sponsorship of conventional war in Lebanon); as such, $T(2,2)$ would set out the collection of doctrine approrpriate to mounting *interjective* missions (a good example is the US Naval operations off the Lebanese coast). In its turn, $T(3,3)$ would refer to the means for effecting an *interdictive* presence, which is the a priori preferred strategy for countering attempts by an adversary to secure a vital interest somewhat remote from the US, while $T(4,4)$ would define no-holds-barred means for defeating attempts by an adversary to attack domestic US interests.

We can see roughly what has been accomplished to this point. First, what might have originally existed as a very large set of integral response programs (context-specific strategic and tactical contingency plans) has now been reduced to a well-bounded and logically ordered set of sixteen alternatives, only four of which are of major generic significance. Second, the entire spectrum of means appropriate to the achievement of any of the strategic postures would be accessible by calling on the tactical set arrayed on the column of interest—for example, interjective doctrine is summarized by $T(i,2)$—whereas the entire array of tactical options pertinent to any generic event is callable by accessing the element of the row of interest (thus, the full set of tactical options available for countering harassment of a client would be indicated by the set $T(1,j)$).

Even at this point, then, there may have been some considerable compression of doctrinal decision premises, this by the conversion to *generic* event, strategic and tactical constructs. Yet there is opportunity for still greater elegance by considering reductions that might take place within Table 5.1 both vertically and horizontally. Consider, particularly, that any tactical initiative that might be mounted within the Naval context would involve specifications on the following dimensions:

- The appropriate US force composition in terms of vessels (by class) and configuration (e.g., a carrier-centered battle group)
- The orders of operation in which these forces may engage (e.g., antisubmarine warfare activities; remote reconnaissance; close airborne surveillance)

- The types of targets that might be acquired (e.g., aircraft, war ships, noncombatant vessels, unmanned sensor platforms)
- The classes of weapons or instruments that can be employed (e.g., only passive means such as jamming; only conventional warheads with some maximum gross yield; nuclear warheads)

These are the elements that, when elaborated, would constitute an *engagement scenario*, with the expected degree of detail increasing as we move from the simpler to the more complex cells of Table 5.1 (from the top-left towards the bottom-right corner along the major diagonal). This implies that in actual practice, higher order engagement scenarios would subsume those of a lower order. For example, the tactical initiatives employed to carry out *interdictive* activities would build upon those appropriate for *interjective* activities; therefore, what would be maintained in $T(3,3)$ would be only those specifications on the above dimensions that are additions to any specifications already present in $T(2,2)$, or perhaps $t(2,3)$. In the same sense, those *interdictive* tactics that might somehow be employed in the face of a lower order threat (say for event-1) would be a subset of those tactics that would be employed in the face of a more complex or perilous event; thus, the engagement scenarios entered in cell $T(3,3)$ would be those that amplify in some respects those that were specified in $t(3,1)$ and $t(3,2)$. In effect, then, we institute a "one-time mention" of any component in the full repertoire of engagement scenarios that is the counterpart on the response dimension to the elimination of redundancies among the set of event determinants.

These parsing operations must of necessity result in an increase in the level of doctrinal discipline—generalized policy and procedural prescriptions, qua strategic/tactical decision premises—that can be maintained by forward-echelon units. The key, again, is the contraction of the storage requirements that occurs in the transition from traditional integrally defined contingency response plans to their compressed primitive equivalents. The net effect is thus the sought-for escalation of the presumptive stand-alone capabilties of lower order organizational elements, i.e., an expansion of the range of events over which rational responses can be expected, even in the absence of any inputs from higher echelon functionaries.[7]

TEMPLATE-BASED OPERATIONS

The basic unit of analysis for actual decision exercises would not in fact be the primitives that we just generated, but rather what are called *templates*. Templates are ordered collections of primitives. In the feedforward context, two types of templates are of central interest: (*a*) *masks*, which provide more or less abstract referents against which real-world events may be compared; masks are thus comprised of selected elements from the population of event-primitives; and (*b*) *scripts*, which serve to define resource/response functions at any desired level of detail, and as such are built up from the set of response-primitives generated earlier.

However, unlike the integral models characteristic of contingency planning constructs, templates are stored in functional form. That is, they are strings of operators that define what particular elements (subset) of the collection of primitives is to be activated, and prescribe the sequence in which they are to be combined, or any other ordering instructions. In the broadest sense, then, templates are the consequence of applying some sort of *synthesis algorithm* that serves to recombine elements that were originally arrived at by the successive reduction of integral event specifications and response plans. But, again, templates are free to take any feasible form and can be constructed at any level of abstraction, whereas the usual contingency planning structure is defined only with respect to a limited collection of discrete referents.

A useful analogy for *masks* is available in terms of the sophisticated graphic programming packages now being marketed. They offer an extraordinary repertoire of construction alternatives, but in effect base all operations on a set of geometric primitives—circles, squares, triangles, etc. These basic geometric elements can be operated on themselves, by defining, for example, the precise radius of the desired circle, or defining the desired relationship between the several legs of a triangle (e.g., $a = b + c$). But, by combining certain of these geometric primitives in certain ways—known a priori to the software, or supplied in real-time by the user—virtually any type of higher order geometric model can be generated, even those strictly putative forms that are relevant to topology or modern algebra. *Masks* (as event templates) would thus be roughly equivalent in implication to those higher order geometric constructs that result from the successive superimposition of geometric primitives. *Scripts*, on the other hand, might be thought to be reminiscent of the many different predefined formations that are so integral to modern professional athletic endeavors, particularly football and baseball. Those associated with the former are perhaps most familiar—the "Prevent Defense," the "Nickel Defense," the "Collapsing Zone," etc. Such formations serve to define the basic structure of a response set that will be employed, with the assignments of specific individuals tailored—in near time—to current intelligence about the players and predilections of a particular opponent. These preset formations thus provide a set of consistent baseline response definitions that, in effect, represent the "boilerplate" of contemporary sports planning.

In short, then, if primitives of the type generated under the structuring provisions may be thought of as providing an *alphabet* for decision support systems, then templates would be *phrases* or even simple sentences. They thus have the effect of in part restoring some of the degree of aggregation of intelligence and doctrine that was lost in the reduction exercises just completed. Recall, however, the dual purpose of the structuring process. First, there was the need to compress decision referents to the point where a great deal of standing intelligence and doctrine might be fedforward to lower level organizational units; second, there was the proposition that the conversion from discrete to continuous formulation of decision premises would increase the expediency with which responses could be generated to events that were different from any that were entered in the original contingency programming structure.

What this would involve in practical terms is clear enough. First, any real-world event that appears for handling would have to be decomposed into a set of rudimentary determinants similar to those contained in the set of event primitives; next, an appropriate, dedicated treatment would have to be formulated by examining the various members of the set of response primitives for that combination that is expected to be most effective for the situation at hand. The net effect is to treat each event as if it were entirely unique and unprecedented, and in effect something of a complete surprise to all involved. From one perspective, this may be seen as the price we pay when we allow elegance, and robustness, to supercede traditional bounded efficiency as a design criterion (this latter leading to the systems that respond, in a more or less optimal way, to some limited number of definite triggering conditions).

But the introduction of templates as the basic unit of analysis and operation has the effect of allowing an optimization-at-the-margin between efficiency and robustness. Consider, again, the template-related operations originally noted in Figure 5.3. Particularly critical is the first of the true template-related tasks, selective synthesis, this effecting the transformation of event and response primitives into masks and scripts, respectively. What is selective here is the basis for the generation of the templates that will be made available at user-installations, given some scarcity of facilities for their storage. There are several different ways of setting priorities, each of which would have unique operational implications:

1. There could be a traditional type of a priori analysis conducted, reminiscent of the usual contingency planning process. In this case, priority would be given to the development of masks that pertain to that set of events/situations that are assigned the highest subjective probability of occurence (or perhaps an objective probability of occurrence, via the employment of some sort of formalistic projection protocol, e.g., a game-theoretic process). The controlling criterion in this scheme is prospective efficiency, per se, in that the only masks that are generated are those likely to be employed most frequently. This, in turn, would tend to translate into expected minimization of average system response time

(the time that elapses between the emergence of an event, its correlation with an appropriate mask, and the identification of a pertinent script).

2. There could be a process followed that is reminiscent of standard distributed data processing conventions. In this case, any installation would be allowed to develop—or be delivered—only those masks that pertain to those decision functions for which it is routinely responsible. This scheme thus perpetuates the traditional distribution of decision prerogatives inherent in hierarchical-bureaucratic organizations. The effect is to somewhat restrict the readiness of the forward or local unit to stand alone. But in practice, two considerations may serve to offset this:

   - Because templated referents are so highly compressed, the amount of actionable information that can be transmitted to forward units over any interval is much greater than where traditional integral models are the medium of expression. This serves to considerably reduce the likelihood of a communications *overload* should it be necessary to substitute some secondary medium (e.g., radio) should a primary communications (e.g., a satellite) link fail. This means that, given indications of an impending network interruption, higher order templates could be forwarded very quickly, and at the same time with considerable security (in that only the ordering or synthesis algorithms are transmitted, not the "intelligence," per se).

   - Alternatively, higher order templates could be stored at the forward sight itself, but kept secured from local access unless certain conditions are fulfilled—i.e., unless a password is fed forward from some higher unit, or unless there is a physical failure of some standing network link or occurrence of jamming, etc.

3. Priority could be given to the development of those masks associated with situations where delay would be thought

to carry the most severe consequences, those events where there is a premium on quickness in the mounting of a response. The fact that templates can be maintained at different levels of aggregation also allows adjustment in the degree of detail in light of required response time; that is, masks associated with the most critical situations would more closely approximate the integral models of contingency planning structures than masks relating to classes of events where slightly longer response times are tolerable. The determination of the degree of aggregation (level of abstraction at which masks are to be maintained) is thus the type of decision that falls quite naturally within the purview of modern system engineering, while this scheme itself reflects the case where the system designer has elected to substitute "expected value of loss" for absolute efficiency as the criterion of interest.

4. There is, finally, what amounts to a quasi-heuristic alternative: to set up a situation where the stream of events to which the system is empirically exposed determines the order in which masks are generated. In this case, we start with "a blank sheet of paper". All events that appear for processing are decomposed into factors similar to those in the set of event primitives; any elements unique to the event at hand will then be added to the set (V). The combination of primitives that defines any event— the set $E\{v\}$—thus represents a potential template $[\{m\}/E]$. After some interval over which the system has been operating, an analysis is conducted that would perform the following:

   - Generate a frequency distribution indicating the number of times each of the potential templates was actually employed; and

   - Enter into the permanent template array $[M]$ those candidates with the highest frequency of employment, until the capacity of the mask storage allotment is filled.

The effect is thus to provide the template-based system with a "learning" capability, a basis for altering the structure of its referent set to accomodate the actual demands on the system. Moreover, there is the opportunity to carry the empirical accomodation function one step further. The degree of aggregation at which the masks are kept could be altered to reflect their frequency of employment, such that the aggregate time to template-based decisions is effectively minimized given some consistency in the distribution of events to which an installation is exposed.

The next major aspect of template-based operations is the *mapping* function that tends to correlate scripts with masks, and hence determines the nature of the responses that will be invoked in the face of actual events. What is called the Notional Mapping function in Figure 5.3 would involve organizational authorities in the generation of a response template appropriate for each of the masks that might be generated under one or another of the above schemes (except for the last case, the "learning" variant, which would proceed at the primitives level in its initial stages). In general, a script would be generated at the same degree of detail as the mask to which it relates. Again, a script is simply an ordered collection of elements drawn from the set of response primitives, such that $S = [\{p\}/M]$

The script gains its real momentum when it takes its place in what is referred to as the Treatment Inventory. Here will be located all ordered pairs of masks and scripts $[T = \{M \times S\}]$ that have been generated to some point in time. Any member of the set of treatment referents $\}t's\}$ could be as simple as a replicate of a script (that is, a more or less abstract set of solution specifications), or could be more elaborate, containing a high level of detail perhaps derived from prior field experience with a class of scripts. Scripts obtained at some point in the past would, for example, contain parametric prescriptions or exact magnitudinal data (e.g., not only set a general formation for the defensive squad to execute, but choreograph the precise moves that each player is to make).

The Treatment Inventory now becomes the primary focus of the template-based decision process which, in great abbreviation, involves the following: the translation of any empirical event into a set of determinants $\{E\}$ that can be compared against the set of masks contained in the set [M]. At this point, one of three outcomes will occur, each of which leads to a different solution protocol:

1. The essential properties of the event may mark it as fundamentally equivalent to some existing event template $(E = M)$. In this instance, there will be some singularly preferred solution that can be identified through simple *association*: that particular $\{t\}$ that relates to $M = E$. Here, then, no new analytical challenges are posed, with the *associative* modality thus restricted to events or problems that are reasonably well precedented, and hence whose treatments are a product of empirical validation and have therefore been carried beyond the level of the generic script;

2. A slightly more interesting situation is the event that is interpretable as a variant on some familiar theme, the case where $E = kM$, should this occur, then the basis for an appropriate solution will generally be a variant on some standing script that, in terms of magnitude of adjustment, is commensurate with the degree to which the event E departs from the template referent M. Hence the *ampliative* modality, where a response to event $E = K [S/M]$. As a rule, this modality would be employed to deal with events intelligible as members of some "class" about which there is some order of general intelligence, some degree of macrodeterminism. To be made executable, however, these script-based solutions would have to be provided with an additional level of detail (via the "parameterization" processes to be described shortly) and;

3. There is, finally, the "worst case," the case where the event in question is one for which no appropriate template has been formulated. The decision makers are restricted to operating at the level of the event and response primitives. They are required to generate a dedicated and entirely unique solution from scratch. It is here that the greatest demands are made on both system elements and users. However, once the *extensive* mod-

ality has been conducted, its results can be fed back to the treatment inventory so that any recurrence can be met using one of the simpler modalities (the ampliative or associative).

Such then are the essentials of template-based decision making. The *event and response primitives* that are available to all organizational units help provide the *robustness* needed in modern decision support systems, by providing the wherewithal to respond to the widest possible range of events that might emerge. On the other hand, the *templates* provide some basis for taking advantage of both a priori and empirical knowledge or experience, and thus seek to introduce some genuine efficiency by acting to consistently *minimize the amount of incremental intelligence and/or analytical effort that must be devoted to event recognition and response generation activities*. It is this latter provision that is most critical in extending the decision support functions that can be provided by highly constrained information facilities, particularly microcomputer-based installations. Finally, when some sort of "learning" provision is installed, there is a basis for making the informational assets of some organizational unit extraordinarily sensitive to the emergent properties of the environment in which it is resident.

The final consideration for this chapter is a task that has been pretty much brushed aside thus far. Particularly in the cases where the ampliative or extensive solution protocols were used, the response that was generated under the template-based process is not sufficiently precise to permit immediate execution. There are some details that have to be added that will demand a quantitative analysis exercise of some sort.

EXPEDITING PARAMETRIC PROCESSES

Ultimately, any organizational resource/response posture becomes intelligible not merely in terms of the broad strategic/tactical premises it entails, but in terms of those specific parameters—numerical or magnitudinal qualifiers—that serve to tailor the initiative to immediate contextual conditions (whether on the battlefield or in the marketplace). As a rule, decisions as to the *parametric* properties of some organizational initiative will generally fall into the domain of quantitative analysis (in terms of the type of feedback and modification mechanisms consistent with the usual *cybernetic* logic). Thus, when focusing on the issue of real-time (or near-term) accomodation to variables in an organization's immediate environment, the appropriate class of decision support facilities will be those numerical processing algorithms derived from traditional operations research, engineering, and the general repertoire of *optimization* techniques (re: statistical control theory, finite-state systems engineering, stochastic processes, dynamic programming, etc.).

A characteristic common to virtually all popular quantitative analysis protocols is the essential fixity of the process steps they entail—the stationariness of their logic—which implies some maximum limit on the number of transactions that can be performed over any interval. A major determinant of this latter factor would naturally enough be the size and sophistication of the computer resources available, and most particularly the way the machine is configured with respect to mathematical operations. Without going into great detail, we can see that when an organizational unit has only microcomputers available, physical limitations and fixed-structure processing algorithms can severely restrict the breadth and depth of the real-time accomodation exercises that can be performed. Moreover, there are really only three ways in which these strictures might be eased in practice:

1. Alter the physical characteristics of the numerical processing function itself. The only really obvious way to do this is to introduce architectural changes of the following sort: (*a*) make a conversion from simple sequential to a *parallel processing* protocol which would attempt to minimize the time required to conduct certain algorithmic exercises by splitting operations among two or more isolated CPUs; (*b*) install a dedicated front-end processor (e.g., a series analyzer) that is optimally efficient in certain orders of numerical transformations,

thus reducing the loadings that will fall on the more general microcomputer.

While these architecture-based remedies are indeed compelling, they are only of long-run significance (requiring capital additions that may likely violate the spatial or budgetary constraints of forward-echelon units). Our attention thus shifts to one or another of the following less exotic remedies:

2. The displacement of traditional fixed-logic algorithms with variable-state processing modalities such as those that might be defined under *simoptimization* logic; and
3. The displacement of traditional numerical processing techniques by *graphic solution* protocols.

These two remedies both exact essentially the same price: the tradeoff of some level of precision in solutions against the expediency of their generation. They thus represent a fall-back position to be employed whenever the demand on local system facilities is such that the only alternative to a reduction in the quality of responses is default—the failure to generate a solution in time to be of any value.

For its part, simoptimization[8] follows quite naturally from the principles of structured design discussed earlier. It is predicated on the generally familiar assertion that the time and resource requirements (system facilities loadings) needed to complete any numerical algorithmic function will generally be determined by the number of state-variables that must have their parameters simultaneously specified, and by the degree of required resolution. Another obvious determinant is the complexity of the processing algorithm itself, the number and nature of the various computational functions entailed in any integral procedure. In effect, then, we have three key dimensions on which processual protocols can be addressed and hence modified:

- *Number of Active State-Variables*. Any reduction in the number of state-variables that require values to be established during any iteration of an algorithm will induce a more than proportional reduction in the time/resources required to complete a transaction;

- *Resolution Level.* Any reduction in the degree of detail to which solutions must be carried will result in a corresponding reduction in the demand on system resources, and hence accelerate the computational procedures; and

- *Degree of Algorithmic Integration.* In general, the aggregate time and resource demands required to arrive at a solution to any well-bounded (i.e., canonically defined) problem can be minimized by the decomposition of the problem—and hence the computational function itself—into a set of subproblems each of which has fewer variables (thus implying fewer integrated procedural steps) than the original formulation.

In great abbreviation, then, simoptimization logic would direct system designers towards the development of computational models that can be modified on these dimensions to accomodate changes in the levels of demand on information system facilities. Simoptimization-based algorithms would alter their essential structure in an attempt to obtain a consistently most favorable compromise between the quality of solutions, the demand on system resources, and prevailing response requirements. Thus, under normal operating conditions, simoptimization solutions might very well be indistinguishable from those that might obtain through routine integral quantitative analysis algorithms.

Should the system come under stress however, then the simoptimization logic would adjust the character of the solution process to avoid complete default: would reduce the number of active state-variables according to some predefined criterion; would reduce resolution levels or increase the level of disaggregation of the algorithm with an eye towards eliminating those steps that are deemed least essential to the process in aggregate.

To some extent, graphic protocols will also tend to result in directed solutions.[9] In all cases, graphic substitutions for numerical algorithms must be considered as expedients, yielding results more quickly and with less expenditure of resources—but almost always exacting a price in terms of absolute accuracy or degree of resolution. This exchange of graphic for numerical protocols has some familiar precedents: it has long been common to solve certain types of linear programming problems by examining the nature of the hyperplanes that are generated by constraints, and then isolating the "corner" solution; in statistical problems, one may often deal with simple time-series by superimposing a hand-drafted curve instead of taking resource to the least-sqaures calculations, an especially useful expedient when the reference data has significant variance; the use of *envelope analysis*—an essentially graphic technique—is increasingly employed as an alternative to the calculus as a basis for portfolio management, for example. Unfortunately, there is relatively little work of a basic nature that has been done on the precise terms of the tradeoff between graphic and mathematical methods, yet such must be thought of as a highly promising method of accelerating throughput in microcomputer installations forced to operate under stress—and as an appropriate point to conclude this inquiry into the role of feedforward technology.

A CLOSING NOTE

To briefly recapitulate, microcomputers are playing an increasingly integral role in modern managerial systems, especially those that are operating under some sort of real-time, command/control technology. The basic integrity of organizations built around such systems thus depends increasingly on the reliability and robustness of the communications configurations that tend to tie together the computer facilities at the various levels of the organizational hierarchy. Where there is a likelihood that such might fail—or, as a competitive asset, be deliberately disrupted—then the microcomputers at the remote, local, or forward-echelon installations must be prepared to stand alone in certain respects. Hence the essential rationale behind the feedforward provisions that have been discussed in these pages.

There is, however, a secondary application of feedforward technology that is perhaps of even greater general interest. Particularly, it provides a basis for distributing relatively elaborate knowledge bases to functionaries who might have only a micro-computer available—physicians, lawyers, forward-deployed military officers, automobile repair stations, etc. When the oner-ous information requirements of most modern professionals are coupled with the physical limitations of their microcomputer installations, they are often forced into an uncomfortable tradeoff—the knowledge base that is forwarded may be either "deep" but very limited in the range of events it can comprehend, or it can attempt to be broad in coverage but must then be relatively "shallow," Neither of the two traditional vehicles for information forwarding—expert systems of the type developed under artificial intelligence methods or interactive computer-aided instructional programs—have been able to resolve this trade-off particularly well. However, if the arguments raised in these pages have any merit, generating highly compressed but adequately rich knowledge bases should prove a challenge tailor-made for feedforward technology.

NOTES

1. There is a less dramatic but perhaps even more pointed example that can be mentioned here. Modern professional football teams rely heavily on their computers, especially as a basis for rationalizing draft choices. The draft is usually held at a location remote from any of the teams themselves, so each must send a representative to this location to exercise its choices. The analytical requirements falling on this local representative are not really very great, as it is the home-based com-puter—in conjunction with the head coach and owners operating it—that will generate the choices. The local representative—linked by telephone or terminal—must merely make them aware of what players have already been chosen by other teams, and then execute the choice passed to him when it is his team's opportunity to make a selection. This local agent is thus not routinely equipped to make any selections on his own volition. As the story goes, one team was unfortunate enough to have its communication link interrupted (and was not able to get the draft authorities to delay the process), such that their local repre-sentative was deprived of higher order instructions during several key rounds. Lacking the basis to make rational selections, he resorted to some basically random selections whose acquisition did not do much to increase the overall competitive posture of the club.

2. For more on this see my "Normative Predicates of Next-Generation Management Support Systems," *IEEE Transactions on Systems, Man, and Cybernetics* 13(3), May/June 1983.

3. Parallel processing would serve to decrease the aggregate time/resource requirements associated with the execution of functions that can be decomposed to some extent (c.f., Harold Lorin, *Parallelism in Hardware and Software*; [Englewood Cliffs, N.J.: Prentice-Hall, 1981]).

4. See, for example, the discussion of relevance vs. actionability of managerial referents in my "The Case for Reactive Management Systems," *IEEE Transactions on Systems, Man, and Cybernetics* 14(1), January 1984.

5. To offset this acceleration of hardware requirements in part, AI practitioners have on the one hand tended to concentrate on increasingly narrowly defined application domains, and on the other to rely increasingly on inputs from the system user or the "man in the loop." This latter has been the preferred recourse when the events to be dealt with are relatively complex, such that the efficiency of the systems depends increasingly on the quality of the inputs or constraints entered by the user. In short, AI expert systems tend to operate best when the user is himself an "expert." Thus there is a further limitation on the relevance of such systems for remote, local, or forward-echelon contexts, for it is precisely there that human expertise can generally be expected to be most scarce.

6. For an elaboration on the employment of state extrema, see the latter portions of my "Reactive Management Systems."

7. As a VCU colleague of mine, Dr. Richard Redmond, has pointed out, this implies the need for local authorities to have some sort of limited data-acquisition facility that would allow them to comprehend the cause of the breakdown in communications. Consider, for example, the case of the commander of a nuclear-armed submarine on remote patrol. The submarine, as one of the three legs of the U.S.'s triadic defense posture, is perhaps also the most generally feared. But the quality of the submarine as a deterrent ultimately reduces to the likelihood of its actually launching its warheads should a nuclear attack destroy the US command/control network; that is, unless the submarine can be presumed capable of acting on its own initiative, a preemptive attack might eliminate the submarine as a putative deterrent. By the same token, the possibility of a breakdown in communication linkages as a sufficient cause for launching is equally unpalatable. This would argue, then, for an onboard set of sensors and rationalizing software that would enable the submarine commander to determine whether or not his isolation is a consequence of a general nuclear discharge, or due to some more innnocent cause.

6

The Role of Decision
Support Systems
in Command and Control

H. Bennett Teates

In a broadly conceived sense, most applications of computers can be interpreted as attempts to improve the quality of decisions. Information systems for the military as well as information retrieval systems for the engineer or business manager can be viewed as attempts to improve the quality of decisions by providing an increased amount of timely information to the decision maker. Computer-controlled production processes and accounting procedures can be viewed as attempts to improve the effectiveness of decisions by providing for the reliable and timely realization of plans previously selected by a decision maker.

Thus, computers are used as aids both in the information gathering stage and in the operational stage of decision-making. In addition, computers are used as aids to the decision process itself. It is in this sense that decision support systems (DSSs), through the advances of technology and the application of the "use-learn-develop" philosophy, are being used to assist military planners in deterministic, probabilistic and inferential decision making.

POSSIBLE SCENARIOS FOR DSSs

Imagine you are a military general in a politically tense area concerned about a possible enemy invasion. From experience, it is estimated that when enemy troops mass at the border, the probability of invasion is 0.75. However, you do not have direct access to information about enemy troops, but must rely on reports of such activity from your intelligence sources. Again, from experience, every time your intelligence sources have reported troops massing, they are really there. Consider that you now receive a report from your sources that enemy troops are at the border. What is the probability of invasion? If you are like most people, you probably answered 0.75. However, the information given is not sufficient to answer the question in the statistically correct way.[1]

Consider a second problem. This time you are a signal battalion commander and it is your task to optimally locate a broadcast transmitter in a line-of-sight communications system so that all of the following constraints are met:

1. All receivers are within range of the transmitter;
2. Receivers are of varying reception sensitivity; and
3. Neither receiver nor transmitter can be located on terrain forward or friendly positions, on terrain hidden from line-of-sight, or on terrain where there is electromagnetic interference with other deployed systems.

How would you accomplish this task?

Again, imagine yourself as a ship commander. Almost hourly your ship receives information about one or more of the hundreds of satellites circling the globe, collecting various types of information. How would you assimilate this plethora of information? Even more importantly, how would you use the information to generate a situation potentially more favorable to your ship and its mission?

Each of these examples is a case in which the command and control decisions involved are best served by the use of computers in Decision Support Systems (DSSs).

BACKGROUND

A command and control (C^2) system is defined as an arrangement of personnel, facilities, and systems for information acquisition, processing, and dissemination employed by a decision maker (DM) in planning, directing, and controlling operations. Figure 6.2, a simplistic representation of this definition, illustrates how the elements of a command and control system support the DM and, in particular, the equality of decision support with intelligence gathering, communications, and information processing.

Over the past decade, computers have come to play an important part in improving the capability of our military forces to gather, process, and disseminate information. Successful applications have occurred most frequently where the computer was used as a control device tightly coupled to some physical process or weapon system. On the other hand, the use of computers to support tactical operations, stratetgic planning, and the projection and evaluation of alternate courses of action have been far less successful and valuable than the designer had intended and the user has expected.

Historically, characteristics of these less successful uses are:

- Very little use of human perception or judgement in a interactive symbiosis with automated processing.
- Attempts to solve in one system all problems the users may enumerate.
- High cost and long period of system acquisition.

Each of the services has spent millions of dollars over the last decade in attempting to acquire tactical command and con-

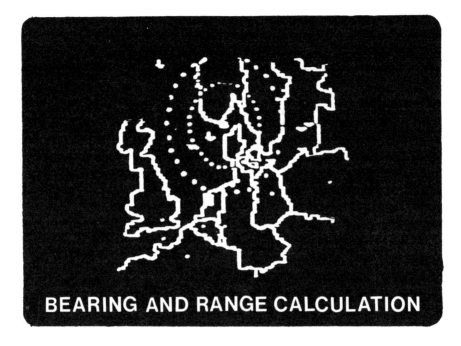

BEARING AND RANGE CALCULATION

Figure 6.2   Representation of the elements of a C^2 system that support the decision maker. (Reprinted from Teates, et al. 1980)

trol systems that would provide centralized information for the decision maker's use in the planning and control of forces. More recently, general acceptance of the position that the acquisition of command and control systems is best served by step-wise progression rather than solving the whole problem at once, combined with the advent of physically small and inexpensive, yet powerful, information processing capability, is resulting in the "roll back" of these characteristics.

Now the trend is to develop an initial capability, put it in the user's hands and enhance the initial capability at a pace that can be understood. This approach is particularly relevant to those portions of C^2 systems that pertain to decision support, as the technology and our understanding of the human decision process have concurrently evolved to where meaningful applications are not only possible, but are actually taking place. Indeed, decision support systems have been developed for the three types of examples that introduced this chapter.

In the first example, the decision maker (DM) is provided with a question or two that assist him in assessing the correct probability of attack or at least cause the DM to carefully consider the basis of his reasoning. In the second, an interactive geographical display with an embedded optimization routine assists the DM in locating the transmitter. In the last example, the information is stored and processed in conjunction with ship's navigation data to alert the DM as to when the ship is susceptible to observation and, for example, when and what type of electronic emissions might be turned on or off.

Each of these DSSs has been developed on "desk-top" computers, each for less than fifteen thousand dollars. (It is worthy to note that these are only examples of the capabilities of these DSSs as each is capable of many other decision support functions). The point is that, although the need still exists for the centralized command and control systems, many command and control decisions can now be distributed out to the point of need and served by available "off-the-shelf" technology.

It is likely that a careful examination of information needs would discover that many C^2 system requirements could be met by small, distributed DSSs; the result potentially being better, more timely decisions, enhanced survivability, and reduced communications.

DECISION SUPPORT SYSTEM CHARACTERISTICS

A central theme of command and control system design is that commanders are more effectively served by "adaptable" information retrieval than by "predesigned" reports. The typical DSS thus aims to provide the decision maker specific information in response to specific requests bearing on a specific decision, in contrast to the general purpose, presequenced-reports-type system. Figure 6.3 illustrates the close interaction required between the computer and the decision maker to have an effective DSS. Additional characteristics of DSSs aim to:

1. "Assist" the decision maker past common human inferential errors and biases (e.g., case #1 cited above).
2. Interactively include the decision maker's judgment and knowledge in the resulting automated output (e.g., case #2 cited above).
3. Provide ease of use and adaptability to accommodate changes in the environment and the decision-making approach of the user.

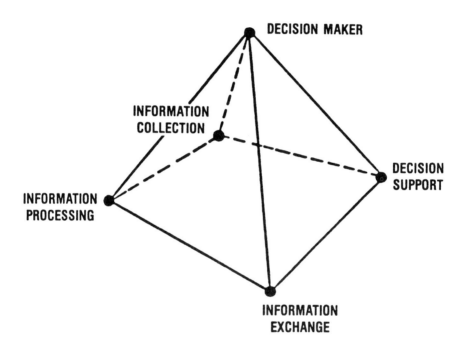

Figure 6.3   Requisite man-machine interaction for an effective DSS

Human Inference

The literature on human inferential errors and biases is largely of recent origin and serves to underscore the need for decision support systems (see Einhorn and Hogarth 1981; Nisbett and Ross 1980; and Tversky, et al. 1980). Whereas human conceptual skills have served us quite well to date, our information processing skills appear to be inadequate (without help) to cope with the needs of an information-heavy environment.

It is a curious fact that although people live in a probabilistic world, few can properly handle even the simplest of problems involving a calculation of probability. People do not possess intuitive "calculators" that allow them to make "optimal calculations." Rather, they use fairly simple procedures, rules of thumb or just plain "gut feeling" in order to reduce mental effort. For example, what is your guess as to the probability that in a room of thirty people, two of them would have the same birthday? Moreover, few people have developed the logical wit or mental tenacity to figure out such problems as the following:

> An employer has three equally qualified candidates for a position—Mr. A, Mr. B, and Mr. C. The employer decides to test the three candidates. He tells them: "I have placed a mark on each of your foreheads. Naturally, you cannot see your own mark, but you can see the mark of the other two candidates. The marks are either black or white; when you see a black mark on anybody's forehead, raise you hand. When you know the color of your mark, get up from your seat. Do not guess." All three men raise their hands, but nobody initially gets up. If you were Mr. C, could you determine the color of the mark on your forehead?[2]

Military decision makers, although concerned with decisions of both large and small consequence, are no less fallible in the use of logic and influence than are other professionals in their areas of expertise. These human foibles can be specifically mitigated through the design and use of DSSs. Indeed, military decision makers, knowing the consequences of poor decisions and rushed by circumstances beyond their control, must often make their decisions under considerable stress.

Interaction of DSS and DM

It is a well-accepted fact that man as an information processor is oriented to better understanding and digesting of information presented in a graphic or spatially related format as opposed to lists of data. In the planning of military operations, particularly, it would be literally impossible to fight a battle without maps and the geographic relationships of friendly and enemy positions and capabilities along with natural terrain or environmental features peculiar to the situation.

By interactively combining the storage, processing, and display power of a DSS with the mental acuity of the military DM for visually presented spatial relationships, the DSS achieves a degree of usefulness greater than the linear sum of its parts. Having previously stored information about friendly and enemy forces and having displayed a map of the terrain with various topographical features, such as roadways, it is a simple matter to extend a computer capability to calculate the route whereby, for example, ammunition could be moved to a critical point in the shortest time or medical supplies could be moved along a route with the greatest total demand.

These are the types of decision aids most commonly conjured up when one mentions decision support, and indeed, ones desperately needed in command and control decision making. Some of the methods that drive these aids include: linear and nonlinear programming, dynamic programming, queuing, inventory, and search techniques. Other analytical techniques that aid the decision maker and derive from potentially having already acquired the base data include: predictions of ammunition supply rates, predictions of transportation needs, conversions of coordinate systems, planning avenues of attack or defense, and similar situations.

Adaptability of DSS

The sophistication of today's information technology and the cost of this technology is such that with some flexibility and urgency in the acquisition process, DSSs could be placed at vital decision-making points today. True, the system may not do all things one would want, but if it does some at a low price, and offers the flexibility to do more as the problems and their solutions are better understood, then much has been gained and little lost.

TECHNOLOGY AND DECISION SUPPORT

There have been many advances in computer-related technology. These advances have been in the form of decreases in price and enhancement of performance and functionality. The power and ubiquity of the personal computer is significant to the emergence of DSSs from the stagnant approaches to command and control support system development.

The power of the personal computer was underscored by the Defense Science Board (DSB) Technology Base Summer Study of 1981. The purpose of this study was to identify and promote technologies that offer "order of magnitude improvement." Examples of technologies identified by the DSB are: very high speed integrated circuits (VHSIC), stealth, optoelectronics, and short-wavelength LASERS. Fourth on the list of the "top ten" was microprocessor-based personal learning aids.

The personal computer is ideally suited for training personnel in procedures, maintenance, weapon laying, leadership, planning, and decision-making. The personal computer has the features, characteristics, and often the capabilities of larger machines. But best of all, it is available to the individual user and can be tailored to meet the specific needs of the user's particular task.

Combined with other emerging technologies (e.g., video tape, video discs, Winchester disks for small computers, bubble memory, fiber optics, and speech analysis and synthesis), the personal computer can be found in numerous pilot projects to demonstrate its cost-effectiveness in training (see Figure 6.4). For example, at Ft. Gordon, it is being used to train soldiers in the maintenance of a complex piece of satellite communications equipment; at Ft. Benning, it is being used to train infantry officers in platoon leadership; at Ft. Leavenworth, it is being used to train officers in combat strategy through war gaming and simulation.

As familiarity with the computer grows from training situations such as these, it is inevitable that the personal computer will become an integral part of operational planning and decision making. Already, demonstrations employing personal computers

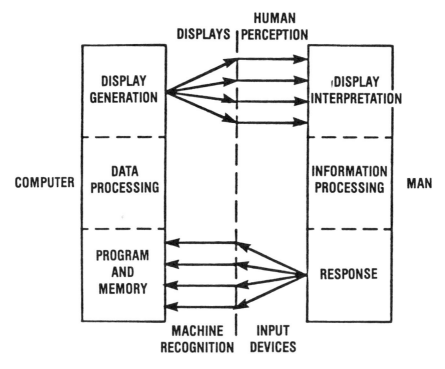

Figure 6.4   Digital and Analog Technology Combined to Meet Decision Support System Needs

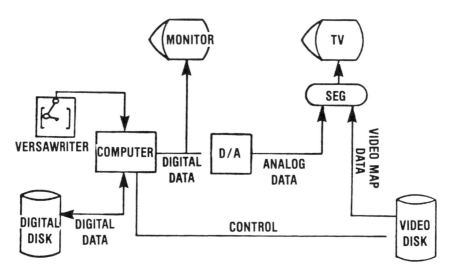

Figure 6.5   AWACS Planner

in specific areas of command and control have been developed by engineers at Georgia Tech for such diverse operations as: planning and locating water points for tactical ground forces, planning and controlling orbit points for the AWACS aircraft (see Figure 6.5), and controlling and monitoring large-scale energy management systems. Each of these projects has incorporated the characteristics requisite of DSS development, namely:

- Direct involvement of the user in the design;
- An initial capability that is real and usable; and
- Built-in interactive changeability.

CONCLUSION

The essence of command and control is decision-making, and it has long been recognized that computers can be used to help make decisions. With advances in technology, better understanding of how decisions are made, and with the application of a design philosophy that builds the user into an interactive man-machine combination at the point of decision, real progress in decision support is being made. The momentum is building, and with appropriate care and reasonable constraint, the coordinated effort of users, developers and researchers can converge in the development of even better DSSs to improve the effectiveness of our military forces and the decision makers who work in them.

NOTES

1. Most people find it difficult to believe the answer is not 0.75. Let

H = hypothesis of being invaded
D = troops massing at the border
R = report of troops massing at the border, and consider the Venn Diagram of Figure 6.1.

Figure 6.1 Venn Diagram

Note that the intersection of H with R is not existent, so that the conditional probability of being invaded given a report of massing at the border is zero. The reason one finds this result so surprising is the common logical fallacy that if R implies D, then D implies R. Although D does occur whenever R is given, the reverse is not necessarily the case. In other words, there may be a number of times that troops massed at the border but were never seen, never reported, *and* never attacked. (From Einhorn 1980.)

2. Mr. C's reasoning should go this way: "If my mark were white, then B would have known his was black since A raised his hand to indicate he could see a black mark. B has not made this deduction, therefore, that situation does not exist. The only alternative situation is that my mark is black—therefore I shall get up. (From Doubleday 1969.) Reprinted with permission of the Armed Forces Communications and Electronics Association (AFCEA)

REFERENCES

Defense Science Board. 1981. Summer Study of Technology Base. Defense Science Board Report.

Doubleday, E. 1969. *Test Your Wits*. New York: Ace Publishing Corporation.

Einhorn, H. 1980. Overconfidence in Judgement. *Annual Review of Psychology*.

Einhorn, H., and R. Hogarth. 1981. Behavioral Decision Theory: Processes of Judgement and Choice. *Annual Review of Psychology*.

Nisbett, R., and L. Ross. 1980. *Human Inference: Strategies and Shortcomings of Social Judgement*. Englewood Cliffs, N.J.: Prentice-Hall.

Teates, B., E. Shanahan, and B. Wise. 1980. Defining and Measuring C^2. *Military Electronics Countermeasures* (May and June), Vol. xxi, no. 6, pp. 41–60.

Tversky, A., D. Kahneman, and P. Slovic, eds. 1980. *Judgement Under Uncertainty: Heuristics and Biases*. New York: Cambridge University Prese, and similar situations.

7

Microcomputer-Based Decision Support for High-Order Corporate Crisis Management

Stephen J. Andriole

THE BACKDROP

Corporate priorities in the immediate and longer range futures will revolve around corporate interests and goals in dramatically changing national and international environments. These environments are and will continue to be characterized by political conflict, resource and energy scarcities, population expansion and maldistribution, increased nuclear proliferation and arms trade, heightened nationalism and especially terrorism, and unstable monetary and economic conditions. As a result of the predominant position that many corporations occupy in the national and international environments, these and other conditions will repeatedly give rise to problems with which they must deal; realistically, some of these problems will evolve into crises of the highest order, that is, crises that will involve human life and enormous amounts of plant and capital, and that occur without much warning.

Given that many corporations will be confronted with national and international problems and crises of all natures, it is imperative that *corporate crisis management* procedures be developed, routinely evaluated, and constantly improved.

Described below are a set of techniques designed to augment existing corporate crisis management procedures. All of the techniques are geared to the high-order corporate crisis. They are, consequently, designed for high stakes, short time, and low anticipation situations. They are also microcomputer-based and grounded in methods developed, tested, and applied in the U.S. intelligence community. The substantive emphases of the computer-based techniques include crisis warning, planning, decision-making, and evaluation.

HIGH-ORDER CORPORATE CRISES

Terrorism

The most catastrophic corporate crises involve threats to the lives of corporate officers, employees, representatives, and their families. Such threats have many origins and natures, including bombings of corporate facilities, hijackings, kidnappings, hostage holdings, barricades, and assassination attempts. Recent U.S. Department of Defense and Central Intelligence Agency statistics indicate conclusively that such threats are increasing dramatically in number and severity. The increase is due primarily to the increasing sophistication of the terrorist threat, the high rate of terrorist success, and the increasing internationalization of terrorist activity.

More specifically, from 1968 to 1979 the number of deaths from international terrorism rose from over 30 (in 1968) to nearly 600 (in 1979). (Total deaths for the 1968-1979 period were 2,700.) Geographically, the number of terrorist attacks since 1968 has been the greatest in Western Europe (over 1,200), Latin America (nearly 900), and North Africa/Middle East (over 500); dangerously high in North America (over 300) and Asia (nearly 200); and surprisingly low in the Soviet bloc (15) and Oceania (19).[1]

Figure 7.1 provides even more evidence of the contemporary terrorist threat. Note that 36.2 percent of all terrorist attacks since 1968 were directed against business executives and corporate facilities and that since 1968 two out of every five international terrorist incidents were targeted against citizens or property. Finally, in 1979, twelve Americans, including one Ambassador, died from terrorist attacks.[2] Much more recently, Iranian "student" terrorists held fifty-two Americans hostage for over fourteen months, citizens were blown up in London, and on and on.

According to all estimates, this dangerous trend in the number of terrorist attacks directed against private citizens and property will continue well into the 1980s. While projections beyond the 1980s are understandably fuzzier, it may well be that terrorism will remain with us for an indefinite period of time, despite strong national and international resolve to discourage it.

Foreign Political Instability

Another class of high-order corporate crises that will continue to confront decision makers is that which results from

Types

EXPLOSIVE BOMBINGS	1,588	(47.6%)
INCENDIARY BOMBINGS	456	(13.7%)
KIDNAPPINGS	263	(7.9%)
ASSASSINATIONS	246	(7.4%)
ARMED ATTACKS	188	(5.5%)
LETTER BOMBINGS	186	(5.5%)
HIJACKINGS	100	(3.0%)
THEFT/BREAK-INS	78	(2.3%)
BARRICADE & HOSTAGE	73	(2.2%)
SNIPINGS	71	(2.1%)
OTHER	87	(2.6%)

Targets

BUSINESS EXECUTIVES/FACILITIES	487	(36.2%)
DIPLOMATIC OFFICIALS/PROPERTY	273	(20.3%)
OTHER GOVERNMENTAL OFFICIALS	217	(16.1%)
MILITARY OFFICIALS/PROPERTY	204	(15.1%)
PRIVATE CITIZENS	166	(12.3%)

Figure 7.1   International Terrorist Incidents by Type, Target, and Percentage: 1968–1979

foreign domestic instability. In the 1970s, for example, vested corporate interests were threatened—and in some cases lost altogether—in Vietnam, Nicaragua, and Iran. More recently, there have been severe problems in Tunisia, West Sahara, Lebanon, El Salvador, Saudi Arabia, Pakistan, and Ethiopia, among others. All of these recent and potential problems and crises threaten corporate interests abroad in unpredictable and dramatic ways. Corporate contingency planning and crisis decision-making procedures must thus develop in perfect harmony with expectations about the likelihood of foreign catastrophes.

International Conflict

In addition to foreign domestic upheavals we can expect numerous international conflicts to occur in the immediate and longer range futures. The Soviet invasion of Afghanistan, the Falkland conflict, and the Israeli invasion of Lebanon are particularly illustrative of the unpredictable and volatile nature of the international arena. In all likelihood, conflicts will develop in the Middle East, Africa, and Latin America during the next five years. Some of these conflicts will be minor and short-lived, but others will have serious regional and even global implications involving the superpowers in at least indirect confrontation.

These international conflicts exert an enormous impact upon international business. Direct impact will take the form of factory, labor, and agreement loss and indirect impact will be felt in response to the inevitable flood of economic and political reactions to the conflicts. Recent examples of direct impact include the loss of markets and plant in Iran, Vietnam, and Lebanon; examples of indirect impact include the cessation of wheat shipments to the Soviet Union and the loss of lucrative Olympic broadcasting contracts—both in response to the Soviet invasion of Afghanistan. More recent is the American attempt to delay construction of the Soviet-European gas pipeline which caused severe problems for more than a few corporations.

Monetary and Trade Instability

Before, during, and after terrorist attacks and intranational and international conflicts, monetary and trade conditions change dramatically. Exchange rates, capital flows, and feverish trade competition all contribute to corporate risk and uncertainty. Frequently, this risk and uncertainty occurs in connection with huge financial interests and responsibilities where urgency and complexity only exacerbate the situation, and where the necessity for successful corporate crisis management is critical. Two examples can be found in Poland and Mexico, where national financial problems have triggered larger international ones.

Domestic Political Instability

As unpleasant as it may be to accept, it is likely that the 1980s will bring some measure of political instability to the U.S. and other highly industrialized nations. Whether caused by outside or indigenous individuals or groups, potential unrest may take many forms, ranging from bombings and hijackings, all the way to assassinations. Persistent inflation, chronic unemployment, and dangerously widening income gaps may well result in terrorism directed at specific corporations.

High-Order Crisis Characteristics

The plans, decisions, and evaluations necessitated by the above high-order corporate crises all involve very high human and financial stakes, all generally occur without warning, and almost always require timely response. The techniques described below are designed to deal with these characteristics.

HIGH-ORDER CORPORATE CRISIS MANAGEMENT TECHNOLOGY

The scope of high-order corporate crisis management comprises both crisis warning and crisis decision making. Three computer-based techniques will be presented. The first, relevant to corporate crisis warning, is a computer program called INFER. The second and third, relevant to corporate crisis decision making, are called OPINT and EVAL.[3]

Corporate Crisis Warning

High-order corporate crisis warning involves the development of models, comprised of data and key indicators, which provide corporate managers with early warnings of important domestic and international events and conditions. Lest there be any confusion about this goal, I am in no way suggesting that specific warnings consisting of dates, events, participants, and consequences can ever be generated; the state of our forecasting methodology prohibits such precision. However, while we cannot generate precise early warnings of specific events and conditions, it is possible to model sets of antecedent events and conditions which, when monitored via estimates regarding their rates of change and likely states at future times, will permit us to generate warnings of events and conditions likely to precede or precipitate a corporate crisis.

Such early warning models come in many shapes and sizes. Some are very complex and rely upon massive amounts of quantitative data and advanced statistical routines. Quantitative-statistical models are expensive to build and maintain; and extremely time-consuming to use. But more importantly, they are usually mistargeted at forecasting such fluid recalcitrant phenomena as political instability, monetary crises, and international conflict. In fact, several methodological assessments have concluded that quantitative-empirical causal and econometric models have failed to reliably forecast any intranational and international events and conditions.[4]

Early warning techniques that rely upon the wisdom and judgment of experienced analysts are often preferred by governments and corporations because they are usually easier to implement and less expensive than quantitative-empirical ones. They are also usually more accurate. But this is not to imply that all qualitative methodologies are superior to quantitative-statistical ones. Unstructured intuition, for example, can be confusing and even dangerous when applied to intranational and international forecasting problems. The argument here is that *structured qualitative methodologies* can be expected to perform at least as well as quantitative ones and frequently much better.

INFER

One structured qualitative methodology, based upon Bayes's theorem of conditional probabilities, is incarnated in the computer program INFER. INFER, developed for the U.S. Department of Defense, involves the development of *influence diagrams.*[5] The diagrams assist decision makers in processing the relevant objective and subjective information that determines the relative likelihoods of the various possible outcomes of a future event. The overall objective of influence diagramming is to ensure that the decision maker's judgments about the probability of a future uncertain event are realistic and consistent with available information relevant to the unfolding of the target event or events.

As Figure 7.2 suggests, influence diagrams are really inference models that recognize a number of key events upon which other events may depend, almost in a chain-reactive fashion.

In the example in Figure 7.2 (of an actual U.S. Defense Department application), it was necessary to determine the likelihood that an evacuation (from Lebanon in 1976) would be necessary and where, in the light of an evacuation, the U.S.

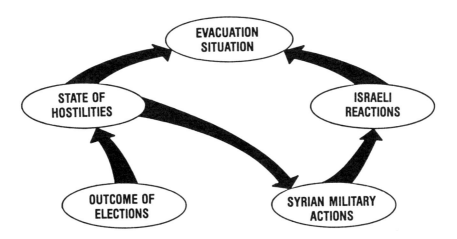

Figure 7.2   Lebanon Evacuation Influence Diagram

Sixth Fleet should be positioned. Assumptions about the level of hostilities in Lebanon had an impact upon forecasts of the number of personnel to be evacuated and whether the evacuation would be calm or violent. However, an assessment of the level of hostilities depended in turn upon the uncertain outcome of the elections upcoming in Lebanon. Additional uncertainties affecting the likelihood of an evacuation concerned what the Syrian armed forces might do and the impact in turn of their actions upon potential Israeli involvement.

The influence diagram enabled intelligence analysts to assess the overall likelihood of an evacuation by assessing the likelihood of the events and conditions that "drove" the overall evacuation likelihood.[6]

Let us look more closely at how the procedure works. For the purposes of this discussion imagine that the evacuation probability was as important to a corporation as it was to the U.S. Sixth Fleet. How would the corporate managers have used INFER? The first step would have involved the assembly of the corporate experts who knew the most about Middle East political affairs generally and the likelihood of the specific evacuation at hand. After an initial discussion which would have identified countless "causal" events and conditions, the experts would have "pruned" the list down to its most diagnostic items. The causal events in figure 7.2 constitute such a pruned list.

But in order to use the influence diagram the corporate experts would have defined each of the events in the diagram according to their possible outcomes. Four possible election outcomes were identified: pro-Syrian, anti-Syrian, unheld because of Syrian intervention, and unheld because of PLO action. The outcomes for the elections were identified first because elections is an "unconditioned" event, that is, unaffected by some other event or condition (see Figure 7.2). The next step would have required the experts to identify the possible outcomes of hostilities *given* the possible outcomes of the elections. INFER would have asked the corporate crisis manager to define hostilities (which, in this case, were defined as possibly decreasing, holding constant, increasing in Beirut, or increasing country-wide) and then assess the probability of each outcome given the occurrence of each possible election outcome. INFER would thus have asked the corporate experts the following questions:

- If the Lebanese elections are held and are pro-Syrian what is the probability of each possible outcome of hostilities?
- If the Lebanese elections are held and are anti-Syrian what is the probability of each possible outcome of hostilities?
- If the Lebanese elections are not held because of Syrian action, what is the probability of each possible outcome of hostilities?
- If the Lebanese elections are not held because of PLO action, what is the probability of each possible outcome of hostilities?

The experts would have assigned numeric probabilities to each of the outcomes (given the possible election outcomes) ranging from 0 to 100 percent, and would have repeated the whole procedure for the other events in the influence diagram. Probabilities for each possible outcome for each of the conditioned events would have been input to INFER given the unconditioned outcomes until all of the events had been assessed. INFER would then have calculated the overall probability of the evacuation based upon all of the subjective probabilities. If any of the experts felt that the overall probability was too high or too low, they could have asked INFER to recalculate the evacuation probability based upon any number of modified probabilities, probabilities that may have been questioned during the initial assessment.

As a system for generating early warnings of impending corporate crises, INFER can be used by specialists in regional and country affairs who might construct diagrams of uncertain events likely to influence the occurrence or nonoccurrence of a particular corporate crisis, such as a kidnapping, a revolution, or a foreign invasion. Probabilities about the likely changes in the uncertain events could then be elicited to generate an overall crisis likelihood, or warning. If the overall crisis probability was considered high enough, then crisis decision-making tools could be used to decide precisely what (and what not) to do in response.

Corporate Crisis Decision Making

When a crisis erupts, time and decision-making support are almost always in short supply. Generally near chaos breaks out and for want of a preconceived plan of action, decisions are often made based upon emotion and fact-free arguments.

Fortunately, a methodology has emerged over the past decade that is tailor-made for crisis situations. The methodology is *decision analysis*, which has its roots in operations research and systems theory. Formal decision analysis is a quantitative method that permits the evaluation of the costs or benefits associated with various courses of action. It involves the identification of alternative choices, the assignment of values for outcomes, and outcome probabilities.

> In the application of decision analysis, a problem is *decomposed* into clearly defined components in which all options, outcomes, values, and probabilities are depicted. *Quantification* in the form of the value for each possible outcome and the probability of those values (or costs) being realized can be in terms of objective information or in the form of quantitative expressions of the subjective judgments of experts. In the latter case, the quantitative expression serves to make *explicit* those subjective qualities which would otherwise be weighted in the decision process, albeit in a more elusive, intuitive way.
>
> Beyond its primary role of serving as a method for the logical solution of complex decision problems, decision analysis has additional advantages as well. The formal structure of decision analysis makes clear all the elements, their relationships, and their associated weights that have been considered in a decision problem. If only because the model is explicit, it can serve an important role in facilitating communication among those involved in the decision process. With a decision problem structured in a decision analytic framework, it is an easy matter to identify the location, extent, and importance of any areas of disagreement, and to determine whether such disagreements have any material impact on the indicated decision. In addition, should there be any change in the circumstances bearing upon a given decision problem, it is fairly straightforward to reenter the existing problem

structure to change values or to add or remove problem dimensions as required.

It should be emphasized that in no sense does decision analysis replace decision makers with arithmetic or change the role of wise human judgment in decision making. Rather, it provides an orderly and more easily understood structure that helps to aggregate the wisdom of experts on the many topics that may be needed to make a decision, and it suports the skilled decision maker by providing him with logically sound techniques to support, supplement, and ensure the internal consistency of his judgments.[7]

Two specific computer-based decision analytic tools are ideal for corporate crisis management use. The first is OPINT and the second is EVAL.

OPINT

OPINT (for Options Screening and Intelligence Assessment) was, like INFER, developed for the U.S. Department of Defense, and has been incarnated as a microcomputer program in a powerful software language (APL). OPINT aids decision makers by enabling them to construct, store, and exercise decision analytic models of complex option selection problems.

Each decision model created by the OPINT user has a unique label, and each is constructed by using the same procedure. A sample OPINT model is shown graphically in Figure 7.3. The format always consists of the following elements:[8]

- The decision—a short label, D, defining the decision problem
- Decision alternatives—a list of the decision alternatives $(D_1, D_2, \ldots D_n)$ available to the decision maker
- An uncertain future event—a key uncertain event, E, that will influence the eventual outcome of the decision
- Event outcomes—a list of event outcomes $(E_1, E_2 \ldots E_n)$ which together define the set of possibilities regarding the occurrence of the future event
- Event probabilities—a vector of probabilities $(p_1, p_2 \ldots p_n)$ associated with the event outcomes, such as p_i represents the probability that event E_i will occur

- Decision outcomes—paired combinations of one decision alternative with one event outcome

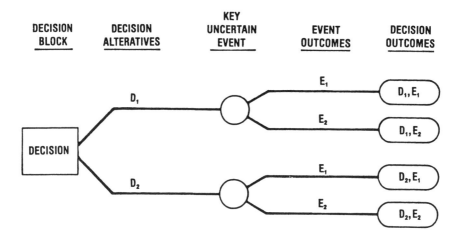

Figure 7.3   An OPINT Decision Model

The next three elements of the OPINT model specify the consequences associated with each decision outcome. The consequeces of outcomes are in the form of relative "regrets":[9]

- Decision outcome criteria—criteria $(C_1, C_2 \ldots C_g)$ by which the decision maker can judge the relative regret associated with each decision outcome
- Criteria weights—a vector of weights $(w_1, w_2 \ldots w_g)$ associated with the criteria, such that w_i represents the relative contribution of criterion C_i
- Regret—a measure of the consequence of an outcome. The total outcome regret is a weighted linear combination of the individual criteria regrets. For each criterion $(C_i$ and for each decision outcome (D_j, E_k), the user must specify a value of regret (r_{ijk}), all as suggested in Figure 7.4.

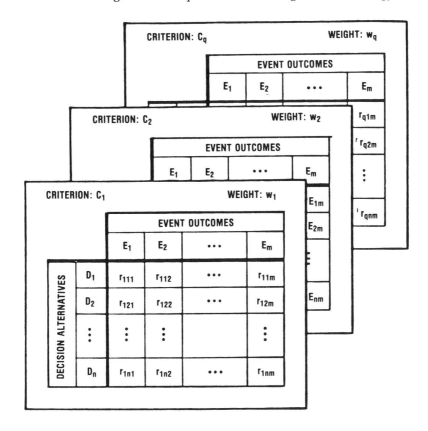

Figure 7.4   Decision Outcome Regret Matrices

The OPINT software system could very easily be used by corporate crisis managers to analyze decision options against sets of specific criteria relevant to the protection of human life, plant, equipment, capital, contracts, and agreements. The necessary input to the system, which consists of option delineation, event probabilities, decision outcome criteria, and regrets, could all be provided by corporate specialists in all of the relevant decision areas. Consequently, many different corporate experts could participate in the management of high-order corporate crises.

EVAL

EVAL is a computer-based decision-aiding evaluation system, also developed for the U.S. Department of Defense, designed to help decision makers solve problems of evaluation under relative certainty, that is, when a problem is not particularly affected by the probability of a key event occurring or not occurring. EVAL can aid corporate decision makers by prescribing a straightforward normative procedure for organizing and analyzing difficult evaluation problems.[10]

EVAL provides a logical evaluation strategy that has several desirable features. First it discriminates among the various alternatives being evaluated, and produces a ranking of the alternatives in terms of the overall subjective values of the decision makers; is also measures the differences among the alternatives.

EVAL models are hierarchical in nature, starting with the overall top-level criterion for which the evaluation score is desired.[11] The factor is decomposed in descending levels from the general to the specific.

As indicated in Figure 7.5, the decision maker must decompose the overall evaluation criterion into its component criteria. Those, in turn, are decomposed until the decision makers cannot get any more specific. When the model is well structured corporate decision makers must make two kinds of assessments: relative utility scores for the various alternatives and relative importance weights for the various criteria, as suggested in Figure 7.5.

Once the model has been structured and the utility scores and importance weights specified, overall utilities for each of the decision alternatives can be produced. The rational user will choose the alternative that has the greatest overall value. Like INFER and OPINT, EVAL permits decision makers to conduct sensitivity analyses, enabling them to play "what if" scenarios against the results of their analyses.

EVAL is applicable to those crisis management situations that are characterized by little uncertainty and many possible decisions. Since EVAL permits managers to evaluate alternatives against an explicit set of criteria, it is possible to assess the desirability of each alternative according to how well it satisfies the criteria identified by corporate crisis managers, criteria

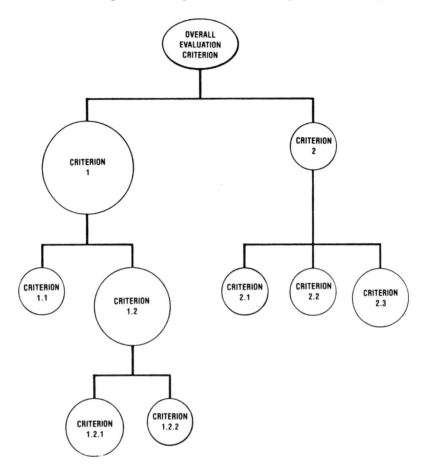

Figure 7.5   An Evaluation Structure

that may be as numerous and substantively diverse as necessary. Also, like INFER and OPINT, EVAL is a computer-based tool which is fast, efficient, and always ready to go.

It is important to once again note what goes into INFER, OPINT, and EVAL and what comes out. All three computer programs rely explicitly upon the subjective judgments of experts and crisis managers. In the case of INFER, the judgments are expressed as (0–100%) probabilities. OPINT also relies upon event probabilities as well as judgments regarding the benefits and "regrets" (costs) connected with each decision option under consideration. EVAL requires the decision maker to identify and rank criteria for evaluating each decision option, and then to score each option vis-à-vis the ranked criteria.

In terms of output, INFER produces an overall crisis probability based upon the probabilities of the events and conditions that the corporate experts designate as likely to influence the occurrence or nonoccurrence of the potential corporate crisis. OPINT produces a benefit/regret-based ranked list of decision options that is grounded in the values that the crisis managers assign to the options, and the probabilities that they assign to a single key event. EVAL produces a ranked list of decision alternatives that not only identifies a "winner" but also measures the distance between all of the alternatives. EVAL also lets the decision makers vary their criteria weights and decision alternative scores, and will generate new lists based upon the changes.

The strength of each software system lies in its ability to organize and structure the expert judgments of crisis managers; at the same time, its output is only as accurate and useful as the input that produces it. If the judgments are uninformed, INFER, OPINT, and EVAL will process them in precisely the same way they process informed ones.

CORPORATE CRISIS MANAGEMENT STRATEGY & TACTICS

INFER, OPINT, and EVAL are the tools by which high-order corporate crises can be managed effectively. But their proper strategic and tactical use is critical to success.

Strategic Corporate Crisis Management

High-order corporate crises almost always occur without any warning at all. Research in crisis management decision making indicates that managers are by and large unprepared when a crisis erupts.[12] *Strategic crisis management* thus involves contingency planning for classes of high-order crises, planning that will enable crisis managers to approach a decision-making problem from positions of analytical strength. *Contingency planning* itself involves identifying key decision makers, listing and modeling decision options, and specifying the criteria for cost/benefit and tradeoff analyses of the options. It also involves the development of influence diagrams that will provide some measure of early warning.

In the case of an OPINT problem, strategic contingency planning involves the structuring of OPINT models for specific kinds of high-order crises, such as hostage situations, political and military coups in countries where corporate interests exist, and monetary crises. Contingency planning for EVAL problems should involve the building of EVAL structures that list and weight necessary evaluative criteria.

This planning will enable corporate decision makers to deal with crises more rationally and effectively. (Interestingly, where governments spend millions of dollars each year to construct contingency plans for all natures, industry often deals with crises in an ad hoc manner.)

The logistics connected with strategic contingency planning for high-order corporate crisis management is straightforward. Generally, an influence diagram or OPINT or EVAL structure can be built in one day, exercised over a period of days, and then "canned" for future use. All of this can be done on a very small portable microcomputer and should involve those likely to be involved in the crisis management episode.

Tactical Corporate Crisis Management

Strategic crisis management is similar to preventive maintenance. But when a crisis erupts, tactical management becomes critical. Since every crisis is unique to some extent, the contingency plans, while enormously useful, will give way to the particulars of the crisis at hand after it erupts. As new information and considerations come to light, the decision models will have to be modified and exercised. In all likelihood, a corporate command center will have to be established. The planning and preparation for emergency situations should include provisions for locating and equipping a room to serve as a command center if a crisis should erupt. As the focal point for operations and the dissemination of information, the command center should be centrally located, equipped with files, maps, corporate personnel data, and communications equipment. The corporate contingency plans, influence diagrams, decision models, and all other aids should be kept in the command center ready for use when needed. Finally, key corporate officials should be familiarized with the crisis management plans, techniques, and command center. They should be prepared to respond to a crisis by managing the command center on short notice, ready to take the required emergency actions.

CONCLUSION

Presented above are a set of ideas that in large part are an outgrowth of an observation of the U.S. defense community's efforts to improve its crisis warning and management capabilities. They are also grounded in a perception that by and large corporations have not invested to upgrade their crisis management capabilities even in the face of the increasing frequency with which corporate crises occur. All of the ideas have been thoroughly and repeatedly tested and applied to real crises. In addition, prior applications have demonstrated conclusively the suitability of the techniques to situations characterized by short time, high stakes, and uncertainty.

Prior planning can enormously prepare corporate crisis managers, minimizing the chaos that inevitably occurs when a crisis erupts. In fact, precrisis-developed warning and decision-making models can often mean the difference between a successfully and unsuccessfully resolved high-order crisis.

All of this is geared to the high-order corporate crisis, which may occur at any time and involve the protection of human life and large corporate financial interests. Hopefully, such crises will occur infrequently as we move into the 1980s. But if they occur with the frequency that has been predicted, we must be prepared to maneuver our way through them effectively.

NOTES

Thanks to Bill Page and Dick Van Orden for many helpful comments and suggestions. Stephen J. Andriole is the President of International Information Systems, Inc., 802 Woodward Road, Marshall, Virginia, 22115, USA.

1. Central Intelligence Agency as cited in *U.S. News and World Report*, November 26, 1981, p. 29.

2. Ibid, p. 29.

3. INFER, OPINT, and EVAL are described in R.M. Gulick, *Documentation of Decision-Aiding Software: Introductory Guide* (McLean, Va.: Decisions and Designs, Inc., February 1980). The computer programs are available from the U.S. Defense Department's Advanced Research Projects Agency's Defense Sciences Office's Systems Sciences Division (DARPA/DSO/SSD) at 1400 Wilson Boulevard, Arlington, VA, 22209, USA. Technical Information about the government-supported computer programs can be obtained from Decisions and Designs, Inc., 8400 Westpark Drive, McLean, VA, 22101, USA, or from the author.

4. See S.J. Andriole and G.W. Hopple, *An Assessment of Political Instability Research Methodologies* (Marshall, Va.: International Information Systems, Inc., September 1982), and J.S. Armstrong, *Long-Range Forecasting: From Crystal Ball to Computer* (New York: John Wiley and Sons, 1978).

5. See Gulick, *Documentation of Decision-Aiding Software*, for more detail about INFER and influence diagrams.

6. For a fuller discussion of this episode see C.W. Kelly, III, S. J. Andriole, and J.A. Daly, "Computer-Based Decision Analysis: An Application to a Middle East Evacuation Problem," *Jerusalem Journal of International Relations*, 5(2): 62–84 (1981).

7. S. Barclay, R.V. Brown, C.W. Kelly, III, C.R. Peterson, J.D. Phillips, and J. Selvidge, *Handbook for Decision Analysis* (McLean, Va.: Decisions and Designs, Inc., September 1977), vi–vii.

8. This section is based upon D.M. Amey, P.H. Feuerwerger, and R.M. Gulick, *Documentation of Decision-Aiding Software: OPINT Functional Description* (McLean, Va.: Decisions and Designs, Inc., April 1979).

9. Ibid.

10. This section is based upon L.B. Allardyce, D. M. Amey, P.H. Feuerwerger, and R.M. Gulick, *Documentation of Decision-Aiding Software:*

EVAL Functional Description (McLean, Va.: Decisions and Designs, Inc., September 1979).

11. EVAL is based upon multiattribute utility theory developed primarily by Professor Ward Edwards of the University of Southern California. See his *How to Use Multi-Attribute Utility Measurement for Social Decision-Making* (Los Angeles: University of Southern California, 1976).

12. See L.A. Hazlewood and J.J. Hayes, *Planning for Problems in Crisis Management* (Arlington, Va.: CACI, Inc., 1976) who report that during the period from 1945 to 1975 the U.S. intelligence community was unprepared for over 58 percent of the crises that occurred, crises that were unanticipated nearly as frequently as they were anticipated. Also see C.F. Smart and W.T. Stanbury, eds., *Studies on Crisis Management* (Scarborough, Ontario: Butterworth & Co., 1978).

III

DECISION SUPPORT
SYSTEM APPLICATIONS

INTRODUCTION

Laboratories are always disconnected from reality. Some are worse than others, of course. In decision support systems labs all over the world interactive systems designers conceive of systems that they sincerely believe will solve nearly all of their intended users' problems. When the system is tested, however, the endless stream of "why doesn't it . . . ?" questions begin. After too many sessions with users the designers throw up their hands in frustration and adopt a "take it or leave it attitude."

There are a variety of approaches one can take to avoid—or at least minimize—tech transfer shock. The *participatory approach* to interactive systems design and development is sound and proven, as is the more recently championed *rapid prototyping approach*, an approach that calls for the iterative development of several systems as a means toward the identification of requirements.

The articles in this part of the book represent efforts to design, develop, test, and transfer decision support systems. The first article by Ruth Phelps documents some Army experiences that turned out well, but not as anticipated. The decision-making tasks involved assessing the likelihood of alternative adversary courses of action, and assessing the impact of new intelligence information upon prior probabilities of important battlefield events. It should be noted that these are especially difficult and important intelligence tasks and the design of a useful decision support system to perform them (better and faster than humans) was a formidable task in and of itself. The results of the experimental applications suggested that the "aids" were not as appropriate for operational use as was hoped; yet, at the same time, were extremely powerful training tools.

The article by Bessent, Bessent, Clark, and Elam describes how microcomputer decision support systems can be used to improve managerial efficiency. The application itself involved the development of a productivity analysis support system (PASS), which is an optimization-based decision support system.

The design of PASS began with an identification of the kinds of questions managers need immediate answers for. They included some of the following:

- How effectively have available resources been used?
- Which aspects of operations can and should be improved?
- What are reasonable goals?
- How much money do we need to perform what services?

Bessent, Bessent, Clark, and Elam describe an application case study of PASS involving the Educational Productivity Council in Texas, a case study with excellent results.

The last article in Part III belongs to Allene K. Cormier, who describes a project involving the networking of decision support systems functions in a high technology organization. Her case study is as informative and encouraging as the Bessent, Bessent, Clark, and Elam one, but reflects a perspective gained only from one who has lived "in the trenches." The value of the Cormier article can be traced to the meticulous approach to systems configuration, training, debugging, and general "hand-holding" necessary to successfully implement a decision support system.

8

Decision Aids For Military Intelligence Analysis: Description, Evaluation, and Implementation

Ruth H. Phelps

The purpose of this chapter is to describe the design and evaluation of two computerized aids for conducting tactical military intelligence analysis for the U.S. Army. Although both aids are based on decision-analytic methodologies (multiattribute utility assessment (MAU) and Bayesian techniques), novel modifications have been incorporated to accommodate the specific user requirements of military intelligence analysts. In addition, because the design of the aids was based on five years of research on the cognitive processes underlying intelligence analysis, extensive user participation and on-site evaluations were possible. The first section of the chapter is devoted to a brief description of the specific intelligence analysis task that was aided with special attention given to the description of the subjective nature of analysis. The second section describes the aids and evaluations. The final section of the chapter discusses the implementation of decision aids.

MILITARY INTELLIGENCE ANALYSIS

The goal of intelligence analysis is to predict enemy behavior. In the tactical arena, intelligence analysts give their best estimates of where the enemy is, the enemy composition (strength and type of enemy units), and what the enemy is both capable of doing and is likely to do. The job is exceedingly difficult because the information to be used is both of unknown validity and reliability. In addition, there are often severe time constraints and personnel limitations. Data are often summarized, then passed on to others for additional analyses, thus allowing errors in the original summaries to be compounded in the later analyses. Although the military is explicit about the goals of analyses, there are few procedures for ensuring that it is carried out logically and systematically. Therefore it was felt that intelligence analysis would indeed be a good candidate for decision-analytic aiding.

In order to understand the process of intelligence analysis, a detailed descriptive study was conducted (U.S. Army, 1984; Thompson, et al. 1984). Because much of intelligence analysis appeared to be subjective, special attention was devoted to understanding the nature of the necessary human judgments. Some of the results of this descriptive study are summarized in Figure 8.1: a simplified lens model diagram of the judgments within the intelligence process (see Hammond, et al. 1980 for a description of lens model analyses). Recall that the goal of intelligence analysis is to predict enemy intent or capability (the right circle in Figure 8.1).; but because the true enemy intent is unknown (left circle, Figure 8.1), the intelligence analyst must make predictions based on information and indicators that serve as cues (center, Figure 8.1). Predictions are accurate to the extent they match true enemy intent, as shown by the arrow in Figure 8.1. Accuracy thus depends on: (1) how reliably the indicators reflect enemy intent and (2) the degree to which the analyst bases predictions on the most reliable indicators. The identification and integration of the indicators into the intelligence estimate depends largely on the personal judgment of the individual analyst.

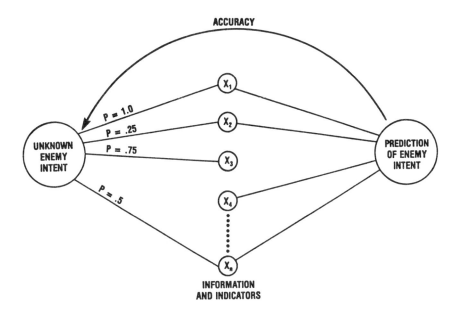

Figure 8.1   Information and indicators are unreliable, as shown by the probabilistic connection between the unknown enemy intent and the indicators (p = probability). Judgment problems occur because indicators that are not connected to enemy intent are sometimes used, e.g., X_4; indicators that are reliable are sometimes not used at all, e.g., X_3.

The subjective nature of intelligence analysis becomes even more obvious when the probabilistic nature of the indicators is considered, as shown in the center of Figure 8.1.There are at least three factors that complicate the analyst's judgment. First, each piece of information reveals the enemy's true intent less than 100 percent of the time; in other words the indicators are unreliable. Second, the analyst may not use some of the indicators regardless of their reliability, as shown by the absence of the line from X_3 to the right in Figure 8.1. Third, some indicators that are not related at all to the enemy intent may influence the analyst's prediction, as shown by the absence of the line from X_4 to the left in Figure 8.1. The subjective nature of the analyst's tasks make the need for systematic procedures (e.g. decision aids) all the more critical.

There are six ways that decision aids can support the judgments made by the analyst. Decision aids can:

1. Provide a framework for organizing the data and information so that it can be applied to any new problem.
2. Provide logical procedures for weighing the importance of both individual pieces of information and categories of information (e.g. terain, enemy reserves). Using a decision aid requires *explicit* evaluation of information so that relevant information is not easily overlooked.
3. Provide logical procedures for integrating analyzed information into a single judgment, prediction, or assessment. Often these are computerized procedures.
4. Provide the analysts with feedback about their own evaluations (e.g., relative importance they placed on different factors or pieces of information; feedback on the robustness of their evaluations). This type of feedback is typically called sensitivity analysis.
5. Provide a vehicle for conducting personal wargaming in order to ask "what if" questions. Computerized aids can store many analyses simultaneously so that analysts can, for example, predict enemy courses of action during both clear and rainy weather. In addition, analyses can be conducted and stored based on assumptions, such as "if blue forces attack, how will that change my prediction of the enemy" or "what if they have three motorized rifle regiments instead of two."
6. Provide a record of each analyst's or group of analysts evaluations. These can be used to: (*a*) evaluate a trainee's analytical strengths and weaknesses, (*b*) compare two different analyst's evaluations and, (*c*) communicate the

background and rationale of an analysis to the commander or supervisor.

Research conducted over the last twenty-five years in both laboratory and military environments has amply demonstrated that the types of predictions required of intelligence analysts are usually difficult and often impossible to make accurately. The most consistent finding of research on human predictions is that errors are not caused by lack of knowledge so much as they are by a difficulty in implementing and using the information that *is* known in a reliable and consistent manner (Adelman, et al. 1983). Thus, decision aids that help analysts to systematically evaluate and integrate information should improve the quality of judgment in the analytical process.

DESCRIPTION AND EVALUATION OF DECISION AIDS

One of the major tasks of tactical intelligence analysis is to evaluate the relative likelihood of enemy options. These options may be to attack or not attack; or once it has been determined that the enemy will attack, the options may be the alternative routes that could be taken during the attack. As discussed in the previous section, intelligence analysts need structured procedures for evaluating such enemy options. Furthermore it was apparent from the U.S. Army's descriptive case study of intelligence analysts that much of analysis is conducted prior to the initiation of battle and analyses are only updated during the battle (U.S. Army 1984). Thus, two decision aids were developed: (1) a multiattribute utility assessment (MAU) aid was developed to help analysts evaluate their static data prior to battle and (2) a Bayesian aid was developed to help in the integration of sequential, dynamic data in the updating of the analysis.

A MAU Aid for Evaluating Enemy Options

Aid Description. The aid for evaluating the relative likelihood of Enemy Courses of Action (ENCOA) before the start of battle is based on MAU procedures. The ENCOA aid is available in two manual versions: one relies totally on paper and pencil and the other uses the HP41C or HP41C-V handheld calculator. It is also available in two computerized versions: one for IBM 5110/5120 computer in APL; and one for the Apple II Plus computer in PASCAL. Complete descriptions can be found by Patterson, et al. (1983) and by Phelps, et al. (1982).

ENCOA assists judgment by breaking down the decision problem (predicting enemy courses of action) into broad tactical factor categories and individual component factors so that each breakdown is more specific than the one preceeding; in other words, a hierarchy of factors is established. Factor categories include Terrain, U.S. Forces, Enemy Forces, Weather, and Risk. These five categories are further divided into the twenty-five individual factors listed in Table 8.1.

Use of ENCOA requires the following five steps:

Step 1. Define COAs. Analysts define which enemy options or courses of action (COA) will be evaluated in the analysis. Usually two to five COAs can be determined.

Step 2. Evaluate COAs. The analyst must evaluate the feasibility to the enemy commander of each COA on each of the twenty-five factors. ENCOA uses a relative scoring system: the best COS (from the enemy's point of view) on a factor is given a score of 100, the worst COA on that factor is given a 0, and other COAs are given intermediate values. Table 8.2 shows a sample analysis; note that the feasibility scores (values) for all factors are listed by each category. Thus in the category *Terrain*, factor 1.1 is ranked 0 for COA_1, 100 for CAO_2, and 70 for COA_3.

Step 3. Evaluate Importance of Factors. Specifying the relative importance or *weight* of the twenty-five factors is done in two phases.

First, the analyst assigns weights to the factors within each category separately. For example, the six factors within the terrain category are assigned weights corresponding to their importance relative to each other. The most important of the six terrain factors is given a weight of 100; the other five factors are given weights proportional to the most important factor (a factor 90

Table 8.1   FACTORS IN ENCOA

I.   Terrain Factors

1.1   Field of fire afforded by terrain fetaures
1.2   Cover and concealment afforded by terrain features
1.3   Mobility provisions due to terrain features
1.4   Rapid seizure or denial of key terrain
1.5   Observation provisions of terrain
1.6   Accomodates natural and artificial obstacles

II.   U.S. Force Factors

2.1   U.S. disposition
2.2   U.S. strength and condition
2.3   U.S. reserves
2.4   U.S. logistic support
2.5   Probable U.S. actions/reactions
2.6   U.S. command and control capabilities/vulnerabilities

III.   Opposing Force Factors

3.1   OPFOR current disposition
3.2   OPFOR strength and condition
3.3   OPFOR reserves
3.4   OPFOR logistic support
3.5   OPFOR command and control capabilities/vulnerabilities

IV.   Weather Factors

4.1   Observation/visibility conditions forecast to exist due to weather
4.2   Cover and concealment conditions forecast to exist due to weather
4.3   Mobility conditions forecast to exist due to weather
4.4   Effect of extreme conditions of forecast weather on personnel and equipment effectiveness

V.   Risk Factors

5.1   Ability to cope with surprises in terms of U.S. strength or U.S. actions/reactions
5.2   Freedom from dependence on forces not under own control
5.3   Freedom from critical dependence on surprise or deception
5.4   Suitability under unexpected adverse weather conditions

Table 8.2   SAMPLE ENCOA ANALYSIS

FACTOR CATEGORY:	VALUES			RELATIVE
TERRAIN	COA$_1$	COA$_2$	COA$_3$	WEIGHTS
1.1 Fields of Fire	0	100	70	20%
1.2 Cover and Conceal	0	30	100	16%
1.3 Mobility	100	10	0	5%
1.4 S/D Key Terrain	10	0	100	25%
1.5 Observation	20	0	100	22%
1.6 Obstacles	0	100	90	12%
Weighted Scores	12	37	88	Total = 100%
FACTOR CATEGORY: US FORCES				
2.1 Disposition	100	0	70	23%
2.2 Strength & Condition	100	20	0	6%
2.3 Reserves	0	100	30	25%
2.4 Logistic Support	70	0	100	13%
2.5 Actions & Reactions	20	100	0	15%
2.6 Command & Control	100	0	90	18%
Weighted Scores	58	41	53	Total = 100%
FACTOR CATEGORY: OPFOR				
3.1 Disposition	0	100	90	10%
3.2 Strength & Condition	0	50	100	35%
3.3 Reserves	0	70	100	30%
3.4 Logistic Support	20	100	80	5%
3.5 Command & Control	0	10	100	20%
Weighted Scores	1	57	98	Total = 100%
FACTOR CATEGORY: WEATHER				
4.1 Observation & Visibility	0	100	80	20%
4.2 Cover and Conceal	100	50	0	30%
4.3 Mobility	10	0	100	40%
4.4 Extreme Weather	0	70	100	10%
Weighted Scores	34	42	66	Total = 100%
FACTOR CATEGORY: RISK				
5.1 US Action/Reaction	0	100	90	50%
5.2 Dependence on other conds	0	90	100	10%
5.3 Dependence on surprise	100	0	10	30%
5.4 Unexpected Weather	0	40	100	10%
Weighted Scores	30	63	68	Total = 100%

SUMMARY

FACTOR CATEGORY	VALUES			RELATIVE CATEGORY WEIGHTS
	COA_1	COA_2	COA_3	
1.0 Terrain	12	37	88	40%
2.0 US Forces	58	41	53	20%
3.0 Enemy Forces	1	57	98	10%
4.0 Weather	34	42	66	5%
5.0 Risk	30	63	68	25%
Total Weighted Scores	26	47	76	Total = 100%

percent as important is given a weight of 90 while a factor half as important is given a weight of 50). Factors within the remaining categories are similarly weighted. (These weights are not recorded in Table 8.2.) Then the weights are normalized so that they sum to 100 within each category, as shown in Table 8.2 under the *Relative Weights* heading.

Second, the weight of each category is determined. This is done by comparing the relative importance of categories for the enemy's mission accomplishment. A weight of 100 is given to the most important category; all other categories are weighted relative to it. Again, the weights are normalized to add up to 100.

Step 4. Calculating Likelihood of COAs. The feasibility scores of step 2 and the relative weights of step 3 are combined to obtain an overall value or worth of each enemy option. These values are obtained by multiplying the feasibility scores (values) by their corresponding weight for each factor, then summing these products for each COA. If the scores and weights are valid and if ENCOA captures the factors most relevant to the situation, the enemy COA with the highest score is the most likely. For the analysis shown in the Summary of Table 8.2, COA_3 has the highest score (76 vs 47 and 26) and is thus most likely.

Step 5. Sensitivity Analysis. When uncertainty enters the picture (and it usually does), it is important to know whether variations in judgment would shift the final prediction of an enemy COA from one option to another—this is sensitivity testing. It systematically tests the sensitivity of the final COA scores to variations in the importance (weights) assigned to factors. For example, an analyst may have entered a weight of 70 for a factor but was really uncertain as to whether that value might just as well have been 60 or 80. The sensitivity analysis calculates the impact of such uncertainty on the rank order of the final COA scores. (Sensitivity analysis is available only in the computerized versions.)

Sensitivity analysis also can be useful when a group of intelligence analysts have conflicting opinions about the importance of particular factors. Sensitivity analysis reveals whether the differences in opinion significantly affect the final prediction. By calculating the importance of differences of opinion, ENCOA reduces emotional aspects of disagreement and encourages analysts to focus only on differences that truly make a difference.

Aid Evaluation. The IBM 5110/5120 computerized version as well as the manual version of ENCOA were evaluated by eleven enlisted intelligence analysts and one officer. All analysts were assigned to an operational Army intelligence unit and had undergone classroom training in military intelligence. The computer was installed in the analysts' office area, personnel were instructed in its use, and workbooks for using ENCOA were delivered. A tactical training exercise complete with background information and maps was provided as a context for conducting their analyses. In addition, analysts were instructed to use ENCOA for any decision problems that arose during their normal course of duties. The computer and materials were left on-site for approximately six months. The goal of the evaluation was to determine the usability, efficacy, and applicability of ENCOA for real-world decision making. The evaluation data consisted of responses to a questionnaire as well as analysis of the intelligence analysts' inputs for the exercise.

The evaluation results showed:

- Acceptance of the computerized aid was contingent upon understanding the algorithms by using the manual aid.
- The aid was viewed as too time consuming to be practical in operational real-time decision making.
- The concept of evaluating the relative importance of factors for discriminating *specific* COAs was exceedingly difficult for the analysts to grasp. There were continual

errors in the assignment of weights: factors on which all COAs were rated the same, indicating no difference in COAs, were repeatedly assigned nonzero weights. The analysts apparently could ignore their previous experience that showed these factors to be important under other circumstances.

- The most intuitively useful aspect of the aid was perceived to be the hierarchical structure of factors. Apparently the analysts had not encountered in their previous training any systematic list of factors relevant for predicting enemy COAs.

- The aid is exceedingly useful for diagnosing weaknesses in an analyst's judgment. Supervisors could easily see where their analysts needed remedial and refresher training. Examination of the weights and values matrix (as in Table 8.2) was the most useful feedback.

A Bayesian Aid for Updating Enemy Options

Description. Once the battle begins and new data are received, the analytic process becomes dynamic and continuous. A prediction of enemy intent, in fact, becomes obsolete as soon as new information must be incorporated; the prediction for one time period becomes the baseline for the next. The BAUDI (Bayesian Aid for the Updating of Dynamic Intelligence) aid, based on Bayesian decision theory, has been developed to help intelligence analysts revise their predictions of enemy intent. BAUDI is available in two completely computerized versions: (1) Apple II Plus computer in the PASCAL language, and (2) IBM 5120 computer in the APL language. (See Adelman, et al. 1982 for a detailed description.)

Bayesian decision theory is a simple mathematical concept that can be used to logically integrate old COA likelihoods with new information to form a revised estimate. It is expressed mathematically by:

$$\underbrace{\frac{P(H_1/D)}{P(H_2/D)}}_{\text{(prior odds)}} \quad \text{X} \quad \underbrace{\frac{P(D'/H_1,D)}{P(D'/H_2,D)}}_{\text{(likelihood ratio)}} \quad = \quad \underbrace{\frac{P(H_1/D',D)}{P(H_2/D',D)}}_{\text{(posterior odds)}}$$

H_1 and H_2 refer to the hypotheses under investigation; D refers to all data collected prior to the newly collected datum, which is represented by D'. The ratio of prior probabilities $P(H_1/D)/P(H_2/D)$ indicates the odds of H_1 to H_2 prior to the newly collected data. The ratio of the conditional probabilities $P(D'/H_1,D)/P(D'/H_2,D)$, called a likelihood ratio, indicates the extent to which the newly collected datum supports each hypothesis. Also, the ratio of posterior probabilities $P(H_1/D',D)/P(H_2/D',D)$ indicates the revised odds of the hypotheses on the basis of all collected data.

A critical feature of BAUDI is that it allows the analyst to disagree with the computer; the analyst can make numerical adjustments to the revised probabilities that seem more consistent with military judgment. BAUDI then recalculates the probabilities to show the analyst the logical implications of any adjustments. The analyst, however, always has the last input, not the computer.

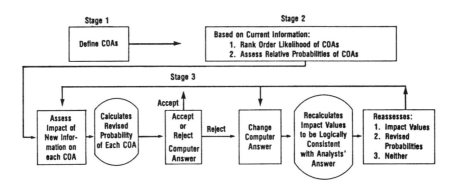

Figure 8.2   The BAUDI steps. All steps in boxes are done by the analyst; steps in ovals are done by the computer.

Figure 8.2 shows the three major stages of BAUDI-aided analysis. The computer itself steps the intelligence analyst through the stages, clearly instructing the analyst on the required inputs and its calculations. The following description of BAUDI procedures assumes the goal of the analysis is to predict enemy COAs.

Stage 1. The analyst defines the number and names of the COAs.

Stage 2. The analyst enters the relative likelihoods of the COAs on the basis of all prior information. This is done by ranking COAs from most to least likely, and then specifying relative probabilities; that is, the analyst assesses how probable the most likely COA is compared to each of the other COAs. Ideally, the analyst would already have determined the relative likelihood of the COAs by using ENCOA before the battle began.

Stage 3. The analyst uses BAUDI to assess both the impact of a new piece of information and the resulting prediction of enemy COAs. For a given piece of information, the analyst first enters a brief identifying title. The analyst then specifies how many times as likely one is to see that information for the most likely COA as compared to each of the other COAs.

BAUDI used Bayes's Theorem to calculate revised probabilities for the COAs; that is, the relative probabilities of the enemy COAs prior to the new information are combined with the *impact* of the new piece of information to give a *revised* assessment of the COA probabilities. The analyst can either accept or, if the aid's answer seems inconsistent with sound military judgment, change these revised probabilities.

If the analyst decides to change the probabilities, BAUDI then recalculates the impact values that would have mathematically generated those probabilities. BAUDI also displays the original impact values (likelihood ratios) so that the analyst can compare them to those calculated from the analysts' newly specified probabilities. The analyst now has the opportunity to change the likelihood ratios if these appear to reflect too much or too little importance of the information being evaluated; if changes are made, BAUDI will recalculate the final revised probabilities.

The iterations continue until the analyst is pleased with the likelihood ratios and revised probabilities for each piece of information, or when there is minimal difference (.05) between the revised and Bayesian probabilities. When new information is received, these revised probabilities become the prior probabilities of the current situation and the analyst need only generate likelihood ratios for the new information in order to obtain the most-up-to-date probabilities for the enemy COAs.

Evaluation. An experiment was conducted to test the efficacy of BAUDI in an Army tactical intelligence context. The task selected was the prediction of the most likely avenue of approach for an enemy attack; the participants were actual Army intelligence analysts. All participants worked through an abridged version of a training exercise. The participant's task was to estimate the posterior probabilities of four avenues of approach open to enemy forces who were attacking U.S. forces. This estimate was to be based on (1) background information about U.S. and enemy composition and disposition, as well as terrain and weather considerations, and (2) ten messages representing intelligence data about enemy actitivy collected sequentially over a two-day period. The messages varied in length and diagnosticity, i.e., the extent to which the message supported one avenue of approach (AOA) over another. Each participant was supplied with a map of the area under consideration, and a transparent acetate overlay so that force composition and disposition, key military terrain features, and reported opposing force activity could be recorded. In short, efforts were made to represent an actual tactical intelligence analysis problem.

Fifteen analysts used the computerized aid to evaluate the messages and formulate a prediction of the relative likelihood of the four avenues of approach. An additional fifteen analysts estimated prior odds, likelihood ratios, and posterior odds but did not use the BAUDI aid.

Although Bayes's Theorem is a normative rule for making intelligence predictions, experimental research in other contexts has shown that people have considerable difficulty making judgments consistent with Bayes' Theorem (Rapoport and Walsten 1972). In general, people revise their final probabilities in the same direction as Bayes's Theorem, but they are too conservative in their revisions, i.e., the revisions are too small. It was hoped that having intelligence analysts use BAUDI would allow them to be less conservative and make predictions more consistent with Bayes's Theorem.

The results showed that all analysts assigned posterior probabilities in the direction predicted by Bayes's Theorem. However, analysts using the aid gave final posterior probabilities that were on the average only 5 percent different from the Bayesian posteriors, while unaided assigned posteriors that were 28 percent discrepant. Thus, the aid did indeed encourage analysts to be less conservative.

As shown in Figure 8.3, analysts using the aid were better able to discriminate the relative probabilities of the four avenues of approach than the unaided analysts. Given the same information, analysts without the aid assigned similar probabilities to all avenues of approach while aided analysts were able to clearly rank order the relative probabilities.

The evaluation of BAUDI demonstrates that use of the aid encourages decision makers to clearly differentiate their options while decision makers not using the aid were unable to differentiate those same options using the same information. Thus, it has been experimentally shown that this aid increases decision-making power of trained military intelligence analysts on a simulated but realistic inference task by encouraging them to be less conservative and to better utilize available information.

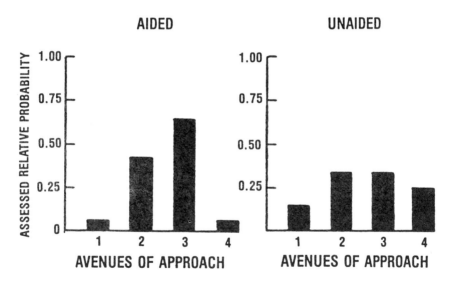

Figure 8.3   Histograms of the relative probability of each of the 4 avenues of approach assigned by analysts using the aid (left panel) and analysts not using the aid (right panel). Note clearer differentiation of avenues for aid users.

IMPLEMENTATION OF DECISION AIDS

Both the ENCOA and BAUDI intelligence aids are being implemented by the Army in the classroom training of intelligence analysts. Efforts to implement them in operational decision-making settings have been painful and unrewarding. Although both aids were designed to improve operational on-the-job decision making, they have been most successfully implemented as training aids due to two factors. First, decision aids tend to be time consuming; it is readily apparent to the user that a seat-of-the-pants decision can be made in seconds while an aided decision is likely to take several minutes to half an hour. Even though the amount of time required certainly decreases with practice, aided decision making will probably always take longer than unaided. Although it is clear to decision analysts that the improved quality of decision making is worth the extra time, this is not accepted by users who have to respond to the time constraints as well as expend the extra cognitive energy required by the decision aids. The second reason that aids are difficult to implement in operational environments is that decision makers often refuse to accept that their cognitive and decision-making skills need aiding at all. Although this may seem to portray decision makers as uninsightful and perhaps egotistical, it is nevertheless an important factor decision aid developers must address. It is also probably a major basis for the proliferation of so-called decision support systems that provide massive data bases with some summary statistics but no support for the thinking or judgmental processes of decision making.

However, neither of these problems seem to reduce acceptance of decision aids by those responsible for the *training* of decision making. Trainers have the luxury of spending more leisurely time to analyze problems and generate solutions; there is less concern with fast answers than with accurate and logical answers. Training is typically more procedure oriented than solution oriented; i.e. they focus more on *how* to do the task than the bottom line answer. Thus, they are more accepting of the amount of time required to use a decision aid as well as grateful for having a systematic set of procedures to solve the problem.

Trainers are also responsible for improving the decision making of others rather than themselves. This decreases the personal threat of needing an aid to help in thinking out a problem; they can always rationalize that the aid is a pedagogical tool and not a cognitive crutch.

The fundamental solution to successful aid implementation is to have the decision maker intimately involved in the design and development of the aid from the beginning. The personal commitment and psychological investment that results from early user involvement will likely be even more important for the achievement of aid implementation than technical accuracy and algorithm sophistication. In some environments, such as high-level corporate policy and decision making in industry and government, close working relationships with the decision makers are possible. However in other circumstances, such as the military, where the decision maker turnover is constant and local policy changes with each new personality, sustaining user involvement in the development process is sometimes impossible. Often the actual user, as a specific person, cannot even be identified; the aid is developed for a job role such as commander, intelligence analyst, logistician, etc. Although the decision problem of such jobs can indeed be accurately captured and modeled, the motivation and commitment of the individual holding the job is not so easily won. This dilemma leads us back to the findings of the aid evaluation described in this chapter: aids are more readily accepted and implemented in training than in operational environments.

The solution to the user involvement problem may lie in implementing aids in training where resistance is least, then fostering student understanding and acceptance of the decision-aiding concepts. When the students become the decision makers in the operational settings, aiding procedures will already be acceptable as analytical tools. Thus the likelihood that they will use available decision aids, as well as support the development of new aids, will be enhanced. Unless the researchers and developers of decision aids devote additional energy and resources to the successful *implementation* of their aids, our field will begin to atrophy from sheer disuse.

REFERENCES

Adelman, L., M. Donnell, and R. Phelps. 1983. *Intelligence Preparation of the Battlefield: Critique and Recommendations.* Alexandria, Va.: U.S. Army Research Institute for the Behavioral and Social Sciences.

Adelman, L., M. Donnell, R. Phelps, and J. Patterson. 1982. An Iterative Bayesian Decision Aid: Toward Improving the User-Aid and User-Organization Interface. In *IEEE Transactions on Systems, Man, and Cybernetics* 12:733–43.

Hammond, K., G. McClelland, and J. Mumpower. 1980. *Human Judgment and Decision Making: Theories, Methods, and Procedures.* New York: Praeger.

Patterson, J., R. Phelps, and J. Hall. 1983. *Intelligence Aid for Evaluating Enemy Courses of Action (ENCOA): Manual for Use of the Apple II Plus and the IBM 5110/5120 Computers.* Research Product 83-10. Alexandria, Va.: U.S. Army Research Institute for the Behavioral and Social Sciences.

Phelps, R., J. Hall, and C. Hoblitzell. 1982. *Intelligence Aid for Evaluating Enemy Courses of Action (ENCOA): Guide for Manual and HP 41-C/HP 41-CV Calculator Procedures.* Research Product 82-6. Alexandria, Va.: U.S. Army Research Institute for the Behavioral and Social Sciences.

Rapoport, A., and T. Walsten. 1972. Individual Decision Behavior. *Annual Review of Psychology* 23: 131–76.

Thompson, J., R. Hopf-Weichel, and E. Geiselman. 1984. *Cognitive Bases of Intelligence Analysis.* Alexandria, Va.: U.S. Army Research Institute for the Behavioral and Social Sciences.

U.S. Army. 1984. *An Introduction to Tactical Intelligence Analysis: Cognitive Preparation of the Battlefield.* U.S. Army Intelligence Center and School, Ft. Huachuca, Ariz.

9

A Microcomputer-Based Productivity Support System for Increasing the Managerial Efficiency of Operating Units

Authella M. Bessent, E. Wailand Bessent, Charles T. Clark, and Joyce J. Elam

Managers of programs and other operating units in the public sector are charged with responsibility for efficient production of their services (Bessent, et al. 1982). In most cases, however, this is an empty requirement since accountability is hampered by a lack of information about how productive such programs are for the amounts of labor, machines, and other resources provided from public funds that the programs use for delivery of their services (Farrell 1957). In addition, a fair and reasonable assessment of productivity must take into account environmental factors that affect a unit's ability to deliver services.

Given the absence of objective information about the unit's productivity, unit managers as well as higher level administrators must make arbitrary judgments about such crucial management decisions as setting goals, assigning personnel, developing work schedules, or developing budgets for increasing productivity. The resulting management situation is like navigating in a fog with no compass—decisions are made on intuition alone.

To support decision making in the areas listed above, a *productivity analysis support system* (PASS) has been developed. PASS is an optimization-based decision support system that distributes its functional capabilities between microcomputers located at the unit manager's site and a mainframe comptuer located at a higher level administrative site. In the next section, the chapter discusses the information requirements of managers faced with the task of productivity analysis that guided the design and implementation of PASS. Then the methodology employed by PASS and its overall architecture is described. This chapter will also discuss the use of PASS in a particular application area—education. Finally, the impact of two years experience is presented.

INFORMATION REQUIREMENTS

Managers of organizations strive to operate their units both efficiently and effectively. A unit is *efficient* if it is achieving levels of outputs (services) that are as high as any other unit when its input levels (resources) are taken into account; an inefficient unit is not achieving comparable outputs. A unit is *effective* if it is meeting targeted output levels. To be both effective and efficient, information is required that can provide a basis for setting goals and responding to changes in resource availability or demand for services. Specifically, unit managers need to know:

- How effectively have available resources been used to deliver the desired services?
- Which aspects of operations can and should be improved?
- What service levels can reasonably be attained given available resources?
- Which organizations, if any, have delivered more services with the same resources?

- If resource levels are decreased by budget cuts, what service levels can be expected from the "best" organizations?
- If more services are demanded or mandated by law, what level of funding is necessary to remain efficient?

The information requirements listed above become the basis for planning more effective and efficient operations. The resulting plans would be feasible since they would be based on the actual performance of a set of similar organizations identified as *pace setter* (efficient) organizations.

Administrators of groups of organizational units (e.g., heads of regional, state, or national agencies) need additional information regarding the distribution of scarce resources to organizational units. Of particular interest are the following:

- How well are subordinate units meeting productivity goals?
- Which distribution of scarce resources would result in the best overall service levels?
- Given existing resource availability, what level of services can be accomplished?

Such information would reduce the occurrences of over- and under-budgeting and -staffing. In addition, it would enable administrators and managers to justify requests for resource increases on the basis of expected efficient performance.

In order to provide the information described in the previous section to operating unit managers and their superiors, PASS was designed in accordance with the following requirements:

1. Employ the most efficient methodology for measuring the efficiency of individual units.
2. Support a centralized function for collecting organizational unit data and performing a set of analyses for each user.
3. Support the users directly by providing capabilities for entering the data required for basic analyses, examining the results of analyses, and performing ad hoc analyses tailored by the user.

The methodology PASS is based on is discussed next, followed by a description of the overall architecture of the system.

Methodology

Measuring the efficiency of multiple input, multiple output nonprofit enterprises has been an econometric problem that has been addressed by several approaches. *Ratio analysis* typically uses a single output measure divided by a single input measure. Organizations frequently rank comparatively high on some measures and low on others, still leaving the problem of an overall assessment unsolved.

Other widely used approaches are based on *regression methods*. Regression equations, which are developed from inefficient as well as efficient units, will be heavily influenced by the most inefficient units and thus may misrepresent input/output possibilities. Consequently, regression methods are not easily used to partition units into efficient and inefficient sets—a major objective of PASS.

Accordingly, PASS employs techniques that take into account all outputs and inputs simultaneously to produce a piecewise linear approximation of an efficiency frontier using efficient units (Charnes, et al. 1978; Clark 1983). A unit is defined as efficient if no other unit is producing more output for the same amounts of inputs. Units that do not lie on the frontier are assigned an efficiency measure based on how far the unit is from the frontier. Different input/output combinations required to place the unit on the frontier are identified. Particular attention has been focused on a new methodology that ensures that this combination represents feasible input levels and realistic output goals for the inefficient organization (Clark 1983).

The determination of an efficiency rating for each unit is accomplished by solving a linear programming model for each unit. If the unit is inefficient, the solution to the model indicates (1) levels of outputs that would result in the unit becoming efficient given the same levels of inputs, (2) the levels of inputs that would result in the unit becoming efficient given the same levels of outputs, and (3) the efficient units that provide the basis for identifying "efficient" input/output combinations. The results depend on both the measurements employed and the selection of comparison units. PASS allows the selection of different comparison sets and measures for custom-tailored analyses (Bessent, et al. 1983b).

PASS Architecture

PASS was designed to be an optimization-based decision support system (Elam and Schneider 1983). The mathematical algorithm that solves the collection of linear programming models described above forms the core of the system. The usability of PASS, however, is dependent on the user's ability to (1) specify the agreed-upon set of input and output measures for the basic analyses, and (2) to use the information created by the solution algorithm in a meaningful way. It was therefore important that PASS provide functions that could be invoked directly by the user. It was equally important that one centralized function (the coordinator) be established to collect the input and output measures from all units to be included in the analysis and to perform basic analyses using a predetermined comparison set and predetermined input and output measures.

To accomplish all of its objectives, PASS was designed to be a distributed system with some functions assigned to the individual users and some functions assigned to the coordinator. The functional capabilities of PASS are described in Table 9.1. PASS is a menu-driven system designed to be operated by the professional seeking an analysis; not by a technical computer expert. The current version of PASS has the user's functions implemented on an APPLE II+ microcomputer and the coordinator's functions implemented on a CDC dual CYBER 170/750.

It is envisioned that PASS will be improved over time as the users and designers gain a mutual understanding of the needs to be addressed by PASS and the potential it provides. The next phase of development is to extend the user's capability to perform specialized "what if" types of analyses on the APPLE microcomputer. Additional functions will be added as the users identify them.

Table 9.1 PASS CAPABILITIES

COORDINATOR SITE

Create data base consisting of detailed information about particular resources and performance measures for each organization over time.

Perform basic set of analyses.

Perform specialized analyses for different comparison sets, different measures.

Produce tabular and graphical reports for current time period as well as comparisons over time.

USER SITE

Capture and verify data on resources and performance.

Find units with better efficiency ratings and/or performance levels that have resouces similar to those of inefficient units.

APPLICATION OF PASS IN THE EDUCATION SECTOR

The Educational Productivity Council (EPC) is a consortium of twenty-five Texas school districts working cooperatively on the problem of educational improvement through state-mandated efficient operations linked to effective practices. By sharing common student test data and information on resources such as expenditures, time allocations for instruction, and professional staffing patterns, the EPC serves a coordinator function for evaluating the relative efficiency of member schools and for supporting decisions made to improve their operations.

Data collected and checked by the member schools using APPLE microcomputers are transferred to the EPC where several programs are executed to produce a data base from which a variety of reports can be generated. The data base contains information on schools within each district, the grade levels to be analyzed within a school (the 3rd, 5th, 7th and 9th grades), and a set of measurements of outputs and inputs for up to three years. Each grade level/year pair has its own unique set of output and input measurements and can be used in any number of efficiency analyses.

Data Base Updates

The data base is updated by two methods. The primary mode is by means of an interactive data collection program for the APPLE. A contact person (usually an administrative staff person) at the local level enters the requested data updates. Data are checked at the EPC office and transmitted to a permanent file accessible by the mainframe computer. The secondary mode is used to update the complete data base resident on the mainframe, correct errors, enter late data, or to modify the data base for special purpose runs; these are accomplished by means of an interactive editing function.

School Profiles

Distributions of input, output, and efficiency ratings for schools indicate how each school's resources, effectiveness, and efficiency compare to schools in the same district and to those in the overall Council. These are available to managers by means of a summary file produced as output of the efficiency analysis (Bessent, et al. 1983b) and by statistical programs that operate on the data base.

Efficiency Analysis Reports   Reports for district managers and for managers of individual schools are sent by mail at the conclusion of each major collection cycle and are available upon request at any time. The reports provide (but are not limited to) the following items:

- The efficiency rating of the school.
- The output and input values employed by the analysis.
- The additional outputs that would be obtained for current inputs if inefficiencies were eliminated.

- Input reduction if inefficiencies were eliminated and no additional output were desired.
- The relative contributions of individual outputs and inputs to the calculated efficiency rating.
- The identification and profiles of fully efficient schools which have input levels similar to the referent school.

Online Search Capability   In addition to the foregoing reports which are routinely supplied to all users, network school members can use an interactive software package (RNKFIND) (Bessent, et al. 1983a) implemented on the Apple II+ to search for schools in the data base that have any specified input and output characteristics. For example, a principal of an inefficient school with a high transient pupil population and relatively few teachers can identify schools with similar problems but that have higher achievement. Then, a direct inquiry to that school can determine how the difficulties were overcome. Similarly, a principal of a school with ample resources can find out how much achievement other well-endowed schools were able to obtain.

Use Made of PASS by EPC Schools

As might be expected for a complex system that has been in development only three years, the use made of PASS by EPC schools varies considerably. At the least, users indicate that reports generated by PASS are routed to building principals as information-only items; but, even there, some principals use the information as a basis for goal setting in their state-required operating plans.

In the most extensive use of PASS (Howard 1982), it is employed by the chief administrator to award merit pay supplements to principals of effective and efficient schools, to set achievement targets for schools, and to review annual budget allocations for the district. At the building level, principals use the results to search for and diagnose sources of inefficiency, to set output targets, to comply with mandated written operating plans, and to investigate operations employed by more efficient schools.

Have schools using PASS improved their efficiency and effectiveness? Like all evaluation, this is hard to show conclusively, but promising findings based on first and second year experience are now presented.

EFFICIENCY AND EFFECTIVENESS IMPACT OF PASS, 1981–1983

Schools using PASS increased both their efficiency and effectiveness during the most recent two years of experience. Effectiveness increases were measured directly by the percent of pupils mastering objectives on a test of basic skills in reading, mathematics, and writing. Efficiency improvement was measured by employing the results of the model that computes efficiency.

Results shown in Table 9.2 indicate gains in effectiveness for both third and fifth grades with EPC schools gaining more than the state average gain. The magnitude of learning gains may not appear impressive, unless one considers that over 300,000 pupils were enrolled in EPC schools and that the obtained average of a 9 percent gain represents a potential increase

Table 9.2 GAIN IN PERCENT OF THIRD AND FIFTH GRADE PUPILS MASTERING BASIC SKILLS OBJECTIVES, 1981–1983

	Third Grade			Fifth Grade		
	Math	Reading	Writing	Math	Reading	Writing
1981 Mean	79.0	81.9	80.4	77.3	74.7	84.8
S.D.	9.3	9.5	11.6	7.3	10.0	7.3
1983 Mean	89.2	89.9	89.6	87.2	84.1	90.6
S.D.	7.9	7.1	8.9	6.7	13.6	6.2
Gain in Effectiveness						
EPC Frontier Schools	+10.2	+8.0	+9.2	+10.1	+9.4	+5.8
Statewide Average Gains	+7.8	+4.5	+7.8	+7.5	+9.3	+2.8

Note: Gains are shown for 45 fifth grades and 39 third grades in fully efficient schools which were in the EPC for the two-year period.

of 27,000 pupils who met competency requirements. It will also be seen in the table that variance decreased in all but one category, indicating that achievement in member schools was not only higher, but it also became more similar.

To obtain evidence of an increase in efficiency for the two-year period, a less direct method was employed. The thirty-nine third grades and forty-five fifth grades in schools that defined the efficiency frontier in 1983 were selected and the efficiency rating for each was recomputed using the 1981 output levels. As shown in Table 9.3, efficiency ratings based on 1981 inputs relative to 1983 outputs showed an average efficiency increase of 8.5 percent.

Since the above result could have been affected by input changes in the same period, a similar calculation was made based on 1983 inputs with 1981 outputs (lower part of table 9.3). Again, new efficiency values were calculated and an average change in efficiency of 10.1 percent for third and fifth grade was observed.

Table 9.3 EFFICIENCY GAINS HOLDING INPUTS CONSTANT

| | | | Efficiency Ratings | | Efficiency Gains |
			Outputs Observed in 1981	Outputs Observed in 1983	(%)
Inputs	Fifth Grade	Mean	88.9	96.9	+8.0
Observed	(n = 45)	S.D.	8.7	3.1	−2.7
in 1981	Third Grade	Mean	87.1	96.0	+8.9
	(n = 39)	S.D.	7.9	4.0	−1.9
Inputs	Fifth Grade	Mean	90.2	1.0	+9.8
Observed	(n = 45)	S.D.	6.7	0.0	−6.7
in 1983	Third Grade	Mean	89.6	1.0	+10.4
	(n = 39)	S.D.	8.5	0.0	−8.5

Thus, when inputs are held constant at either the 1981 or the 1983 levels, an increase in efficiency of about 9 percent was found, in addition to the increase in effectiveness.

To cite an example of the results obtained by a school district that has been a consistent participant in the EPC, Garland Independent School District has experienced an average increase of 12.6 percent in basic skills learning along with an increase in efficiency. All thirty-one schools in Garland were inefficient in 1981 and eleven became fully efficient in the two year period. In a similar case, Round Rock School District, which had no efficient schools in 1981, gained to 66 percent of its schools being efficient during a period in which the district experienced a 7 percent increase in achievement with a growth rate of 17.8 percent (1408 pupils). The districts were both heavily involved in EPC activities and one used the results of the analysis as a basis for awarding merit pay to principals (Howard 1982).

Of course, many other factors offset outcomes in schools, and no claim is made that use of PASS alone accounts for the difference. Administrators of member schools were motivated to improve their operations—that is a condition for membership. But without the decision support provided, their task would have been much more difficult.

REFERENCES

Bessent, A., W. Bessent, K. Chan, C.T. Clark, and J. Elam. 1983a. *Using RNKFIND Code (Version 1.0) to Find Organizational Sub-Units With User Specified Characteristics.* Research Report EPC 016. Educational Productivity Council, The University of Texas, Austin.

Bessent, A., W. Bessent, C.T. Clark, and J. Elam. 1983b. *Constrained Facet Analysis of the Efficiency of Organizational Sub-Units with the CFA Code (Version 1.0).* Research Report EPC 015. Educational Productivity Council, The University of Texas, Austin.

Bessent, A., W. Bessent, J. Kennington, and B. Reagan. 1982. Productivity in the Houston Independent School District. *Management Science* 28 (12):1355–67.

Charnes, A., W.W. Cooper, and E. Rhodes. 1978. Measuring the Efficiency of Decision Making Units. *European Journal of Operational Research* 2 (6): 429–43.

Clark, C.T. 1983. Data Envelopment Analysis and Extensions for Decision Support and Management Planning. Ph.D. diss. Graduate School of Business, The University of Texas, Austin.

Elam, J., and R. Schneider. 1983. Optimization-Based Decision Support Systems. *Program Manager* (Spring), Vol. xi, no. 9, pp. 18–27.

Farrell, M.J. 1957. The Measurement of Productive Efficiency. *Journal of the Royal Statistical Society* 120 (part 3).

Howard, W. 1982. *Summary of Remarks on Administrative Uses of Efficiency in the Round Rock Independent School District.* Research Report EPC 005. Educational Productivity Council, The University of Texas, Austin.

10

Microcomputers and Decision Support System Networks: A Case Study

Allene K. Cormier

Microcomputers can potentially play an important or even vital role in most decision support systems. To achieve the full benefits that microcomputers can offer, however, requires that decision support system architectures be designed to incorporate them in a systematic and preplanned way. How they should be incorporated (or whether they should be) is a decision that must be made on a case-by-case basis, carefully considering the particular circumstances of each implementation.

This chapter discusses the potential effects that the incorporation of microcomputers into the design of a decision support system could have on the major issues related to the system implementation and system utility. The discussion focuses on actual experiences with a specific decision support system, which reflect the perspective of the project manager who was responsible for the implementation of the system in its pilot form. In addition, at the conclusion of the pilot project, a user survey was conducted that was designed to provide feedback to support decisions concerning future aspects of the system implementation.[1] In lengthy personal interviews, approximately one third of all pilot system users were asked about their usage of the system, their assessment of its overall utility, their views on the system's functions, applications, and user services provided, and their suggestions for system changes or enhancements.

The remainder of this chapter is organized as follows. First, the stage is set with a discussion of the corporate and system environment into which this pilot decision support system was introduced, with a description of the particular characteristics of the system itself, and with an outline of the implementation approach, including the methods of user training and assistance.

This is followed by a description of postimplementation usage patterns of the management, staff, and secretaries. The pros and cons of the chosen implementation strategy and the implementation issues that have significant corporate implications are then discussed.

The chapter concludes with a discussion of why the majority of the most essential ingredients for a successful system implementation would benefit from the addition of microcomputers to the system network, and why the minority would not.

THE SYSTEM ENVIRONMENT

The corporation in which this system was implemented is involved with research, development, engineering, and scientific activities. It primarily supports a wide range of government programs including those of defense and national security, transportation, advanced information systems, energy, and the environment. It has a total of approximately 4000 employees, and they are primarily located in two sites that are 500 miles apart.

The two sites are, to a large extent, engaged in work that does not require a great deal of collaboration between the two. Only the administrative and financial activities require coordination. As a result, they operate quite independently of one another. The decision to implement a decision support system, and the selection of the specific system, was done by our site without consultation of the other site. In fact, the other site had, during the time period that this system was being chosen, decided to undertake a similar project. They had selected, and were making plans to install, an entirely different decision support system that had been developed by a different vendor, and which was incompatible with the system selected for our site. This decision, as will be discussed later, affected some user's perceptions of the utility of the system.

The concept for this system began to evolve when a computer and telecommunications steering committee was formed. A major committee task was to determine what future computer and telecommunications capabilities the site needed in order to support both internal and client-related needs and activities. The committee had senior management representatives from all of the major organizations at the site. The committee's final recommendation involved the phased implementation of a pilot "target system" concept which included experimentation with "electronic office" and management decision support systems. The corporate executive vice president subsequently approved and funded the recommendation. The fact that the system was both conceived and blessed by the consensus of senior management, and that corporate overhead funding was supplied to finance it, was extremely significant. High-level commitment and corporate overhead funding are both extremely crucial elements in the acceptance and success of a corporatewide information system.

THE SYSTEM'S CHARACTERISTICS

The specific decision support system software was leased from a vendor and enhanced by the corporation. The system's character is such that the applications that the leasing corporation develops may be added to the system menu in a way that appears to the users to be part of the system itself. The major capabilities of this menu-driven system as it was developed by the vendor and enhanced and implemented by the corporation included:

- *Communications functions* (electronic mail), with "notes" and "messages" for informal communication, and document distribution for formal documents such as memos, letters, and technical reports.

- *Document preparation*, including initial creation, editing and formatting, filing and retrieval, printing and distribution. It is important to note here that a complete corporatewide word-processing network already existed and was being used by virtually every secretary, and that the decision support system's document preparation feature was in no way similar to, from a user's standpoint, nor compatible with, the corporate word-processing system. This, as we shall see, made the system less useful for many users.

- *Calendar* for personal or conference room scheduling.

- *Management support applications,* including a weekly project cost-reporting system, a proposal pricing and budget system, an excused employee absence reporting system, a system maintained by the personnel department that allowed managers to request to interview potential applicants for positions that they had advertised, and a resume-tracking system that was developed for one specific division. The resume-tracking system monitored potential candidates for hire, and it included a list of the individuals with whom each candidate was to interview, the up-to-date status of which of the scheduled interviewers the candidate had seen, and each interviewer's rating of the candidate.

- *Information distribution applications,* including an online site telephone directory, a weekly site calendar of events (which included meetings or briefings of some broad interest), divisional calendars of events (which included items of interest that were more limited to each respective division), an application that presented abstracts of recent project publications, and a newsletter published by the library (containing recent additions to the collection, items of interest, etc.).

All users of the system also had access, through their terminal and a local area network, to other corporate computational facilities. Those facilities included many other applications, programming languages, access to other computer systems and Arpanet, and the computer center of the corporation's other site.

THE IMPLEMENTATION APPROACH

The implementation plan for the pilot system included two phases (following a three month initial installation, testing, and debugging period, which was accomplished with approximately fifty users, consisting of both the system support staff, and willing individuals who were representative of the different types of managers, professionals, secretaries, and administrative personnel in the corporation). The users that were given access to the pilot system during the first phase were all senior to midlevel managers and their secretaries (approximately 130 new users in total), and this phase extended over a fifteen-month period. Each manager was given a terminal and a system account; however, each secretary was only given an account. Most of the secretaries had access to the system through their word processors (by emulating the appropriate terminal type), but some had no feasible means of using any terminal to gain access (they were expected to use their boss's terminal when it was free).

The Phase 2 implementation extended system access to two entire technical departments, involving approximately sixty users, and extending over an eight-month period. One terminal was installed in each staff office (which varied between having either one or two occupants), a terminal was installed in each manager's office, and those secretaries who did not have the means to access the system via their word processing terminal were given terminals as well.

Subsequently the "experiment" was declared a success by the management, and full scale implementation is currently underway. Eventually all staff members will have access to the system.

User Training and Assistance

Introductory training sessions were offered to all users. The sessions included a discussion of the terminals and basic information about all of the system's functions (except document preparation). Training for mangement and their secretaries was accomplished during a one to two hour session in the manager's office with both the manager and the secretary in attendance. Members of the two departments were trained in groups, with approximately four staff members at a time using two terminals. In addition, specialized document preparation training was offered to those who requested it.

A user's guide was written by the system support staff, as the vendor documentation was totally insufficient. In addition, the applications developed within the corporation needed to be properly documented and explained to users. The user's guide was distributed to users one week prior to training.

User assistance was provided via telephone and a system ID used specifically for that purpose. Users could either call and discuss their questions or problems with the system instructors, or they could send a question, suggestion, etc., to the ID using electronic mail.

POSTIMPLEMENTATION USAGE PATTERNS

Management Usage Patterns

Overall, managers found various uses for the decision support system. All managers used the system at least once a day, and most used it more frequently. More than three quarters accessed the system in the morning and stayed connected all day, while a few of the more infrequent users connected and disconnected themselves to the system as needed. Electronic mail and management support applications constituted the core of their use.

Electronic mail: All managers checked their "in-baskets" at least once daily, and most more frequently. About half reported that they used the system to send messages as well as to receive them. The others typically only received mail via the system, rarely sending messages themselves. These *reactive* users, however, would at times use the system to directly reply to messages sent to them. Most of them were motivated to access the system primarily because their superiors occasionally used it to communicate with them. As one user told me, "I get embarrassed when my bosses send me a message and I don't respond immediately." These reactive users reported that their communications needs were often local and best served by face-to-face contacts, or that the other modes of communication that were available to them (telephone or intercom) served them satisfactorily.

The other group, the *proactive* users, experimented with the system to a greater extent. Some reported that they felt comfortable using the system for all types of communication, while others felt that they restricted their use of the system's mail feature to less critical types of communication. These users found that electronic mail offered them certain advantages not available with other methods of communication. They reported that using the system saved them time by eliminating the wait and inconvenience of unanswered telephone calls, and that it was particularly convenient for sending messages either before or after regular working hours, or for contacting people who are otherwise difficult to reach. Some appreciated being able to keep selected people informed without having to directly interact with them. Others appreciated having a way to communicate with superiors in a convenient but nonobtrusive manner.

Managers felt that there were several factors that limited their use of electronic mail. While a few did feel that they used the system for communications as much as they ever would, others felt that they had not changed their work patterns to incorporate regular use of electronic mail, i.e., that it was not totally a habit yet. The limited network of users was a constraint on the use of this feature. The necessity of distributing many things to both system and nonsystem users was a duplication of effort. Some active users suggested that limited or intermittent usage on the part of other users constrained their use of electronic mail; the uncertainty of whether these potential mail recipients would collect their mail in a timely fashion was a deterrent. The fact that some secretaries did not have easy access to a system terminal often tended to limit their manager's use of the system. Also, many managers felt that using electronic messages for sensitive issues was not appropriate. The wording of an electronic message, particularly a sensitive one, is a complicated matter since tone of voice cannot be used to temper it.

The most frequently cited effects on managers' work activities among the active users of the system's electronic mail feature were changes in the pattern and nature of communications. Active mail users reported making fewer telephone calls, keeping more people regularly informed (or at least doing so more conveniently), and a tendency to communicate with additional people. Reported additions to a manager's communication network often included people several steps up or down the management heirarchy (beyond immediate supervisory relationships) or people organizationally or physically removed from them.

Calendar: Less than a quarter of the managers made any use of the calendar function. Most felt that the function was both tedious and time consuming to use. Some believed that their nonuse was a matter of habit, yet others believed that they and their secretaries would both keep a paper calendar anyway, and that using the system for this would simply mean that there was a third calendar to keep updated. Some felt that the nonportability of an online calendar is a deterrent to its use.

Document preparation: On the whole, managers were not regular users of the document preparation feature. Generally, they felt that the nature of their work did not require it and that their current secretarial support adequately provided for their needs. Some, however, did use the feature to prepare short memos, particularly those users who were skilled at touch typing.

Management support applications: Managers believed that these applications, along with electronic mail, were unquestionably the most valuable parts of this system. The project cost-reporting system was used the most heavily. Managers felt that having access to weekly updates of project cost information was extremely valuable, especially at key points in project activities.

Information distribution applications: Less than a quarter of the managers used the information distribution applications. The application that they did use frequently was the online site telephone directory, which they, like other users, tended to utilize as a locator/search system, rather than simply as a telephone book (the directory could be searched by first or last name, telephone number, office number, employee number, etc.).

Desired enhancements: Managers felt that they would like to see the system immediately enhanced in two major ways. First, they wished to see expanded management tools included in the system. They felt that the system tools that they were currently using provided useful information, but they expressed a need for tools that would allow them to manipulate both the data they already had access to, as well as other new types of useful management data. A project scheduling tool was of particular interest. The ability to customize the accessed data to suit their particular needs was also important.

The second category of enhancements that the managers believed would serve to make the system more useful could be classified as administrative support functions. They felt that many administrative functions could be performed using the system, including the ordering of documents, making travel and purchasing requests, ordering supplies and furniture, etc.

Staff Usage Patterns

The professional staff used the system less than the managers; however, this could have been more due to two fairly crucial problems, rather than to a lack of usefulness of the system itself. The first, and perhaps foremost, problem was that the staff members in the department were physically located on one floor of a single building, and the majority of the department's work was done by individuals working independently or in groups comprised solely of department personnel. Staff members felt that they had no need to use the system to communicate or coordinate with their co-workers; they could just as easily walk next door or down the hall to talk with them directly. Those individuals in the department who regularly worked with people in other divisions (which were physically removed) could potentially use the system, but the people with whom they were working had no access to the system. The second problem was that the area in which the staff members were located had, throughout the entire time that they had had access to the system, been plagued by frequent network failures, which at times resulted in severely limited service.

To the extent that the professional staff did use the system, their activities focused on document preparation. They also found that the availability of a terminal for data processing purposes was a major asset. Their use of electronic mail was much less frequent than that of managers.

Electronic mail: Only approximately half of the staff members who used the system regularly checked their in-baskets daily. The remainder checked them only once or twice a week. Less then a quarter of them sent messages. The majority of the staff felt that the availability of electronic mail had little or no affect on their work. Whether their limited use of this feature was primarily due to their office configuration, which was previously discussed, or whether staff members of this type of corporation would never make significant use of electronic mail is not clear; however, based upon staff behavior in other parts of the corporation, it seems that the former is the case.

Document preparation: Over half of the staff used document preparation regularly. They used it to prepare documents, memos, and briefings. However, due to the incompatibility between this system and the corporate word-processing system, draft versions of a document or memo were prepared by the staff using the system, and it was then given to a secretary who rekeyed the material using the corporate word-processing system. As stated in the implementation description, all of the secretaries who supported these department staff members had system accounts and terminals, however, they preferred to use the word-processing system because they were more familiar with it, and because they felt it was easier to use.

Overall, the staff felt that the document preparation feature was by far the most useful part of the system to them; they felt that writing was faster using the system, and they liked the independence of being able to prepare a draft themselves. They often gave draft versions of a document that they had prepared using the system to the appropriate reviewers so that one round of comments could accompany the document when it went to the secretary for the first time. They felt that this resulted in fewer revision cycles and thus less work for them. Secretaries stated that they preferred working from a typed draft, and felt that they were more productive in doing so.

Other system features: The staff made little or no use of the other system features. Most felt that they had no need to keep a calendar, and those who did shared the management view that the calendar feature was too cumbersome and tedious to use. Staff rarely had any need for the management support applications, and less than half of the staff used the distribution applications regularly, although more than half felt that it was a good idea for a decision support system to include such applications. The site telephone directory was the most popular of these applications, and again, it was used primarily as a locator.

Desired enhancements: The staff felt that there were two major areas of the system that needed further development. First, they felt that more data-processing tools should be available at the corporate computer center (which they had access to through their terminals), and that all of the tools should be more user friendly. Specifically, they suggested the addition of an easy-to-use calculator function, a spread-sheet system, a data base management system, and a statistical analysis system. The second category of desired enhancements was the addition of friendlier interfaces with the other computer systems to which they had access. They felt that the access path (via the local area network and gateways) to these resources was extremely tedious and unforgiving, and that no good documentation existed that explained the laborious procedures.

Secretarial Usage Patterns

Secretarial use of the system seemed to depend highly on their management's use, or nonuse, of the system. In most cases, if the manager that the secretary supported did not make significant use of the system, neither did the secretary. In cases where the manager was an active user of the system, but used it quite independently of his or her supporting secretary, the secretary might or might not make any use of the system, depending upon her own inclination toward doing so, whether she had access to other word-processing tools, and whether or not she used the system to communicate with either professional staff members that she supported or other secretaries. Finally, in cases where the manager actively used the system "through their secretary," the secretary quite naturally made frequent use of it.

PROS AND CONS OF THE IMPLEMENTATION STRATEGY

Overall, irrespective of the selected implementation strategy, the relative success of the system depended to a large extent on two independent conditions mentioned earlier. The first was the fact that senior management agreed by consensus to implement the system, and the second was that corporate overhead monies were allocated to fund it. A corporatewide implementation of such a system requires the commitment of senior management to both use and support it in order to give it a fair trial, and funding via overhead rather than project monies ensures that the system is universally accepted, and not rejected out of hand because of local, project-related funding fluctuations and shortages.

As to the implementation strategy itself, giving senior level management access to the system first had its pluses and minuses. On the positive side, this strategy allowed for reasonably widespread acceptance of the system quickly, i.e., it was introduced to every part of the corporation from the start, which made all organizations feel included in the initial experimentation with decision support systems. In addition, peer pressure played a part in encouraging reluctant managers to, at a minimum, utilize the system for electronic mail. No one wanted to be embarrassed by not responding to an inquiry that was made via the system, especially if the inquiry was from a vice president.

On the negative side, this implementation strategy did not allow a critical mass of any cohesive working group to have access to the system, therefore making it much less valuable to its initial users than it might otherwise have been. As I mentioned earlier, managers used the system to talk to each other and to access budgeting and project data, but felt limited in the ways in which they could use the system. Those individuals with whom they worked most closely were not yet users. They felt that the majority of their time was spent interacting with members of their own division, or to some extent, with managers at the other corporate site (whose decision support system was not compatible with this system), as opposed to the managers of other divisions.

Choosing to first implement the system throughout an entire division, whose work concentrated around a few projects, would have been a better choice from the standpoint that probably a much greater percentage of the staff's work could have been done using the system than was the case with the lateral management implementation. Applications could have been developed that were tailored to the specific needs of the projects that the division was involved with, and they could have been implemented prior to giving any users access to the system. A combination of the fact that a division implementation of this type would most likely guarantee that the users had a greater need to communicate with one another (and would hopefully find the system useful for their coordination and communications), and the fact that applications tailored to the specific needs of the division would be especially useful, would seem to indicate that there are compelling arguments for designing an implementation strategy that includes giving early system access to such an organization.

CORPORATE IMPLEMENTATION ISSUES

Four areas of concern emerged during this project that a corporation intending to implement a decision support system should give specific consideration to if it intends that the system provide routine support to work operations.

The first falls into the category of *user considerations*. The general feeling among all of the users of this system was that more attention needed to be paid to user services and support. Users felt very strongly that some type of user training is mandatory with decision support systems, particularly if the system is being introduced to nondata processing users. A good number of users felt that the training that they had received was not sufficient for two reasons. First, they felt that the training was not as long and detailed as it should be, and second, that it was not tailored to the variable needs of new users. They also felt that the documentation was not adequate. As a result, they often felt stranded when problems occurred. Users often had no choice but to call the help number and hope that someone would answer their call and would be able to assist them.

This is not a problem that will soon be corrected in this organization. The "controlling majority" of the senior managers responsible for the implementation of the system remain adamantly opposed to both training and user support, and will neither lobby for, nor support, adequate budget requests for staff members to do these jobs. They feel that if any manager or staff member is not intelligent enough to learn the system with little or no assistance, that they have no business working at the corporation anyway! That attitude had prevented adequate user training and documentation development from the start, as there were too few system support staff members to do the required tasks, and this situation continued to negatively affect the implementation throughout.

With a decision support system, adequate training is necessary in order to make people feel comfortable enough with the system to begin incorporating it into their daily work activities. Then, once the system is well integrated in the user's daily routine, and the user becomes dependent on its being there, someone needs to be available at all times to help the user solve the problems that he or she encounters with the system. Furthermore, these methods of both initial and follow-on user assistance must be easy to use. The users must be able to solve their problems quickly so that they may complete their tasks on schedule. If they are unable to complete their tasks due to these difficulties, and if this occurs often to many users, an angry and disillusioned user population will soon emerge. This leads to the next point.

There are a number of *system considerations* that are extremely crucial if an automated decision support system is to play an integral role in the daily work activities of its users. First, the service must be reliable if users are expected to depend on it. It must be available to use at virtually all times during working hours, and either planned or unplanned interruptions in service should be nearly nonexistent. Second, the architecture must be sufficient and appropriate to the users' and corporation's needs. Specifically, there must be sufficient numbers of terminals and printers, and they must be strategically located; there should be sufficient integration among corporate computer applications; and the system must be sufficiently portable to support the considerable out-of-the-office work that is done. Third, any type of modification that is made to the system, regardless of whether it is maintenance or enhancement related, must be implemented in a way that does not disrupt daily use. System changes should be coordinated with users before they are finalized; they should only be periodically implemented and done so en masse during nonworking hours; and, to the greatest extent possible, they should be compatible with larger future plans and systems.

If an automated system is to become an integral part of the corporation's operations, consideration must be given to adapting *corporate procedures and operations* to take advantage of the system's capabilities at an organizational level. Administrative and finance-related procedures would probably be the first candidates for change. As with automating other types of tasks, care should be taken not to duplicate online the processes that heretofore were done in a manual fashion, or to disregard a potential application out-of-hand because on the surface it appears that something such as a required signature or a particular format precludes its automation. All of the users of this system agreed that the fewer administrative tasks they were required to do the better, and the more that an automated system could shorten the amount of time they spent on this type of work, the more helpful it would be.

The fourth area of corporate concern involves *privacy considerations*. Procedures for handling sensitive material on a decision support system must be developed. Many managers felt that sensitive information such as personnel data was being provided, reviewed, and communicated via the system, and that adequate safeguards were not built into the system to permit this.

THE USE OF MICROCOMPUTERS
IN THE SYSTEM

Could the incorporation of microcomputers in this architecture have affected the critical issues involved in user acceptance and system usefulness?

There are six characteristics of this implementation (among those discussed thus far) that were the most influential in gaining user acceptance of the system, and that made some aspects of the system useful and other aspects not so useful. These will be detailed below with discussion following regarding whether the incorporation of microcomputers into the system network could have positively affected these characteristics. The first four characteristics discussed are ones that would have benefited from the addition of microcomputers.

Something for Everyone

For any system implementation to be successful, the overall value of the system must be perceived by its prospective users to be high enough to warrant their investment of time and effort to use it. Specifically, it must be able to meet some necessary portion of the varied needs of the different types of users, and the varying needs of the individuals which constitute those types. This system had a little bit to offer everyone (with the exception of only some portion of the secretaries).

As discussed earlier, managers found electronic mail and the management support applications helpful enough to warrant their use of the system, and most of the staff found that document preparation created enough incentive for them to utilize the system, but because of the secretaries' inclination to use the corporate word-processing facilities rather than this system, they primarily found the system useful only if they used its' communications functions. If it had been feasible to incorporate the corporate word-processing capability into this system, probably virtually every secretary would have used it (and the corporation would have saved money be eliminating duplicate facilities). If the system had been enhanced to include more administrative support applications, even more of the secretaries' needs would have been met.

Could the incorporation of microcomputers in the architecture of this system have affected the overall value to its users? First of all, it is clear that all of the applications of a system of this magnitude could not be supported solely by microcomputers, given their current capacities and capabilities. In fact, numerous hosts specializing in different kinds of applications are required.

However, given the existence of such hosts, the addition of microcomputers connected to the local area network could have made this system more valuable to its users, particularly in the areas of unique user needs and application customization. Applications could easily have been developed (either by the central support staff or by the users themselves) that would allow managers to use microcomputers to access and download data from the appropriate hosts, and then to manipulate that data in the different ways desired by the different managers.

Some members of the professional staff would have found that a microcomputer would have better served as their system terminal because it would have allowed them to obtain and use applications that were valuable to their work, but that were not in great enough demand to warrant their being host based and available to all users. Microcomputers would have also given these staff users more control over the availability of some automated tools, as such microcomputer-based software could have been puchased independently by individual departments, without their needing to go through the corporate computer center bureaucracy in order to obtain them. Some might argue, however, that allowing users to both develop and obtain software applications for themselves could lead to corporate computer chaos (with an unruly and unnecessary proliferation of microcomputer applications and peripherals), and as a result, to higher overall corporate costs, than would otherwise be the case with host-based systems that incorporate a more modest, but adequate level of user responsive capabilities.

The projected potential improvements to both the quantity and quality of the corporation's products, and the effect that these tools might or might not have on the overall quality of the working environment for the staff, must be weighed against whether or not it is felt that incorporating microcomputers into a decision support system network would lead to redundant capabilities and unnecessary escalating costs. This decision must certainly be made on a case-by-case basis by each corporation.

Accomodating Both Sophisticated and Novice Users

The second characteristic, which actually may have as great an effect upon the success of a system as any, is classified as *user responsiveness*. First of all, the system must be easy for inexperienced or casual users to operate, yet it must also allow sophisticated users to operate the system using powerful commands, quickly bypassing the tedious menus and processes that are available for the naive user.

This concept has been given a great deal of attention in the literature for a number of years, with some writers claiming that ease of use and powerful commands (which may be used with both simple and advanced functions) are mutually exclusive concepts in system design, and other writers attesting that combining these concepts into a single system is indeed feasible. The opponents also claim that even if a system could be designed that incorporated both of these concepts, the practicalities of the increased amount of time and effort that would be necessary to design such a system would make the resulting price of the product too high. However, the proponents argue that such a design is indeed possible, and that the reasons for not doing so in the past revolve around the fact that programmers have designed systems without the help of either users or user-oriented representatives, and that most system developers are simply too short sighted to realize that the investment of a bit more time and money would result in a system that would be an order of magnitude more appealing to its users. (This author tends to agree with those who proport that designing such a system is possible and economically feasible.)

All users of the system described in this chapter ardently felt that every feature of a decision support system must adequately serve both new and experienced users in order for them to fully integrate it into their working lives, and to make maximum use of what the system had to offer. They pointed out that all experienced users are new users at one time, and in fact, that any individual is typically, at any given point in time, both experienced with some subset of features, yet inexperienced with another subset, given that a system with such broad capabilities would never be applicable in total to a single user.

Other aspects that apply to the user responsiveness of implementation design are initial and ongoing *user training, user documentation,* and *user assistance.* These activities must be carefully planned and constantly reevaluated, and they must be adequate in size and scope to serve the using population, increasing over time in proportion to the increase in the numbers of users. This is an area that this company paid far too little attention to. As a result, the users often cited inadequate training and support as significant reasons for their under-utilization of the system. The final aspect of user responsiveness, which evolved as critical in our implementation, was the insistence on the part of users that all system changes and enchancements be *upward compatible* to the maximum extent possible. Not surprisingly, they had no desire to even occasionally be forced to relearn aspects of the system.

As to the potential effects that the use of microcomputers could have on these user-responsive related issues, it seems that user training, documentation, and assistance would be unaffected, as would the ability to make system changes and enchancements upward compatible. However, micros might very well be used to simplify the user interface. That is, the task of combining the elements of ease-of-use with powerful sophisticated commands and capabilities might be easier with microcomputer user nodes, primarily because the users could have more control over the selection of individual applications, which would allow them to select those that best suited their needs as either casual or sophisticated users; and further, because they would have the choice of customizing their tool to suit their needs if desired.

Adequate System Availability

Another characteristic that has a significant impact on the success of a decision support system implementation is system availability and reliability. The system must be available at virtually all times during the "real" working hours of the corporation, which probably extend beyond "nine to five." Maintenance should only be applied during off hours, and much attention should be paid to making the network reliable. There is a real advantage in employing microcomputers as user nodes to avoid such downtime. If a sufficient number of applications were micro based, a pause in network or host service would not equate to everyone being "dead in the water." It has also been my experience that the reliability of microcomputers is superior to that of almost any other piece of such a network. If this is true, it would also mean that the microcomputers would be less likely to fail themselves, giving their users even greater reliability than a standard terminal on an individual basis.

Portability was also often cited as an important but inadequate feature of our pilot network. Users mentioned not only the inability to take system-based work home easily, but also the inability to easily gain access to the netowrk while traveling on business. It was possible to borrow dial-up terminals from the computer center for use at home or on trips, but doing so either tied up the individual's home telephone, or resulted in considerable long distance phone charges (as we had no access to long distance leased telephone lines). It is certainly reasonable that microcomputer user nodes would allow work to be taken home more easily, given the scenario that the individual had a compatible micro at home, which these days is not out of the question. However, there is no doubt that having the capability at home would cost the employee a good deal of money or, if the corporation were willing to fund either part or all of the employee's workstation, would result in nontrivial costs to the corporation. Portable microcomputers that are compatible with those in the network might be a reasonable, although not inexpensive, solution for travelers; however, they would still need to dial in to the network if they needed to use electronic mail.

System Privacy

Many managers expressed a great deal of concern over the amount of care that they felt needed to be taken with the incorporation of sensitive personnel, project, or costing data into such a system. They felt that this system did not possess adequate security procedures to make them comfortable enough to be willing to use it for such matters. They did not like the idea that such data might be "sitting out there in their account" just waiting for an intruder to access it (in reality, intruding on their accounts would have been extremely difficult; however their perception of the situation was of primary importance). Microcomputers could be extremely beneficial in helping to overcome this fear. Managers could access the sensitive information from the host, download it to their micro, and when they are not using it, put it on a floppy disk and lock it up if they so desired. For the most part, the managers were not as opposed to having the data on the host, just as long as it was not in their account (where they felt responsible for it). They also believed, to some extent, that the data was primarily sensitive because of its particular association with their organization, as opposed to a conglomeration of this data pooled on a host somewhere.

A Critical Mass of Users

The "critical mass" element is one of the two aspects of this implementation that would have remained unaffected by the incorporation of microcomputers. As discussed in the section examining the pros and cons of our implementation strategy, the pilot user groups did not contain any substantial networks of individuals who needed to frequently and routinely communicate and coordinate with one another in order to do their jobs. Electronic mail is only useful as long as an individual sends and receives (or at a minimum receives) enough messages to make it worth his or her while to routinely check the in-basket. In our case, there was enough electronic mail traffic among most managers that they both used the feature and found it to be helpful to them; however, they felt that the network of individuals available for them to communicate with via the system was limited. Implementing the system throughout their respective divisions would have greatly enhanced the value of this application to them.

In contrast, the pilot staff users never constituted a critical mass, therefore this function was not of any particular use to them. In addition, there was certainly not a critical mass of users as applied to any other feature of the system. For example, no staff members ever electronically mailed to one another documents that they had drafted using the system, nor did managers ever route data from the management support applications among themselves.

The critical mass element, as it affects the implementation strategy of a decision support system, is architecturally independent assuming that each user has adequate access to a terminal connected to the network. This element is simply one that must be carefully and thoughtfully considered by the staff designing the strategy for the introduction of such a system.

Top Management Support

The final, and extremely important, characteristic of this implementation was senior management's collective belief that the idea for the acquisition, development, and implementation of the system was theirs. There was a significant amount of pride involved in finding the system to be useful. This element would have remained constant regardless of the selected system architecture.

SUMMARY

All in all, adding selected microcomputer user nodes to this decision support system network would have positively affected the majority of the ingredients required for a successful implementation, and would not have negatively affected the remainder. Overall, the result would have been a more usable and better accepted system.

NOTES

Judith S. Dahmann, who has a doctorate in sociology, and who has had much experience with evaluating the effectivenss of computer information systems, brought the needed insight to the task of structuring the interview guide such that the information we collected was meaningful, and further aided in structuring the analysis of the data collected. Parts of this article are based upon an internal corporate paper that we coauthored that specifically discusses the user survey in detail.

IV

DESIGN, EVALUATION, AND IMPLEMENTATION ISSUES

INTRODUCTION

How do you know if your decision support system is any good? How do you know if it is doing what it is supposed to be doing? How do you know which of the many commercially available microcomputer decision support systems will best serve your needs?

This part of the book deals with these and related issues. The opening article by William B. Rouse entitled, "Design and Evaluation of Computer-based Decision Support Systems," offers an "integrated design and evaluation methodology based on a top-down view of human decision making and decision aiding." He outlines a design process that considers types of decision-making tasks, situations, and strategies as integral to the design and subsequent evaluation processes. The evaluation process itself should focus, according to Rouse, on compatibility, understandability, and effectiveness. He then describes at least two ways to conduct such an evaluation.

The article by Leonard Adelman and Michael L. Donnell describes a case study that yielded a number of important insights. Like Rouse, they focus on structured evaluation, but unlike Rouse, they describe the results of a detailed empirical evaluation that involved a number of expert users, several evaluative scenarios, and a methodology—multiattribute utility assessment—that itself has been used to drive decision support systems.

Hopple's article deals much more with design than evaluation. He focuses on the psychological baggage that users bring to the decision support process, and upon the difficulty of building systems compatible with the cognitive problem-solving strengths and weaknesses of users. Given that humans are suboptimal information processors, and that computer-based problem solving is "unnatural" at best, should we expect very much from our decision support systems? Or should we design them from the cognitive ground up, forsaking emphases on function and friendliness in favor of emphases on cognitive style, preferences, and performance? These questions illustrate the flavor of the important issues raised by Hopple.

The articles in Part IV suggest that there are still a lot of unanswered questions about decision support systems design and evaluation. Hopple alerts us to the importance of cognitive compatibility, while Rouse, Adelman, and Donnell suggest that before releasing a decision support system one should test it thoroughly to make sure that it is supporting the right decisions in the right way.

It should also be acknowledged that careful design and structured requirements analysis are often the "poor relations" in interactive systems design and development. How often have we heard complaints in the workplace about how time-consuming and tedious structured requirements analyses are? How often have we heard disparaging comments about cognitive overkill? All of the articles in this book suggest that if we are to develop successful microcomputer decision support systems then we must adopt a highly systematic and structured analytical approach to the process, an approach that is also consistent and verifiable. If we follow these general guidelines then our chances of success are substantially improved.

11

DESIGN AND EVALUATION OF COMPUTER-BASED DECISION SUPPORT SYSTEMS*

William B. Rouse

Advances in computer and communications technology, as well as population growth and evolving organizational forms, are resulting in increasingly complex systems. Because of the many components and relationships among elements in these systems, very information-rich situations tend to arise. In addition, the large-scale nature of these systems can present the possibility of large losses of money, and perhaps lives, if these systems are not operated, maintained, and managed appropriately. This trend toward very complex and often high-risk systems has substantially increased the need for and interest in

*An abbreviated version of this chapter appears in the *Proceedings of the First USA-Japan Conference on Human-Computer Interaction, Honolulu, Hawaii, August 1984.*

decision support systems for aiding humans in decision making and problem solving.

It is quite natural to suggest that the computer technology that prompted this trend can also provide the means for assisting human operators, maintainers, and managers in coping with it. To a great extent, computer-based decision support systems represent the only viable approach. However, the computer is not quite the panacea that everyone would like.

For quite some time, there has been an implicitly shared assumption in the technological community that the introduction of computer-based systems is inherently a good idea. In recent years, this assumption has been shown to have a limited range of validity. For example, it has been found that shifting procedural information from hard copy to computer-generated displays can degrade performance unless appropriate aids are provided (Rouse and Rouse 1980; Rouse, et al. 1982). Similarly, it has been found that additional information on bibliographic data base structure (made feasible by computer technology) can degrade performance without additional aiding (Morehead and Rouse 1983). Therefore, computer-based approaches are not always inherently better.

The implication of this conclusion is *not* that alternatives to computer-based approaches should be sought. Instead, the implication is that computer-based decision support systems must be carefully designed and evaluated if the anticipated benefits are to be realized. The purpose of this chapter is to propose an overall approach to design and evaluation.

An overall methodology is needed for two reasons. First, design has to be systematic if one is to avoid producing ad hoc aids, with the concomitant potential for repeating previous mistakes. Second, a methodology is needed whereby design and evauation are pursued, to the extent possible, in parallel. Such a parallel approach will allow necessary modifications to be identified while it is still possible to implement them. This will make the design and evaluation process more efficient as well as more effective.

This chapter presents an integrated design and evaluation methodology based on a top-down view of human decision making and decision aiding. The discussion begins with an outline of a design process that explicitly considers types of decision-making tasks, situations, and strategies as well as forms of information, prototypical messages, and adaptive aids. The discussion then proceeds to outline a multilevel approach to evaluation. Finally, the chapter concludes with a brief summary of applications and implications.

DESIGN METHODOLOGY

While decision support systems can be designed to aid humans in a wide variety of tasks and situations, this variety is not as great as one might imagine. It easily can be argued that there is a limited set of general tasks and situations that is sufficiently robust to describe the domain of virtually any decision support system. Such a "standard" description allows one to prescribe analytically the types of strategy, forms of information, and prototypical messages associated with an aid. This results in the normative view of design advocated in this paper. The presentation in this section draws heavily from Rouse and Rouse (1983) and Rouse, et al. (1984).

Decision-making Tasks

A recent review of the literature on decision support systems (Rouse and Rouse 1983) led to the conclusion that virtually every aid discussed is aimed at supporting one or more of three general decision-making tasks: 1) situation assessment, 2) planning and commitment, and 3) execution and monitoring.

Situation assessment is required when the information received by humans differs from their expectations in other than an acceptable manner. The unexpected deviations prompt humans to question the validity of their a priori assumptions regarding the status quo. This questioning leads to information seeking in search of an explanation of what has happened, is happening, or may happen. As the phrase implies, the goal is to assess the underlying situation that produced the unexpected information.

Given an explanation of the new situation, the next general task is *planning and commitment* which involves generating, evaluating, and selecting among alternative courses of action relative to criteria that reflect tradeoffs between possibly competing objectives (e.g., maintaining normal operations vs. ceasing operation to isolate a problem). In many systems, alternative plans are readily available in terms of formal procedures for dealing with particular situations. Further, humans' training may, in effect, prescribe the course of action they will take and, therefore, alternatives need not be actively considered. However, when situations arise that were not anticipated in the design of the procedures, or situations arise that are unfamiliar because they were not considered in the design of the training, humans can be required to pursue planning and commitment. In such situations, humans' decision-making and problem-solving abilities, as well as their breadth of experience, are likely to be crucial.

The third general decision-making task, *execution and monitoring*, involves implementing the plan selected, observing its consequences, and evaluating deviations of observed consequences from expectations. Most of humans' activities are dominated by execution and monitoring. The vast majority of the time, differences between observations and expectations are minor and, consequently, situation assessment or planning and commitment are not required. However, when they are required (i.e., deviations are unacceptable), the role of humans becomes central to resolving any potential problems.

While siutation assessment, planning and commitment, and execution and monitoring are the general decision-making tasks of interest, they are somewhat too broad in scope to provide an operationally useful categorization of functions of decision support systems. Therefore, these three general tasks were further subdivided to yield the thirteen tasks shown in Figure 11.1.

Two aspects of this figure are of particular note. First, execution and monitoring tasks are shown at the top of this figure to emphasize that these tasks constitute decision makers' most frequent activities. Further, situation assessment as well as planning and commitment are unnecessary unless deviations from expectations are unacceptable. The second aspect of this figure

EXECUTION AND MONITORING
1. IMPLEMENTATION OF PLAN
2. OBSERVATION OF CONSEQUENCES
3. EVALUATION OF DEVIATIONS FROM EXPECTATIONS
4. SELECTION BETWEEN ACCEPTANCE AND REJECTION

SITUATION ASSESSMENT: INFORMATION SEEKING
5. GENERATION/IDENTIFICATION OF ALTERNATIVE INFORMATION SOURCES
6. EVALUATION OF ALTERNATIVE INFORMATION SOURCES
7. SELECTION AMONG ALTERNATIVE INFORMATION SOURCES

SITUATION ASSESSMENT: EXPLANATION
8. GENERATION OF ALTERNATIVE EXPLANATIONS
9. EVALUATION OF ALTERNATIVE EXPLANATIONS
10. SELECTION AMONG ALTERNATIVE EXPLANATIONS

PLANNING AND COMMITMENT
11. GENERATION OF ALTERNATIVE COURSES OF ACTION
12. EVALUATION OF ALTERNATIVE COURSES OF ACTION
13. SELECTION AMONG ALTERNATIVE COURSES OF ACTION

Figure 11.1   General Decision-making Tasks

that should be noted is the fact that eleven of the thirteen tasks involve *generation, evaluation,* and *selection*; this distinction is important to later discussions in this chapter.

Definitions and detailed examples of each of these thirteen tasks are presented by Rouse and Rouse (1983) for command and control situations, and by Rouse, et al. (1984) for process control situations. Thus, this taxonomy of decision-making tasks has a wide range of applicability, in part because the synthesis of this taxonomy benefited greatly from previous efforts in this area (Rasmussen 1976; Wohl 1981; Rouse 1983).

Decision-making Situations

The choosing of decision-making tasks to be supported, as well as identification of the information requirements that must be met to support these tasks, depends on the types of decision-making situations in which the aid will be employed. There are three general classes of situations of interest. These classes can be described in terms of familiarity and frequency.

Most situations are *familiar* and *frequent*. They are familiar in that the possibility of their occurence has been anticipated. They are frequent in the sense that considerable experience has been gained in dealing with them. For such situations, decision makers usually "know" what to do; upon observing the situation, the course of action is apparent.

Familiar and *infrequent* situations usually do not allow for such immediate action because the humans involved do not have much experience with these types of situations, although the possibility of their occurrence was anticipated. As a result, a course of action may be hypothesized immediately, but a variety of information is collected before this course of action is implemented.

Unfamiliar and *infrequent* situations are such that they are not anticipated by the decision maker and, by definition, seldom if ever previously experienced. As a result, the appropriate course of action is not at all obvious. Further, available procedures may be inadequate or even inappropriate for coping with the situation. Therefore, decision makers have to rely on knowledge that goes beyond situation-specific experiences and job aids.

As shown in Figure 11.2, not all of the thirteen decision making tasks are relevant to the three types of situation. Since *familiar and frequent* situations are such that the decision maker "knows what to do," alternative information sources, explanations, and courses of action need not be considered (thus the two *no's* in column one of fig. 11.2). Thus, the four execution and monitoring tasks are usually the only applicable tasks.

Familiar and infrequent situations require that the situation be verified prior to action. The verfication process is likely to require consideration of sources of verifying information. However, once the situation is verified, alternative courses of action need not be considered (thus the *no* in planning and commitment in fig. 11.2). Therefore, decision making proceeds immediately to execution and monitoring.

Unfamiliar and, by definition, *infrequent* situations are likely to require the full range of decision-making tasks. In the process of synthesizing a course of action, the decision maker will usually have to consider a variety of hypotheses and options. This process tends to be far removed from "knowing what to do."

Decision-making Strategies

As might be expected, decision makers approach the three types of situations quite differently (Rasmussen 1983; Rouse 1983). *Familiar situations* call upon humans' pattern recognition abilities, and decision-making strategies tend to be *symptomatic* in the sense that observed patterns of informtion are mapped directly to appropriate courses of action. Therefore, information to support this type of strategy should be pattern oriented and, in particular, utilize patterns that are stereotypical for the population of decision makers of interest.

At the other extreme, *unfamiliar situations* call upon humans' analytical reasoning abilities, with the result that decision-making strategies tend to be *topographic* in the sense that structural relationships among elements of information are explicitly considered. Information to support topographic strategies should be structure oriented and emphasize causal or functional relationships. This will allow the *tracing* of unfamiliar patterns that is typical for topographic strategies, rather than

DECISION-MAKING TASKS	TYPES OF SITUATION		
	FAMILIAR & FREQUENT	FAMILIAR & INFREQUENT	UNFAMILIAR & INFREQUENT
EXECUTION & MONITORING	YES	YES	YES
SITUATION ASSESSMENT	NO	YES	YES
PLANNING & COMMITMENT	NO	NO	YES

Figure 11.2   Relevance of Tasks to Situations

the *mapping* from patterns to courses of action that is usual for symptomatic strategies.

Familiar and infrequent situations are likely to result in *mixed strategies*. Execution and monitoring will primarily be approached symptomatically while some aspects of situation assessment may require a topographic approach. This does not necessarily imply that topographic or structural information be explicitly displayed. In familiar situations it is quite likely that decision makers will have complete knowledge of the relevant structural information (i.e., will have a good "mental model"). However, in order to use this structural information to assess the situation, the information that is displayed must be consistent with a topographic approach. Therefore, aggregated patterns would be inappropriate. Instead, displays should show disaggregated elements of information that allow decision makers to trace patterns through their mental models of causal or functional relationships among these elements of information.

Forms of Information

The distinction between *aggregated patterns* and *disaggregated elements* is important for determining how the state of the system should be displayed. The term *state* is used here to denote the set of physical, economic, organizational, and environmental variables that is sufficient to describe the current status of the system, as well as serve as input for any projections of the future status of the system.

For symptomatic strategies, system state should be displayed as an aggregated pattern. Some types of display are excellent for emphasizing patterns. For example, colorgraphic pie charts of economic information for a business, or circular profiles of physical variables for an engineering system, are oriented toward pattern recognition. In general, displays intended to present an "overall impression" are pattern oriented.

In contrast, topographic strategies require that the system state be displayed as disaggregated elements. This is due to the fact that particular variables (e.g., temperatures, inflation rates, employee turnover rates) are usually needed to trace through causal or functional relationships. This allows the decision maker in an unfamiliar situation to determine "why" the current system state has emerged; for familiar situations, this question is unnecessary.

Displays that explicitly depict both structural relationships and the variables associated with each element of the structure are good choices when disaggregated elements are needed. For example, a display indicating resource flows (e.g., raw materials, finished products, and capital) in a production and distribution system, or mass and energy flows in an engineering system, provide support for topographic strategies. Of course, as noted earlier, the structure of the system need not be shown explicitly if it is reasonable to assume that decision makers' mental models of this structure are sufficiently accurate and accessible for this purpose.

Another consideration relative to the form of information is the extent to which information about future system states is needed. *Current* information (which may include information related to past system states) is sufficient for familiar and frequent situations because the decision maker "knows" what will happen. In contrast, unfamiliar and infrequent situations often require *projected* information, particularly for those tasks in the planning and commitment category. The intermediate type of situation (i.e., familiar and infrequent) may also be benefited by projected information for the purpose of verifying that the situation is likely to evolve as hypothesized.

Thus, forms of information can be described in terms of two dichotomies: 1) patterns vs. elements, and 2) current vs. projected. The appropriateness of different forms for alternative combinations of tasks and situations are shown in Figure 11.3. From this figure, one can see that the choice of task and type of situation dictates the strategy, which in turn dictates the form of information and, hence, the choice of how information should be displayed (e.g., pie charts vs. trend graphs vs. tables).

Of course, the extent to which the resulting choices are appropriate depends on having correctly specified tasks and situations. With regard to situations, this can be somewhat difficult because familiarity and frequency are defined, at least partially, relative to particular individuals. Therefore, it is quite possible

DECISION-MAKING TASKS	TYPES OF SITUATION		
	FAMILIAR & INFREQUENT	FAMILIAR & FREQUENT	UNFAMILIAR & INFREQUENT
EXECUTION & MONITORING	CURRENT PATTERNS	CURRENT PATTERNS	CURRENT PATTERNS & ELEMENTS
SITUATION ASSESSMENT	——	CURRENT PATTERNS & PROJECTED ELEMENTS	CURRENT & PROJECTED ELEMENTS
PLANNING & COMMITMENT	——	——	CURRENT & PROJECTED ELEMENTS

Figure 11.3   Appropriate Forms of Information

that a given situation will be viewed as familiar by one individual and unfamiliar by another.

This possibility usually results in designers hedging by providing more information than strictly required, "just in case" particular individuals need it. This hedging also tends to occur when decision makers are asked about what information they need. Numerous studies (see Rouse and Rouse 1984 and Morehead 1984 for reviews) have shown that operators, managers, commanders, researchers, and others tend to overspecify their information requirements. Decision makers apparently find some "comfort" in additional and perhaps redundant information. Unfortunately, this can become a problem when display space is limited.

There appear to be two viable ways of dealing with this problem. One is to view the information requirements that emerge from the top-down analysis espoused in this paper as *minimum requirements*. Additional information is acceptable to the extent that clutter, confusion, and other human factor incompatibilities are not likely to result. An alternative approach to dealing with overspecification of information requirements is to *adapt* the decision support system to particular decision makers. This approach is discussed in some detail in a later section of this chapter.

Prototypical Messages

Form is only one attribute of the information provided by decision support systems. Of greater importance is *content* (i.e., the "what" as opposed to the "how"). Specifying the content of a decision support system's displays (i.e., the variables to appear) independent of any particular application is virtually impossible. However, it is possible to specify the nature of the *messages* that must be transmitted to support each task and situation.

This approach requires that one define a set of *prototypical* messages that are relevant to a range of applications. Considering the thirteen decision-making tasks discussed earlier, it was noted then that eleven of these tasks can be classified by one of three terms: 1) generation/identification, 2) evaluation, and 3) selection. For each of these terms, a farily general set of prototypical messages can be formulated. This set of prototypical messages is elaborated on in Rouse et al. (1984); unfortunately, space limitations do not allow presentation of this material here.

However, the genesis of this set of messages is fairly straightforward. Messages for generation/identification are simply expressed in terms of alternative information sources, explanations, and courses of action. Messages for selection are also quite easy to envision, simply specifying the alternative that should be selected. Evaluation is much more complicated because evaluation can be relative to deviations, confidence, consequences, resource requirements, or comparisons of alterantives.

Given this set of prototypical messages, one is in a position to be much more specific about how an aid might support each of the thirteen decision-making tasks. Succinctly, in order for an aid to support a particular task, it must provide at least one of the prototypical messages associated with the task. Of course, while this set provides the alternative messages, the choice of which alternatives are most appropriate depends on the particular applications.

The top-down approach presented here for specifying a set of messages provides an alternative means for dealing with the traditional problem of defining information requirements, which is typically pursued in a bottom-up manner (i.e., "up" from activity primitives rather than "down" from overall objectives). Once the messages/information requirements have been defined, one is in a position to determine display elements and formats, dialogue structures, etc. Considerations of these issues is beyond the scope of this chapter. The interested reader is referred to Frey, et al. (1984), which basically picks up where this chapter leaves off.

Adaptive Aids

It was noted earlier that the familiarity characteristics of situations are likely to be dependent on the particular individual who is to be supported by the aid. As a result, strategies, and hence appropriate forms of information, are likely to vary with individuals. Ideally, therefore, the nature of the aiding as well as the human-computer interface should be adapted to individual users.

A recent report presents a framework for characterizing adaptive decision aids (Rouse and Rouse 1983). Beyond the typical characteristics of type of decision task (i.e., the thirteen discussed earlier) and level of decision aiding (i.e., ranging from cautions and warnings to expert advice), the framework involves four key attributes which are summarized in Figure 11.4.

The *form* of adaptation relates to the question: What is adapted to? This question can be answered at several levels. At the highest level, adaptation can be relative to the *task* or *user*. At lower levels of detail, adaptation can involve a *class* of tasks or users, a particular *member* of a class, or the *state* of a particular member. Virtually any aid is adapted (albeit offline by the designer) to a class of tasks or users. Thus, the key distinction here is between adapting to members (e.g., particular users) versus states (e.g., specific situations) at particular points in time.

The *mode* of adaptation concerns the question: Who does the adapting? There are three possible answers to this question: 1) *designer*, 2) *user*, and 3) *aid*. A further aspect of the mode of adaptation is whether it is done *offline* or *online*. Any adaptation by the designer is, by definition, performed offline while users and aids usually adapt online. Designer-offline adaptation typically involves classes of tasks and users, and can be viewed as the special case of nonadaptive aiding.

The *method* of adaptation relates to the question: How is the adaptation done? In general, adaptation involves measurements that are manipulated using models such that modifications of various types may result. A continuum of modifications is possible. The highest level modification is the *allocation* of tasks (e.g., does human or computer select among courses of action?). A lower level modification involves *partitioning* of a task (e.g., human chooses goal and computer controls system to achieve this goal). The lowest level modification involves *transformation* of a task (e.g., abstracting of a display from a physical to a functional representation).

The *means* of communication concerns the question: How is information transmitted? This refers to the manner in which

FORM OF ADAPTATION: WHAT IS ADAPTED TO?

	CLASS	MEMBER	STATE
USER	1	2	2
TASK	1	2	2

MODE OF ADAPTATION: WHO DOES THE ADAPTING?

	DESIGNER	USER	AID
OFFLINE	1	2	3
ONLINE	4	3	2

METHOD OF ADAPTATION: HOW IS THE ADAPTATION DONE?

	ALLOCATING	PARTITIONING	TRANSFORMATION
MEASUREMENTS	2	2	2
MODELS	2	2	2

MEANS OF COMMUNICATION: HOW IS INFORMATION TRANSMITTED?

	DIRECT	INDIRECT	INFERRED
EXPLICIT	2	3	3
IMPLICIT	3	2	2

Notes:

1 = always combined
2 = frequently combined
3 = seldom combined
4 = never combined

Figure 11.4   Four Attributes of Adaptive Decision Aids

measurements are made and the ways in which users and aids inform each other of the status of the decision-making process. Communication can be either *explicit* or *implicit*. Explicit communication may involve specific displays and controls, standard dialogs via keyboard or voice, or natural language via keyboard or voice. Implicit communication can be accomplished using unobtrusive but *direct* observations, *indirect* measurements, or *inference* via models.

The previously noted report on adaptive aids (Rouse and Rouse 1983) discusses the above attributes in great detail with a variety of examples. In addition, command and control decision making is described in terms of the thirteen decision-making tasks discussed earlier. This description is used, in conjunction with the framework for adaptive outlined in this section, to identify opportunities for aiding in general, and possibilities of adaptive aiding in particular.

Summary

The approach to design presented in this section espouses a top-down view of decision support systems. By specifying the types of situation of interest, one defines the possible tasks of interest as well as the expected strategies. The situations, tasks, and strategies dictate the appropriate forms of information. Tasks also define the alternative prototypical messages that might be provided. Given the types of message and the general forms they should take, one is in a position to proceed with detailed design such as prescribed by Frey, et al. (1984). Finally, since the perceived characteristics of situations and the resulting decision-making strategies are often very sensitive to differences among individuals, it may be appropriate to consider adaptive aids in terms of the attributes that were briefly outlined above.

EVALUATION METHODOLOGY

The use of the word *evaluation* is somewhat problematic because its colloquial usage allows a very broad range of interpretations. One common use of the word evaluation is as a synonym of *demonstration*. From this perspective, evaluation simply involves turning the system on and seeing if, for example, the display appears and basically looks something like that the designer intended. This type of evaluation gives one an overall impression of a system, but provides no definitive information on performance. For this reason, within this chapter, evaluation and demonstration are by no means synonymous.

Industry tends to dichotomize evaluation into verification and validation. *Verification* is the process of demonstrating that hardware has been fabricated and software programmed as designed. In other words, verification involves determining that design drawings and other documentation have been accurately translated into an end product.

In contrast, *validation* is the process of assessing the degree to which a design achieves the objectives of interest. Thus, validation goes beyond asing whether or not the system was built according to plans; validation asks whether or not the plan was a suitable means for achieving the end specified by the design objectives. This type of evaluation can be difficult because it involves assessing the products of synthesis (i.e., design) rather than the products of translation (i.e., fabrication and programming). Nevertheless, validation is the type of evaluation emphasized in this chapter.

Levels of Evaluation

It is quite useful to approach evaluation of decision support systems in terms of three types of issues (Rouse 1984). The first type of issue is *compatibility*. The nature of physical presentations to the user and the responses expected from the user must be compatible with human input-output abilities and limitations. Succinctly, regardless of the overall design objectives, users have to be able to read the displays, reach the keyboard, etc. Otherwise, there is a great risk that the value of higher level design features (i.e., the decision aiding) will be hidden amidst compatibility deficiencies.

However, a system that is compatible with human abilities and limitations is not necessarily understandable. Thus, the second type of issue is *understandability* in the sense that the structure, format, and content of the user-system dialog must result in meaningful communication. In other words, the messages displayed by the system must be interpretable by the user, and the messages that the user wants to transmit to the system have to be expressible. If a user can read the menu of options and reach the touch panel to select an option, but the options available are meaningless, then the effort invested in assuring compatibility will have been wasted to the extent that there is a lack of understandability.

Therefore, the designer of a decision support system must assure that it is compatible and understandable. However, while compatibility and understandability are necessary, they are not sufficient; the designer must also assure *effectiveness*. A decision support system is effective to the extent that it supports a decision maker in a manner that leads to improved performance, results in a difficult task being less difficult, or enables accomplishing a task that could not otherwise be accomplished. Assessing effectiveness obviously depends on defining appropriate measures of performance, difficulty, etc.

In summary, evaluation of a decision support system involves assuring that the system is compatible with human input-output abilities and limitations, understandable in terms of the messages transmitted, and effective in the sense that design objectives are achieved. In general, these three levels of evaluation cannot all be performed simultaneously. Instead, a multiphase evaluation is needed, the nature of which depends on the approach employed.

Approaches to Evaluation

There are two fundamentally different approaches to evaluation. If a prototype system and population of potential users are available, and if time and resources allow, an *empirical evaluation* can be performed. In contrast, if the system only exists in terms of design documentation, or the population of potential users is not yet available, or time and resources are constrained, then an *analytical evaluation* will have to suffice.

The implication of this contrast is, of course, that empirical evaluation is preferred to analytical evaluation. This is due to the fact that analytical evaluation is inherently limited in that design objectives, concepts, and details may be carefully and systematically reviewed, but they are not tested. In a sense, an analytical evaluation can *verify* the tenability of a design, but cannot *validate* the design in terms of having achieved the design objectives. Nevertheless, analytical evaluation can be a very efficient means for providing an assessment of a decision support system's potential for effectiveness. Further, analytical evaluation may be necessary if an empirical evaluation leads to the conclusion that a design is not acceptable.

Analytical Evaluation

It is possible for an analytical evaluation to be very straightforward. If an analytical process, such as outlined earlier in this chapter, has been used to design the decision support system, and the use and results of that process are well documented, then one need only audit the lines of reasoning and resulting design decisions from which the system emerged. Unfortunately, such information is seldom available. The evaluation problem, therefore, becomes one of attempting to verify that a design is consistent with objectives that are usually only vaguely defined.

Clearly, this is almost an impossible task. However, it is feasible if a design framework can be developed such that any decision support system can be viewed as if it was designed using this framework. The design process outlined earlier can serve this function (Rouse, et al. 1984). This process enables one to proceed from design objectives (i.e., situations and tasks) to information requirements (i.e., types and forms of message) to detailed design (i.e., particular displays). The detailed review of displays can be performed using a guide such as that developed by Frey and his colleagues (Frey, et al. 1984).

The analytical evaluation process proposed in this chapter proceeds in a top-down manner from effectiveness, to understandability, to compatibility. As noted earlier, effectiveness is the degree to which a decision support system enables achievement of design objectives. To the extent that effectiveness can be assessed analytically, the design process espoused in this chapter assures effectiveness. Further evaluation requires empirical testing.

A decision support system is understandable if information communicated to decision makers is meaningful to these individuals. To assess understandability, one must first determine the knowledge required of decision makers in order for them to understand the messages displayed. Once these knowledge requirements are identified, one must then assess the extent to which decision makers can be expected to have this knowledge. Any knowledge that is lacking can be designated as presenting a potential limit to understandability.

The author and his colleagues (Rouse, et al. 1984) have developed a method for performing this type of analysis. Using a taxonomy of knowledge requirements, each type of message is considered as it is manifested by the decision support system. Knowledge requirements in the categories of *display* (e.g., coding), *command* (e.g., dialog), and *system* (e.g., functions) are then identified. The extent to which decision makers have this knowledge is then determined on the basis of their overall training, likely experience, training specific to the decision support system, and access to sources of information other than those supplied by the decision support system. One particularly useful output of this process is identification of aspects of training for use of the system that should be augmented.

Analytical evaluation of compatibility is reasonably straightforward. A variety of checklists are available, some of which are fairly general while others are targeted at particular application domains. A variety of these checklists is reviewed by Frey and coworkers (Frey, et al. 1984). The design methodology proposed in their volume is such that compatibility is assured if the method is followed.

Empirical Evaluation

While analytical evaluation is necessarily top-down because it proceeds from design objectives to the resulting product, empirical evaluation must be bottom-up because it requires decision makers to interact with the product rather than the objectives. Therefore, compatibility must be considered first; otherwise understandability and effectiveness may be moot points. For example, it is unreasonable to attempt an assessment of the understandability of messages if the level of incompatibility is such that the messages are too small to read. Similarly understandability must be assessed prior to effectiveness because it is unreasonable to try to determine if a less than fully meaningful message is useful.

Empirical evaluations are also more efficient if compatibility is pursued first, followed by understandability, and finally effectiveness (Rouse 1984). This is due to the efficiency of the evaluation methods that are best employed for each of the three levels of evaluation. In general, the cost and sophistication of appropriate evaluation methods increase as one proceeds from compatibility to understandability, and so on. Therefore, one should try to address and resolve compatibility issues early with the faster, less expensive methods; one can then deal with the understandability and effectiveness issues, which require slower, more expensive methods, unhampered by compatibility problems.

The author has proposed a multimethod approach to dealing successively with the compatibility, understandability, and effectiveness (Rouse 1984). *Paper evaluations* (e.g., checklists) are recommended for compatibility. Both static and dynamic features of a decision support system can be evaluated in this manner. This type of evaluation is equivalent to the analytical assessment of compatibility noted earlier, with the one exception that it usually involves the actual system rather than design documentation for an eventual system.

Part-task simulator evaluations are suggested for assessing understandability. A part-task simulator is a device that roughly approximates the real system of interest in terms of appearance, static and dynamic characteristics, and range of decision-maker activities required. A wide range of part-task simulators is possible, delimited on the low end by static mockups and, on the high end, by full-scope simulators (see below).

The primary objectives of part-task simulator evaluation is to assess understandability by determining if decision makers can comprehend the messages transmitted to them by the decision support system and, if decision makers can communicate their desires and perhaps intentions to the system. This message orientation is based on the approach to design discussed earlier and, to an extent, the analytical approach outlined above for evaluating understandability; the key difference is that empirical evaluation involves assessing the meaningfullness of messages for particular decision makers during actual use of the part-task simulator. Hunt (1984) discusses two case studies where this approach was utilized.

Full-scope simulator and/or *real system evaluations* are recommended for effectiveness. A full-scope simulator is a high-fidelity replica of a real system that allows decision makers to experience virtually the full range of system behaviors, without waiting for all these behaviors to occur in the normal course of events or endangering anyone by initiating the situations of interest in the real system. In general, full-scope simulators are the preferred way to assess effectiveness whenever the potential cost or danger of using the real system for evaluation is unacceptable. (Interestingly, as more and more real systems become computer based, the difference between full-scope simulator and real system may simply be one of the positions of a mode switch.)

As noted earlier, effectiveness can be defined as the degree to which design objectives are achieved. This determination reqires that one define measures of effectiveness, as well as criteria whereby one can decide about the acceptability of any particular set of measurements. This is a complex issue that cannot be treated adequately in the space allowed here. The reader is referred to Rouse (1984) for a thorough discussion related to decision support systems, as well as Henneman and Rouse (1984) for measurement issues in the area of decision making and problem solving.

Summary

There are three primary evaluation concerns: *compatibility, understandability,* and *effectiveness*. These are two fairly different, yet complementary, ways of approaching these concerns. As shown in Figure 11.5, one way is *top-down analytical evaluation* which involves viewing a decision support system as if it were designed using the design process proposed earlier in this chap-

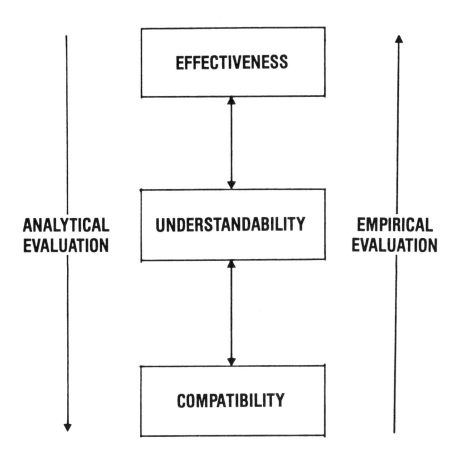

Figure 11.5   Approaches to Evaluation

ter; if the system actually was designed using this process, than analytical evaluation is quite straightforward. The second way is *bottom-up empirical evaluation* which involves first assuring compatibility (via paper evaluation) and then assessing understandability and effectiveness (via part-task and full-scope simulator evaluations, respectively). For more information and guidance on evaluation of decision support systems, see Rouse, et al. (1984) for analytical evaluation and Rouse (1984) for empirical evaluation.

CONCLUSIONS

This chapter has outlined an integrated methodology for design and evaluation of computer-based decision support systems. Most of the design-oriented aspects of the methodology were drawn from Rouse and Rouse (1983) and Rouse, et al. (1984); most of the evaluation-oriented aspects were drawn from Rouse (1984) and Rouse, et al. (1984). Obviously, a brief chapter can only provide, at best, an overview of three comprehensive reports totaling 350 pages. Thus, emphasis was placed on the overall structure of the methodology, as well as the key concepts that provide the basis of the approach.

Various aspects of the methodology have been applied, or are being applied, in several different domains. Design of decision support systems in the area of command and control systems, and in the area of process control (e.g., nuclear power plants) are two examples. Evaluations of several process control aids have also been pursued. An evaluation of a computer-based training system is a current application of the methodology.

All of these applications have led, or are leading, to new insights into how the design and evaluation methodology should be modified and extended. Thus, the presentation in this chapter is, in many ways, a status report on an evolving technology. Much research and experience is needed if the methodology is to mature and be widely used. Such efforts are absolutely necessary if the design of decision support systems is to move beyond the "gadgetry" phase that so often predominates in domains where rapidly evolving technologies are applicable.

ACKNOWLEDGEMENTS

The perspective espoused in this chapter emerged from the author's involvement with a variety of people and projects. Several of the author's colleagues at Search Technology Inc. contributed to these efforts, including R.M. Hunt, S.H. Rouse, P.R. Frey, and M.E. Maddox. J. Rasmussen of Riso National Laboratory in Denmark provided many keen insights. S. Ward of the Aerospace Medical Research Laboratory, J.F. O'Brien of the Electric Power Research Institute, and J. Jenkins of the Nuclear Regulatory Commission provided research support as well as valuable comments and suggestions. W.H. Sides, R.A. Kisner, and P. Haas of Oak Ridge National Laboratory and J.G. Wohl of ALPHATECH, Inc. also contributed timely and useful reviews of various aspects of this work.

REFERENCES

Frey, P.R., W.H. Sides, R.M. Hunt, and W.B. Rouse. 1984. *Computer-Generated Display System Guidelines*. Vol. 1, *Display Design*. Palo Alto, Calif.: Electric Power Research Institute.

Henneman, R.L., and W.B. Rouse. 1984. Measures of human problem-solving performance in fault diagnosis tasks. In *IEEE Trans. Systems, Man, and Cybernetics* SMC-14 (1), pp. 267–278.

Hunt, R.M. 1984. *Computer-Generated Display System Guidelines. Vol. 3, Applications of Volumes 1 and 2.* Palo Alto, Calif.: Electric Power Research Institute.

Morehead, D.R. 1984. The Value of Information in Simulated and Real Search Environments. Ph.D. diss., Georgia Institute of Technology, Atlanta.

Morehead, D.R. and W.B. Rouse, 1983. Human-computer interaction in information seeking tasks. *Infor. Proc. and Mgt.* 19(4): 243–53.

Rasmussen, J. 1976. Outline of a hybrid model of the process plant operator. In *Monitoring Behavior and Supervisory Control*, ed. T. Sheridan and G. Johnansen, 371–83. New York: Plenum Press.

——— 1983. Skills, rules, and knowledge; signals, signs, and symbols and other distinctions in human performance models. In *IEEE Trans. Systems, Man, and Cybernetics* SMC-13(3): 257–66.

Rouse, S.H., and W.B. Rouse. 1980. Computer-based manuals for procedural information. In *IEEE Trans. Systems, Man, and Cybernetics* SMC-10(8): 506–10.

Rouse, S.H., W.B. Rouse, and J.M. Hammer. 1982. Design and evaluation of an onboard computer-based information system for aircraft. In *IEEE Trans. Systems, Man, and Cybernetics* SMC-12(4): 451–63.

Rouse, W.B. 1983. Models of human problem solving: detection, diagnosis, and compensation for system failures. *Automatica* 19(6): 613–25.

——— 1984. *Computer-Generated Display System Guidelines.* Vol. 2, *Developing an Evaluation Plan.* Palo Alto, Calif.: Electric Power Research Institute.

Rouse, W.B., P.R. Frey, and S.H. Rouse, 1984. *Classification and Evaluation of Decision Aids for Nuclear Power Plant Operators.* Report No. 8303–1. Norcross, Ga.: Search Technology.

Rouse, W.B., and S.H. Rouse. 1983. *A Framework for Research on Adaptive Decision Aids.* Report No. AFAMRL-TR-83-082. Aerospace Medical Research Laboratory, Wright-Patterson Air Force Base, Ohio.

——— 1984. Human information seeking and design of information systems. *Info. Proc. and Mgt.* 20(1): 129–38.

Wohl, J.G. 1981. Force management decision requirements for Air Force tactical command and control. In. *IEEE Trans. Systems, Man, and Cybernetics* SMC-11(9): 618–39.

12

Evaluating Decision Support Systems: A General Framework and Case Study

Leonard Adelman and Michael L. Donnell

Microcomputer decision support systems (DSS) hold great promise for improving decision making because the decreasing cost of hardware and the increasing power of software are making it possible for decision makers to use microcomputer DSS to help them think about the many interrelated characteristics of the individual decisions facing them, and thus improve the performance of the cognitive aspects of the decision-making process. Indeed, this book contains a number of important examples of how microcomputer DSS can improve the decision making process; Adelman (in press) and Sprague & Carlson (1982) provide two of many other examples. Yet, caution is warranted regarding the overall value of DSS. DSS are not more a panacea for decision making than management information systems (MIS) are for information management. Just as scientists are studying the conditions that lead to the successful and unsuccessful application of MIS (e.g., see Adelman 1982; Ginzberg 1978; Shycon 1977), they must begin studying the conditions that lead to the successful and unsuccessful application of DSS. To do so requires a rigorous evaluation approach.

The purpose of this chapter is to present such a rigorous DSS evaluation approach and to show how it was applied in a single case study. The general framework presented herein addresses issues regarding (1) the interface between the DSS and its potential user(s), their organization, and the larger competitive environment in which they reside; (2) the various measures for assessing the DSS's effectiveness; and (3) the realism of the evaluation setting.

A three phase evaluation approach is proposed, composed of a *technical* evaluation phase for "looking inside the black box"; an *empirical* evaluation phase for rigorously assessing the DSS's impact on performance; and a *subjective* evaluation phase for obtaining users' opinions regarding the DSS's strengths and weaknesses. The case study presents the procedures for, and results of, implementing the general evaluation framework and three phase evaluation approach. Although the framework was developed primarily for use by DSS designers and evaluators, it should also help potential DSS users assess the extent to which different DSS meet their needs.

GENERAL FRAMEWORK
FOR DSS EVALUATION

Figure 12.1 is a pictorial framework for considering issues relevant to the design and evaluation of DSS. As noted by Adelman, et al. (1982), these issues arise at the three interfaces (sets of arrows) represented within Figure 12.1. The first interface is between the DSS and the user (DSS/U). Here the issue is the extent to which characteristics of the DSS facilitate or hinder its usability. The second interface is between the user (and DSS) and the larger decision-making organization (U/DMO) of which both are a part. Here the issue is to what extent the DSS facili-

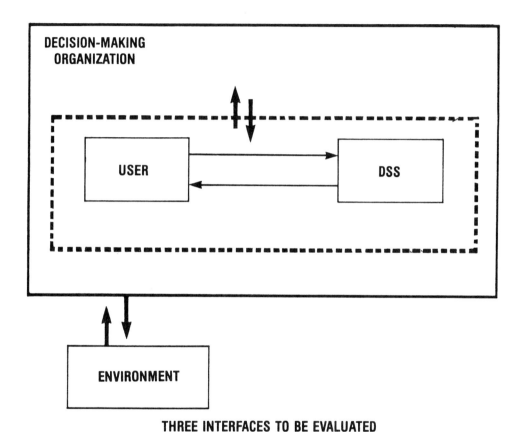

Figure 12.1 Pictorial framework for considering issues relevant to the design and evaluation of design support systems. Three interfaces are to be evaluated.

tates the decision-making process of the organization. The third interface is between the decision-making organization and the environment (DMO/ENV). Here the issue is whether or not the DSS improves the quality of the organization's decision making.

These three types of interfaces—DSS/U, U/DMO, and DMO/ ENV—are, of course, by no means independent. In fact, they are "nested": Interface 2 (U/DMO) effectiveness is necessarily influenced by Interface 1 (DSS/U) effectiveness, and Interface 3 (DMO/ ENV) effectiveness is necessarily influenced by the effectiveness of the other two interfaces. Nevertheless, the three types of interfaces do have different implications for evaluation, particularly in terms of measures of effectiveness, which justify their use as a general framework for discussing DSS evaluation.

Measures of Effectiveness (MOEs)

If an evaluation is to be effective, the evaluator must decide in advance what is to be examined. This is done by identifying one or many measures of effectiveness (MOEs) which are designed to answer the evaluator's questions. Ideally, these MOEs are objectively measurable and quantitative variables that will describe the effectiveness of the DSS. In the present case, however, the term MOE will also include subjectively measurable variables that result in a qualitative rather than quantitative description. The only restrictions are that each MOE must be measurable and that it should be expected to correlate (positively or negatively) with the overall effectiveness. (i.e., utility) of the DSS.

Table 12.1 presents the MOEs used in the application presented later in this chapter. This application was designed to evaluate five different DSS prototypes developed for U.S. Air Force tactical decision making. The MOE categories were designed to be as general as possible so that the same MOEs could be used to evaluate each prototype. To accomplish this, the authors refined and expanded the hierarchy of evaluation criteria developed by Sage and White (1980) and tried to use as many of the criteria as possible that were used earlier in the contract when deciding which DSS prototypes to develop in the first place. Other MOEs could, of course, be used in an evaluation depending

Table 12.1   Hierarchy of Measures of Effectiveness (MOEs) and Number of Questions Assessing Bottom-Level MOEs

0.0   Overall Utility (6)

1.0 DSS/User Interface	2.0 User-DSS/Organization	3.0 Organization/Environment
1.1 Match with Personnel	2.1 Efficiency factors	3.1 Decision Accuracy (8)
1.1.1 Training & technical background (3)	2.1.1 Time	3.2 Match between DSS's technical approach and problems's requirements (7)
1.1.2 Workstyle, workload and interest (4)	2.1.1.1 Task accomplishment (3)	3.3 Decision process quality (2)
1.1.3 Operational needs (5)	2.1.1.2 Data management (2)	3.3.1 Quality of framework for incorporating judgment (2)
1.2 DSS's characteristics	2.1.1.3 Set-up requirements (2)	3.3.2 Range of alternatives (2)
1.2.1 General	2.1.2 Perceived reliability under average battle conditions (2)	3.3.3 Range of objectives (2)
1.2.1.1 Ease of use (4)	2.1.2.1 Skill availability (3)	3.3.4 Weighing of consequences of alternatives (2)
1.2.1.2 Understanding (3)	2.1.2.2 Hardware availability	3.3.5 Assessment of consequences of alternatives (3)
1.2.1.3 Ease of training (2)	2.2 Match with Organizational factors	3.3.6 Reexamination of decision-making process (3)
1.2.1.4 Response time (2)	2.2.1 Effect on organizational procedures and structure (2)	3.3.7 Use of information (3)
1.2.2 Specific	2.2.2 Effect on other people's position in the organization	3.3.8 Consideration of implementation and contingency plans (2)
1.2.2.1 User interface (2)	2.2.2.1 Political acceptability (2)	3.3.9 Effect on group discussions (3)
1.2.2.2 Data files (3)	2.2.2.2 Other people's workload (2)	3.3.10 Effect on decision makers' confidence (2)
1.2.2.3 Expert judgments (2)	2.2.3 Effect on information flow (2)	
1.2.2.4 Ability to modify judgments (2)	2.2.4 Side effects	
1.2.2.5 Automatic calculations (2)	2.2.4.1 Value in performing other tasks (2)	
1.2.2.6 Graphs (2)	2.2.4.2 Value to SAC or other services (2)	
1.2.2.7 Printouts (2)	2.2.4.3 Training value (2)	
1.2.2.8 Text (2)		

Note: Numbers in parentheses are number of questions used for assessment of the DSS in a short-answer questionnaire.

on the characteristics of the DSS and the concerns of potential users.

As can be seen, the MOEs presented in Table 12.1 are organized into a hierarchy such that the three uppermost levels represent the three interfaces in Figure 12.1; the topmost level of the hierarchy represents the DSS's overall utility on value. Each of the three uppermost levels of MOE categories is subdivided further until it is easy to identify distinct measurable MOEs. By assuming that each terminal node in the hierarchy could be translated into an MOE, the task of evaluating a DSS is translated into one of assigning scores to the bottom-level nodes of the evaluation hierarchy. (The numbers following each node or criterion refer to the number of questions used for assessment of the DSS, discussed in the section on subjective evaluation later in the chapter.) By then weighing the relative importance of the MOEs and MOE categories moving up the hierarchy, one obtains an explicit, retraceable process for evaluating the overall value and relative strengths and weaknesses of the DSS.

MOEs assessing the quality of the *DSS/User Interface* are divided into two major groups of criteria: those that assess the match between the DSS and potential user's background, workstyle, and operational needs; and those that assess the adequacy of the DSS' characteristics. This latter group is composed of general DSS characteristics, such as its ease of use and response time, and specific characteristics, such as the adequacy of the DSS's data files, graphic displays, hard copy capabilities, and text.

MOE's assessing the quality of the *User-DSS/Decision-making Organization Interface* are divided into two major groups of criteria: those that assess the DSS's efficiency from an organizational perspective, and those that assess the DSS's fit into the organization. Organizational efficiency criteria include the amount of time it takes to use the DSS to accomplish the task it is supporting (this is distinctly different than its response time), data management and set-up time requirements, and, pertinent to the present application, the DSS's perceived reliability and supportability under battle conditions. Criteria explicitly focusing on the DSS's potential effect on organizational procedures, other people's work, the flow of information, and its value in performing other tasks were used to assess the DSS's fit into the organization for which it was developed.

MOEs assessing the quality of the *Decision-making Organization/Environment Interface* are grouped into three major criteria: the perceived quality of decisions obtained using the DSS; the extent to which the DSS's technical approach matches the technical requirements of the task; and the extent to which the DSS improves the quality of the decision-making process. This last group of criteria is quite broad, ranging from the extent to which the DSS helps the user survey a wide range of alternatives and objectives, to the degree to which the DSS increases or decreases the user's confidence in the decision.

DSS Evaluation Procedures and MOEs Collection

In general, the quality of the evaluation of a DSS (e.g., the reliability of the scores in the bottom level of the evaluation hierarchy) depends on two things: (1) the types of measures of effectiveness (MOEs) of the evaluation factors that are used; and (2) the "realism" of the experimental simulation of each interface. With regard to the MOEs, there are three types of collection procedures to consider: subjective judgment, expert observation, and objective measurement. *Subjective judgment* requires users to score their experiences, usually by answering a questionnaire following use of the DSS. *Expert observation* also involves subjective judgment, only this time on the part of nonparticipating observers of the DSS users and experts in the area the DSS was developed to support. *Objective measurement* is usually associated with empirical experimentation and comparison. Objective empirical measurement is usually considered the most valid and, therefore, preferred type of data to collect. Unfortunately, experimental comparison of objective measurements is often a very costly data collection process. As a result, expert observation and subjective judgment are frequently relied upon to examine most of the evaluative factors.

DSS Setting

Before the MOEs for a DSS can be collected and analyzed, it is necessary to construct a setting in which the DSS can be operated. The setting might simply be a laboratory experiment with a mock problem, or it might be a full-scale field trial. Such settings differ in terms of their "fidelity" or similarity to the expected operational setting, the amount of experimental control that they provide, and their costs. Thus, the choice of a setting can be a difficult one.

Figure 12.2, adapted from Adelman, et al. (1981), depicts the situation that prevails when one attempts to conduct an assessment of effectiveness. The first part of the figure, labeled *Target Setting*, represents the expected operational setting for the DSS. Of course this setting will not be available for evaluation purposes unless the DSS is actually placed in the organization. In lieu of the target setting, it is therefore necessary to construct a test setting within which the evaluation can proceed.

One of the most fundamental dimensions over which test settings can vary is their degree of fidelity to the target setting.

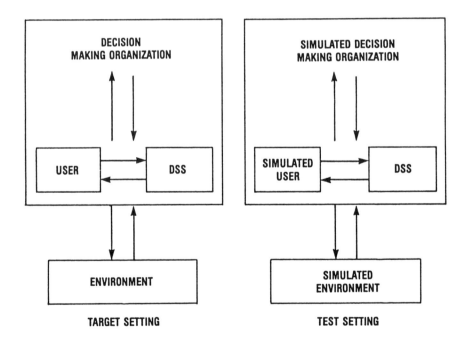

Figure 12.2   Notional Representation of the Setting for Aid Evaluation

The simulated environment, the simulated DMO, and even the simulated user can range between being only superficially accurate to being accurate in great detail. By itself, high fidelity is, of course, desirable in any evaluation setting, but it is expensive. Besides increased dollar costs and evaluation time, fidelity introduces an additional cost in terms of loss of experimenter control. This means that on the one hand it may be increasingly difficult to obtain the desired measures, and on the other hand these measures will be increasingly susceptible to influences that are extraneous to the evaluation context. Even if one is successful in eliminating extraneous influences from the evaluation, there will be increased difficulty in specifying and controlling causal relationships in a high-fidelity setting. Thus, a tradeoff is established between fidelity and costs such that, depending on the objective of the evaluation, it may be desirable to simulate parts of the target setting.

This concept of fidelity, and the tradeoffs it implies, can be further examined by considering four settings: the four combinations involving either high or low fidelity for the organization and environment, as shown in Figure 12.3. The additional settings provided by low fidelity for the user are not examined because a user who can operate the DSS is required for any evaluation.

SETTING FIDELITY	TYPE OF EVALUATION	INTERFACE EXAMINED	QUESTION EVALUATED	EXPERIMENTER COST	CONTROL
LOW ENVIRONMENT LOW DMO	LABORATORY	DSS/U	DA USER COMPATIBILITY	LOW	HIGH
HIGH ENVIRONMENT LOW DMO	LABORATORY	DSS/U	DA COHERENCE & COMPLETENESS	LOW	HIGH
LOW ENVIRONMENT HIGH DMO	GAMING SIMULATION	U/DMO	DA COMPATIBILITY WITH DMO	MODERATE	MODERATE
HIGH ENVIRONMENT HIGH DMO	FIELD TEST	DMO/ENV	DA EFFECT ON DMO PERFORMANCE	HIGH	LOW

Figure 12.3   Summary of Alternative Evaluation Settings

*DA - Decision Aid

Of the four settings, *the low-fidelity environment and low-fidelity organization* is the most austere. Such a setting is well suited to DSS design questions concerning its user compatibility. These questions are primarily concerned with the DSS-User interface and, therefore, need not concern themselves with characteristics of the decision-making organization, or even the true environment. Since so little simulation effort is required, this setting can be implemented in a carefully controlled laboratory experiment.

The *high-fidelity environment and low-fidelity organization setting* can also be conducted in a laboratory setting, but this setting serves a different purpose. In this setting, great attention is paid to providing the user with realistic data about the environment, realistic options, and realistic scenarios, but the decision-making organization through which the user would interact with this environment is only superficially implemented. Thus, it is possible to investigate the coherence, completeness, and accuracy of the information provided by using the DSS without going the additional step and ascertaining whether it will improve the organization's performance. It is important to note that a DSS can improve decision accuracy but, because of detrimental organization dynamics, not improve organizational performance.

The *low-fidelity environment and high-fidelity DMO setting* provides the means to answer questions about the interface between the user and the decision-making organization. In this setting, less concern is devoted to constructing realistic problems and more concern is devoted to simulating the lines of communication and authority within the DMO. Since a simulated DMO is outside the scope of most laboratories, this type of setting is better thought of as a gaming simulation. Although the departure from the laboratory is necessary to assess how the DSS will fit into the organization, or be tailored to fit better, it implies decreasing experimenter control and increasing costs.

Finally, *the high-fidelity environment and high-fidelity DMO setting* is the most accurate setting, virtually requiring a field test with a realistic and well-implemented problem scenario. This accuracy is obtained at a high cost, but is necessary to fully answer questions about DSS effects on organization performance. Since questions about the organization/environment interface are the ultimate questions concerning the DSS's effectiveness, field tests of this sort are a highly desirable precursor to the full-scale implementation of the DSS.

Three-phase Evaluation Approach

Clearly, the choice of an evaluation setting interacts with the type of question that one hopes to answer, and the resources available to perform the evaluation. Nevertheless, all evaluation settings are generally capable of supporting a rigorous evaluation approach comprised of technical, empirical, and subjective evaluation phases. The *technical* phase focuses on evaluating the DSS from both an algorithmic (internal) perspective and a systemic input/output (external) perspective. The goal of the technical evaluation is to identify system problems prior to and during the use of the DSS by representative users, and to suggest software modifications to correct these deficiencies. The *empirical* evaluation phase, in contrast, focuses on obtaining objective measures of the DSS's performance. The goal of the empirical phase is to assess, for example, whether persons make significantly better or faster decisions or use significantly more information working with rather than without the DSS. Finally, the *subjective* evaluation phase focuses on evaluating the DSS from the perspective of potential users. The goal of the subjective evaluation phase is to assess whether the users generally like the DSS; what they consider to be its relative strengths and weaknesses; and what changes they would suggest for improving it.

The next section describes a successful application of this three-phase evaluation approach. In many ways, this application represents an illustrative summary of the above framework. The focus was on developing a carefully controlled setting in which the DSS would be evaluated empirically through an experiment; consequently, we developed a laboratory setting with a high-fidelity environment and a low-fidelity decision-making organization so that we would have maximum experimenter control. Evaluation participants solved representative problems with and without the DSS; consequently we were able to obtain objective

MOEs for task performance and speed. And questionnaires were used to obtain subjective data for the MOEs presented in Table 12.1; consequently, we were able to address design and evaluation issues at each of the three interfaces in our general framework.

APPLICATION OF GENERAL EVALUATION FRAMEWORK AND THREE-PHASE APPROACH

Over the twenty-four-month period from September, 1981 to September, 1983, PAR Technology was the prime contractor to the Rome Air Development Center (RADC) on a contract designed to develop five DSS prototypes for Air Force decision making. Four tasks were performed on this project. Task I was a detailed study of the functions performed in the domain of interest. The study was performed with a view toward defining potential aiding situations in which the technologies of Artificial Intelligence, Decision Analysis, and Operations Research might be applied to aid decision making. In Task II, twenty-eight proposed DSS prototypes were subjected to a two-phase utility analysis and to a cost-benefit analysis in order to identify the five prototypes for development on the project. These five DSS prototypes were developed by the project contractors in Task III, and evaluated in Task IV. This chapter overviews the evaluation of a DSS prototype developed by PAR called DART, which is an expert system (see Figgins, et al. 1983), to assist in activity node identification.

The activity node identification process is extremely difficult to perform because of the varying nature of the nodes of interest and the tremendous volume of available relevant data. Because of limited time and potential information overload, experience has become an increasingly important factor in the activity node identification process. There are, however, few analysts with the necessary activity node identification experience. An expert system DSS prototype represented a means of capturing activity node identification expertise, and making it available to inexperienced analysts. The DART prototype was to contain enough expert knowledge to identify (with a degree of certainty) thirteen different types of activity nodes. More importantly, the DART prototype had to be capable of effectively communicating the rationale for the identification, for it was to support the analyst's decision-making process, not replace it. The results for each of the three evaluation phases are now considered, in turn.

Technical Evaluation

The technical evaluation of the DART DSS prototype took place at PAR's corporate headquarters in New Hartford, New York, in late January, 1983. The technical evaluation focused on the system characterisitcs of DART's many modules. These modules are represented in Figure 12.4 from a functional perspective. The most visible portion of the system is the Executive, which assists the user in managing the aid. The Executive consists of:

- The Inference Engine
- The Advice Interpreter
- The Model Manager
- The Display Manager

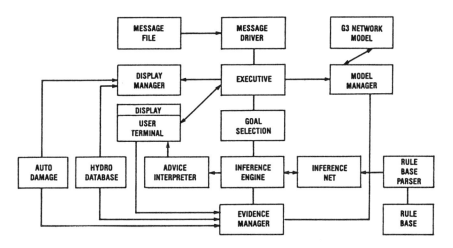

Figure 12.4   DART Functional View

Based upon a selected goal hypothesis (one of the thirteen identifiable activity nodes), the Inference Engine accesses that portion of the Inference Network that will analyze the pertinent, available information concerning the goal. The rules contained in this selected segment of the Inference Network use the data (or evidence) found in the message and associated degrees of belief from the Evidence Manager to identify the most likely activity node. The Advice Interpreter advises the user of the degree of belief for this identified activity node. Additionally, the user can consult the Advice Interpreter for the evidence used in reaching this decision. Once advised, the user can call the graphics display via the Display Manager or call the Model Manager to update the activity node identification model. The Display Manager provides the means to display terrain data; the Model Manager places identified activity nodes on this terrain. The Message File and Driver provide a time-sequenced list of reports that the analyst can use to correlate multiple reports of the same activity node, thereby increasing the confidence in the identified activity node.

In brief, the evaluation team concluded that, from a technical perspective, the DART prototype contained all of the modules necessary for a consultative expert system to support the activity node identification, decision-making process. The experts who participated in the empirical and subjective evaluations supported this position, for although they recommended many improvements, they neither recommended additional modules nor deletions of those already developed for the DART prototype.

Empirical Evaluation

The goal of the empirical evaluation phase was to objectively assess whether DART significantly improved the accuracy of analysts performing the target identification process. To accomplish this goal, an experiment was performed. The three independent variables were (1) whether the analyst was experienced or not in activity node identification, (2) whether the analyst performed the activity node identification task with or without DART, and (3) which of two different activity node identification problems the analyst performed. The dependent variable was the quality of the analyst's solution to the activity node identification problem.

The test setting for the empirical evaluation was created concurrently with the performance of the the technical evaluation. An isolated room fourteen by twelve feet was used for the unaided condition. A smaller room with a computer terminal and DeAnza display, both of which were linked to a VAX 11/780 system was used for the aided condition. (Note: Operational versions of DART and the other DSS prototypes are to be tailored for military microcomputers on subsequent procurements at the government's discretion.) Both test areas had 1:500,000 and 1:250,000 scale charts of the geographic area of interest used in the activity node identification problems.

The participant's task for each of the two problem scenarios was to identify ground components of opposing forces moving in a specified direction over the area of interst on the basis of message data. The problems differed in the number of each of thirteen possible activity node types and the available message data. In the first problem there were 100 messages; in the second problem there were 80 messages. Each participant had 1 1/2 hours to perform each problem regardless of whether he worked with or without DART. The activity nodes identified by each participant were placed on acetate and overlaid on the large wall map representing the geographic area for which the problem scenarios were created. Since a correct solution existed for each scenario, it was possible to determine the number, location, and type of correctly identified activity nodes. Using this information and looking at the acetate overlay map, the experts then rated the quality of each participant's solution for each scenario on a 0 to 10 scale, where higher scores meant a better solution. Qualitative ratings were required because all misclassifications were not equally detrimental; the solution's quality depended on an analyst's judgment as to the importance of the type and location of the misclassifications. Each participant's solution was coded by letter to minimize the expert's ability to identify its author.

The empirical and subjective evaluations were conducted at PAR's corporate headquarters in New Hartford, New York, over two four-day periods in February and March, 1983. The subjects for the first session were RADC personnel who had no activity node identification experience; these four participants are referred to as nonexperts. The subjects for the second session were U.S. Air Force analysts with considerable activity node identification experience; these three participants are referred to as experts. The subjects were provided through the cooperation and courtesy of different Air Force agencies. Although the sample size was small for an empirical evaluation, it was as large as possible given prior Air Force commitments. Larger sample sizes have been used by the authors in empirical evaluations of other DSS prototypes (e.g., see Adelman, et al. 1982).

Nonexperts' results. The primary value of the session with the nonexperts was identification of the following three necessary modifications to the test conditions and the DART user interface. First, the nonexperts did not have enough hands-on training in using DART; consequently, the experts' schedule was modified to provide more training. Second, DART was slow and cumbersome to use because it required the user to update the Model Manager and Display Manager after each message by sequentially accessing a number of menus; consequently, DART was modified to give the user the ability to automatically update the Model Manager and Display Manager after each message, thereby making DART much faster to use. And third, the message flow in the unaided participants' task was found to be unrepresentative of the analyst's actual environment; consequently, the message flow was modified for the session with the experts so that it better represented the analyst's actual environment. The results of the session with the nonexperts were, however, not included in the empirical and subjective evaluations of DART because so many changes were made to the test conditions and DART user interface between sessions that, prior to the session with the experts, the evaluation team concluded that it was inappropriate to combine the results of the two sessions.

Experts' session. The schedule for the DART evaluation session with the experts proceeded as described below over the four-day evaluation period. Monday morning was dedicated to providing a technical overview of DART so that the experts would understand how DART performed activity node identification. On Monday afternoon and most of Tuesday, the experts received hands-on training in using DART. This was accomplished by providing each expert with two 1 1/2-hour training sessions on DART. The DART test scenarios were completed by the experts on Tuesday and Wednesday. Two of the experts worked the first scenario in the unaided condition, and one used DART. In contrast, two experts worked the second using DART and one worked without it. This arrangement ensured that each expert had used DART to solve one scenario, and that there were three aided and three unaided solutions in total. On Thursday, the experts rated the quality of the three solutions generated by the experts for each scenario. The experts' ratings were based on the number, location, and type of both correctly and incorrectly identified activity nodes. The participants also completed the evaluation questionnaires and discussed their impressions of DART's strengths and weakness with members of PAR's evaluation team and RADC personnel monitoring the contract.

Experts' results. The experts quality ratings of the experts' solutions, and the conditions under which they were generated, are presented in Table 12.2. The higher the number, the better the quality rating. Pearson product-moment correlations (r) were calculated to determine the extent of agreement among the three experts' ratings. Pearson product-moment correlations can vary from $+1.0$ indicating perfect agreement to -1.0 indicating perfect disagreement; a value of zero indicates that there is no relationship between the ratings. The Pearson product-moment correlations were computed by combining the ratings for both scenarios thereby creating a sample size of six (instead of three) and, in turn, greater confidence in the results. The Pearson product-moment correlations between the quality ratings of experts E1 and E2, and E1 and E3, and E2 and E3, were .94, .93, and .97 respectively. All three correlations were statistically significant at the $p/.01$ level, thereby indicating that there was considerable agreement among the experts' quality ratings of the solutions.

Scenario #1					Scenario #2				
GOB	E1	E2	E3	Mean	GOB	E1	E2	E3	Mean
A (Unaided)	3	5	3	3.67	A (Aided)	6	8	7	7.0
B (Unaided)	8	8	8	8.0	B (Unaided)	9	9	9	9.0
C (Aided)	5	7	7	6.33	C (Aided)	7	8	8	7.67

Table 12.2   The Experts' Quality Ratings of the Experts' Solutions

The mean quality rating and the sample size for each of the four cells in the 2 (Aid) x 2 (Scenario) design for the experts' solutions are presented in table 12.3. As can be seen, there are only three observations each in the Aided-Scenario I and Unaided-Scenario II cells. This occurred because, since only three experts participated in the evaluation, two cells of the design could only have one participant if each expert was to (1) perform each scenario only once and (2) work both with and without the aid. The Aided-Scenario I and Unaided-Scenario II conditions, and the expert who worked them, were randomly selected by the evaluation team. Table 12.3 shows a sample size of three observations for these two cells because each of the three experts independently evaluated the one expert's solution. The Unaided-Scenario I and Aided-Scenario II cells have a sample size of six observations because each of the three experts independently evaluated the two experts' solutions for these two cells.

A repeated measures t-test, where the experts were the repeated measure, was used to statistically determine whether, on the average, (1) experts performed better aided than unaided and (2) if performance was significantly better for one scenario than the other. (Note: An Analysis of Variance was not used because, due to the small and unequal sample sizes for the cells, analysis of the Aid x Scenario interaction was not warranted.) There was no statistical difference in the mean scores for the aided and unaided conditions; experts performed equally well working with DART as without it. Mean performance was, however, significantly better for Scenario II than Scenario I (t =

	Scenario I	Scenario II	$\bar{x}$
Aided	N = 3 6.33	N = 6 7.33	N = 9 7.00
Unaided	N = 6 5.83	N = 3 9.00	N = 9 6.89
$\bar{x}$	N = 9 6.00	N = 9 7.89	N = 18 6.95

Table 12.3 Mean Quality Ratings and Sample Size for the Four Cells of the 2 (Aid) x 2 (Scenario) Design for the Experts' Ground Orders of Battle

2.34, $df = 4$, $p < .05$). This may have been due to practice effects because Scenario II was performed after Scenario I. This hypothesis is unlikely, however, because the experts indicated that both tasks were quite representative of their actual environment. A more likely explanation is that Scenario II was easier than Scenario I.

An additional analysis was performed in an effort to better understand why there was no difference in the performance of experts working with and without DART. In particular, the evaluation team counted the number of mistakes the experts made for the thirteen different activity nodes in the two scenarios, both with and without DART. Although no statistical tests were performed because of the small size for each target, examination of the mean scores suggests that aided experts were better than unaided experts in identifying certain activity nodes, and worse in identifying others. This suggests that (1) DART's rule-based, expert system for identifying certain activity nodes needs improvement, and (2) that such improvement would result in experts performing the test scenarios better with DART than without it.

Subjective Evaluation

The subjective evaluation of DART was comprised of the experts' answers to two questionnaires. The first questionnaire was of a short-answer format with the questions designed to assess qualitatively the MOEs presented in Table 12.1. The second questionnaire was of an open-ended format that gave the experts an opportunity to indicate, without any prompting from the evaulation team, what they perceived to be the strengths and weaknesses of the DART prototype and to recommend improvements to it. We will only present the results obtained from the first questionnaire in this chapter for two reasons. First, there was general agreement between the answers to the two questionnaires; consequently, it is unnecessary to present the results to both of them here. Second, the short-answer questionnaire had been standardized so that, except for substantive changes unique to DART, the same questionnaire could be used to assess participants' impressions of the strengths and weaknesses of each of the five prototypes developed on the contract; consequently, the short-answer questionnaire represents the first step in developing an empirically based measurement instrument that can be used by other people evaluating decision support systems.

The short-answer questionnaire had 121 questions. Most of the questions assessed the bottom-level MOEs in Table 12.1; however, six questions directly assessed overall utility (node 0.0 in Table 12.1), two questions directly assessed decision process quality (node 3.3 in Table 12.1), and three questions each assessed the quality of the training sessions and the test scenarios (neither of which are MOEs). All questions required the participant to respond on a ten-point scale from 0 (very strongly disagree) to 10 (very strongly agree), with 5 being "neither disagree nor agree." There were two or more questions for each MOE criterion in an effort to achieve greater confidence in the criterion scores.

The number in the parentheses to the right of each bottom-level MOE in Table 12.1 indicates the number of questions assessing that criterion. The actual number depended on the availability of previously written questions assessing the criterion (e.g., from Sage & White 1980), the ease in writing "different-sounding" questions for the criterion, and its depth in the hierarchy. Half the questions for each criterion were presented in each half of the questionnaire to eliminate sequence ordering effects. In most cases, a high score indicated good performance, but typically for one question measuring each criterion, a low score indicated good performance in an effort to ensure that the participants paid careful attention to the questions. A prototype's score on a bottom-level criterion was the mean score of the participants' responses to the questions assessing it. Values for criteria moving up the hierarchy were the mean score for the criteria below it.

It is important to make two technical notes at this point. First, by averaging lower level criterion scores to obtain upper level criterion scores, one is giving each MOE criterion equal weight in the hierarchy. Although it is quite possible that people may think certain criteria are more important than others, members of the evaluation team thought it inappropriate to give differential weights to the criteria at this time. Second, there is an alternative approach to obtaining the scores on the upper level criteria. Specifically, one could have taken the average of the scores to all the questions assessing each upper level criterion. For example, to obtain a score for criterion 1.2, one could have averaged the scores for all the questions assessing criteria 1.2.1 and 1.2.2 instead of just averaging the mean scores for criteria 1.2.1 and 1.2.2 as we did. The alternative approach would have given greater weight to criterion 1.2.2 because there were more questions for criterion 1.2.2 than for 1.2.1. Again, because we did not want to differentially weight the MOE criteria, we rejected this approach.

On the basis of the six questions directly asking about its utility, DART received a mean score of 8.22 on the ten-point scale. On the basis of the evaluation hierarchy, DART received a mean overall utility score (node 0.0) of 7.36. The DSS/User Interface received the highest mean score [$\bar{x}(1.0) = 7.81$] of the three interfaces. The User-DSS/Organization Interface [$\bar{x}(2.0) =$

7.17] and Organization/Environment Interface [$\bar{x}(3.0) = 7.09$] received comparable scores. The experts' subjective evaluation scores for all of the criteria in the MOE hierarchy are presented in Table 12.4.

SUMMARY/CONCLUSION

The purpose of this chapter was to present a general framework for evaluating decision support systems, and show how it was applied in a single case study. The framework addressed issues regarding (1) the interfaces between the DSS and its potential user(s), their organization, and the larger environment in which both reside; (2) the various measures for assessing DSS effectiveness; and (3) issues regarding the realism of the evaluation setting. This framework naturally led the authors to propose a three-phase evaluation approach composed of a technical evaluation phase for "looking inside the black box;" an empirical evaluation phase for rigorously assessing the DSS's impact on performance; and a subjective evaluation phase for obtaining users' opinion regarding the DSS's strengths and weaknesses. The case study presented the procedures for, and results of, implementing the general evaluation framework and three-phase approach for an Air Force DSS prototype to support opposing force utility node identification.

In concluding this paper, we would like to emphasize that the general evaluation framework and approach presented herein not only satisfy the short-term objective of rigorous DSS evaluation, they address the long-term objectives of (1) developing empirically based measurement instruments and (2) collecting empirical data on the factors affecting DSS success and failure. These long-term objectives are essential if we are to learn how better to design, develop, and implement decision support systems. For example, Adelman (1983) has outlined statistical analyses for using the short-answer questionnaire to address both long-term objectives. Regarding the former, effort is underway to measure the psychometric characteristics of the questionnaire. Reliability will be measured by both correlating the answers to a test-retest administration of the entire questionnaire

Table 12.4 Experts' Subjective Evaluation Scores on Criteria in the MOE Hierarchy

	0.0 Utility (i.e., potential for implementation)
— Based on 6 questions	8.22
— Based on the MAUA criteria hierarchy	7.36

1.0 DSS/User Interface — 7.81

Criterion	Score
1.1 Match between DSS and personnel	7.93
1.1.1 Match with training and technical background	8.44
1.1.2 Match with work style, workload, and interest	7.08
1.1.3 Match with operational needs	8.27
1.2 DSS's characteristics	7.68
1.2.1 General characteristics	8.46
1.2.1.1 Ease of use	8.56
1.2.1.2 Transparency (i.e., user understanding)	7.78
1.2.1.3 Ease of training	8.83
1.2.1.4 Response time	8.67
1.2.2 Specific characteristics	6.90
1.2.2.1 User interface	7.67
1.2.2.2 Types of data files	6.56
1.2.2.3 Expert judgment stored in DSS	6.84
1.2.2.4 Ability to modify judgments	6.88
1.2.2.5 DSS's automatic calculations	7.16
1.2.2.6 DSS's graphs	5.84
1.2.2.7 The need for hard copy	(9.33)
1.2.2.8 DSS's text	7.33

2.0 User-DSS/Organization Interface — 7.17

Criterion	Score
2.1 Efficiency Factors	6.65
2.1.1 Speed	6.55
2.1.1.1 Time required for task accomplishment	7.11
2.1.1.2 Time required for data management	6.20
2.1.1.3 Set-up time requirements	6.33
2.1.2 Perceived reliability under battle conditions	6.50
2.1.3 Perceived supportability under battle conditions	6.91
2.1.3.1 Skill availability	7.56
2.1.3.2 Hardware availability	6.25
2.2 Match between DSS and organization	7.69
2.2.1 Effect on organization procedures	7.0
2.2.2 Effect on other people's position	7.42
2.2.2.1 Political acceptability	7.67
2.2.2.2 Other people's workload	7.17
2.2.3 Effect on information flow	8.17
2.2.4 Side effects	8.17
2.2.4.1 Value in performing other tasks	7.50
2.2.4.2 Value to SAC or other services	8.33
2.2.4.3 Training Value	8.67

3.0 Organization/Environment Interface — 7.09

Criterion	Score
3.1 Decision Quality	7.58
3.2 Technical Soundness (Match between DSS's tech. approach & analysts' tech. requirements	6.52
3.3 Decision Process Quality (based on 10 attributes)	7.18
— Based on 2 questions	(7.83)
3.3.1 Framework incorporating judgment	6.83
3.3.2 Survey range of alternatives	7.33
3.3.3 Surveu range of objectives	6.83
3.3.4 Weighing consequences	7.33
3.3.5 Assessment of consequences	6.67
3.3.6 Reexamination of decision-making process	7.11
3.3.7 Use of information	7.78
3.3.8 Implementation	7.50
3.3.9 Effect on group discussion	7.11
3.3.10 Confidence	7.33

to some of the nonexperts, and by calculating a split-half reliability score correlating questions measuring the same criterion with each other, over all participants. The construct validity of the questionnaire will be measured by relating, probably qualitatively, the criterion scores generated by the questionnaire with the strengths and weaknesses listed by the participants in the open-ended questionnaire. The internal consistency of the questions measuring each criterion will be represented by the mean interitem correlation. And a hierarchical cluster analysis is proposed for determining (1) which questions correlate most highly with each other; (2) whether highly correlated questions are measuring the criterion they were supposed to measure; and (3) whether the criteria are grouping together hierarchically in the same manner as in the originally developed hierarchy (Table 12.1). The results of such psychometric analyses are required in order to develop an empirically based general questionnaire for evaluating DSS performance characterisitics.

Regarding the second long-term objective, the short-answer questionnaire permits the use of a multiple regression analysis to estimate statistically the relative importance the experts placed on the different MOE criteria when evaluating the five Air Force prototypes. The experts' mean scores for the individual criterial represent values on independent variables. (The total sample size of experts and the results of the proposed cluster analysis will affect the selection of these independent variables.) The experts' mean scores for the six questions assessing overall utility (node 0.0 in the hierarchy) represent values on the dependent variable. A multiple regression analysis can be used to estimate the predicatability of the experts' utility judgments and identify those criteria that had the greatest effect on it. Such empirically derived results should not only assist in refining the five prototypes, but help guide future DSS design and development, the ultimate goal for developing a rigorous approach for DSS evaluation.

ACKNOWLEDGMENTS

The authors would like to thank all government and contractor personnel who made the evaluation of DART possible. The evaluation effort was supported by RADC Contract #F30602-81-C-0263. The writing of the paper was supported in part by RADC Contract #F30602-83-C-0154. The authors would like to thank Second Lieutenant Delores Clark, Mr. Frank Sliwa, and Mr. Yale Smith of RADC, and Mr. Kerry Gates of PAR for their helpful comments on earlier versions of this manuscript. The views and conclusions expressed in this paper, are, however, those of the authors and should not be construed in any way to represent an official position of PAR, RADC, or any military agency.

REFERENCES

Adelman, L. 1982. Involving users in the development of decision-analytic aids: The principal factor in successful implementation. *Journal of the Operational Research Society* 33: 333–42.

——— 1983. A psychological approach to evaluating decision support systems. *Human Factor Society Proceedings* 1: 492–95.

——— 1984. Real-time computer support for decision analysis in a group setting: Another class of decision support systems. *Interfaces* Vol. 16 no. 3, pp. 17–26.

Adelman, L., M.L. Donnell, J.F. Patterson, and J.J. Weiss. 1981. *Issues in the Design and Evaluation of Decision-Analytic Aids*. Technical Report TR 81-1-304. McLean, Va.: Decisions and Designs.

Adelman, L., M.L. Donnell, R.H. Phelps, and J. F. Patterson. 1982. An iterative Bayesian decision aid: Toward improving the user-aid and user-organization interfaces. In *IEEE Transactions on Systems, Man, and Cybernetics* SMC-12: 733–42.

Figgins, T., S. Barth, and K. Gates. 1983. *DART Functional Description*. Contract #F30602-81-C-0263. Rome Air Development Center, Griffiss Air Force Base, New York.

Ginzberg, M.J. 1978. Steps toward more effective implementation of MS and MIS. *Interfaces* 8: 57–63.

Sage, A.P., and C.C. White, III. 1980. *Evaluation of two DDI decision aids developed for DCA:C140*. Document No. 33737-W114-RU-00. Falls Church, Va.: TRW Defense and Space Systems Group, January.

Shycon, N.H. 1977. All around the model — perspectives on MS applications. *Interfaces* 7: 40–43.

Sprague, R.H., Jr., and E.D. Carlson. 1982. *Building Effective Decision Support Systems*. Englewood Cliffs, N.J.: Prentice-Hall.

13

Psychological Issues in the Design and Development of Decision Support Systems

Gerald W. Hopple

The naked decision maker no longer exists. Extrasomatic decision-aiding, -supporting, and -facilitating mechanisms have proliferated, leading to the popularization of a family of acronyms like MIS (management information systems) and DSS (decision support systems). Of the various CBIS (computer-based information systems) competing for attention, DSS are the newest and the most challenging. They build on but go well beyond the classical MIS in scope and function. However, the challenge also poses a danger to the DSS professional—the potential hubris of assuming that a DSS will be a *decision-making* rather than a *decision-supporting* machine. This chapter is concerned with a more mundane but nevertheless vital theme of DSS design and development: the adaptation of psychological findings to the process of building such extrasomatic systems. The failure to fit the machine-based system to the human who uses it—and the need to exploit the very different strengths of electronic computers (and systems residing in such machines) and biocomputers or people—would doom a DSS from the outset. Clearly, however, as this suggests, there are things that machines do better than people, and psychology provides evidence about what falls into this category. The psychology of DSS design and development therefore highlights the human-machine fit and the division of labor issues.

OVERVIEW

Decision supporting is a fuzzy concept. Some vendors have oversold DSS, and others have latched onto the label as a buzzword to describe computer-based systems that are not DSS. Watson and Hill's (1983, 82) definition effectively specifies the essential nature of a DSS: "an interactive system that provides the user with easy access to decision models and data in order to support semistructured and unstructured decision-making tasks." MIS, in contrast, deal with structured tasks and put greater relative emphasis on data than models. On the CBIS continuum, there is clearly a gray area at the boundary between MIS and DSS, but there is a discernible difference. The DSS emphasis on decision models, the critical criterion for "knowing one when you see one," makes the psychology of DSS design and development both different from and more challenging than the parallel MIS process.

Blanning (1983) is quite correct, however, in pointing out that behavioral or psychological research on DSS is an outgrowth of the earlier work on the design of MIS. Both emphasize the impact of personal, environmental, and MIS or DSS characteristics on decision making. How to design a DSS is very much a function of these three clusters of variables.

The centrality of psychology to the design and development of any CBIS is hardly controversial. Terms like "human factors" and "ergonomics" attest to this. However, the typical decision aid or MIS attempts to compensate for the well-known shortcomings of the intuitive scientist by building in automatic error-checking procedures and otherwise gently prodding or forcefully pushing the user into the correct pathway. The problem is not so straightforward with DSS. Whereas a decision aid may be designed to help a user structure a problem and derive a probabilistic assessment, a DSS is ultimately concerned with supporting decisions about planning, resource allocation, or some other functional area. Typically, the decision context is poorly structured or unstructured. There is no right answer that can be reached via the application of an embedded algorithm—particularly when the task is unstructured. A DSS can and should incorporate constraints derived from formal logic and work on judgement and inference (e.g., inferences 1 and 2 are incompatible, this compound probability is impossible, etc.), but the DSS is much more than a tutor and an information system (although it incorporates tutorial and data base functions). A DSS is comprised of one or more decision models that emanate ultimately from the user; if the model is imposed on the user, he or she will not use the system. A corporate planning model, a typical DSS, is in this sense very unlike a financial planning model, a typical MIS.

THE BUILDING BLOCKS OF THE PSYCHOLOGICAL DESIGN AND DEVELOPMENT PROCESS

How the typical DSS differs from its less autonomous (and complex) CBIS cousins will be spelled out in the next section. At this point, it is important to flesh out the three components of the DSS design framework: the user; the environment in which the system is used; and the DSS itself.

The DSS User

Personal characteristics refer to the distinctive traits of the individual user. *System targeting* is the first phase in any interactive computer-based problem-solving system design and development process, and *user profiling* is a key aspect of the system targeting task (Andriole 1983). An obvious and commonly used dimension is user experience (whether the user is naive, experienced, or scientific-technical, for example).

But users can also be profiled in more psychologically meaningful ways. People differ, for example, in how they collect and process information. Cognitive and social psychologists have identified a number of such dimensions for classifying users.

Cognitive style is a particularly common dimension. In a useful literature review of the area, Ragan, et al. (1979) identified ten cognitive variables that exemplify elements of cognitive style:

- *Field Dependence-Field Independence*: an analytic as opposed to global manner of perceiving.
- *Impulsivity-Reflectivity:* Reflective subjects consider hypotheses longer and are usually correct upon choosing a response; impulsive individuals tend to select the first response that occurs to them and are usually incorrect.
- *Visual-Haptic*: The visual perceptual type is said to use his or her eyes as the primary sensory intermediaries, while the haptic is said to use his or her eyes ony when necessary and relies mainly upon kinesthetic and body orientation.
- *Leveling-Sharpening*: Levelers tend to incorporate new ideas with old memories, and blur the original image; sharpeners can add new ideas as well as holding on to the old image.
- *Constricted-Flexible Control*: individual differences in reference to susceptibility to distraction.
- *Breadth of Categorization*: an individual's preference for broad versus narrow categorization.
- *Scanning*: an individual difference reflected in extensiveness and intensity of attention deployment.
- *Tolerance for Unrealistic Experiences*: individual differences in willingness to accept perceptions that are at variance with normal experiences.
- *Cognitive Complexity-Simplicity*: differences in an individual's tendency to construe the world in a multidimensional and discriminating manner.

- *Conceptualizing Styles*: individual differences in categorization of stimuli with perceived similarities or differences; utilization of consistent conceptualization approaches in concept formation.

These variables suggest ways to present computer-generated information and enhance human-computer interaction. For example, users high on the visual dimension would benefit from the use of graphical output and query systems, just as "scanners" would feel comfortable with abbreviated display formats.

A specific component of cognitive style, *integrative complexity*, has been studied in a number of real-world and laboratory experiments (Schroeder, et al. 1967; Streufert and Streufert 1978; Tetlock 1984). The integrative complexity coding system, originally developed for scoring open-ended responses to a semiprojective test designed to measure individual differences in integrative complexity, has proven to be a flexible, easily operationalized, reliable, and valid methodological tool.

Operationally, *differentiation* refers to the number of characteristics or dimensions of a problem that are taken into account analytically. A highly differentiated approach, for example, would recognize that different corporate policies can have multiple—and sometimes contradictory—effects that cannot be readily classified on a single evaluative dimension of judgment. In contrast, a decision maker at the simple pole of the differentiation continuum might analyze policy issues in an undifferentiated way by placing options into "good" and "bad" policy categories.

Integration concerns the development of complex connections among differentiated characteristics. Differentiation is therefore a precondition for integration. The complexity of integration depends on whether the user perceives the differentiated characteristics as operating in isolation (low integration), in first-order or simple interations (the effects of A on B depend on levels of C, moderate integration), or in mulitple, contingent patterns (high integration).

On the 7-point integrative complexity scale, scores of 1 reflect low differentiation and low integration. Scores of 3 reflect moderate or high differentiation and low integration. Scores of 5 reflect moderate or high differentiation combined with moderate integration. Scores of 7 show both high differentiation and integration. Scores of 2, 4, and 6 represent transition points between adjacent levels.

Several points should be stressed from the perspective of relating this kind of research to typologies of DSS users. First, there have been many empirical studies of people making judgments and decisions in the real world, particularly with respect to foreign policy makers. All of the research supports the inference that there is considerable variation across the cells of the integrative complexity typology.

Second, it should be emphasized that the complexity coding system highlights the cognitive structure, not the content, of expressed beliefs. For example, Tetlock (1984), in his study of the relationship between cognitive complexity and political ideology in the British House of Commons, found that members could be simple or complex in advocating any kind of political position. The fact that the cognitive complexity construct is not biased for or against any particular view of the world is important to underline because of the need to avoid assigning value judgments to the content of positions taken in the light of the individual's level of cognitive complexity.

A third point that should be stressed is that it is unwarranted to assume that integratively complex analysis is "good" and "simple" analysis is "bad." This is hardly the case invariably. Complex analysis may end up being too subtle and tentative to be of value for decision making. Simple analysis—if it is grounded in a careful and rigorous problem-solving process—may be able to cut through the dense underbrush and illuminate the critical facets of an issue area or problem. Where a user falls on the contiuum says little about the quality of his or her analytical processes.

Fourth, integrative complexity can be viewed as both a personality or cognitive trait (an enduring, stable individual characteristic) and a situationally based response. For example, extensive research (Raphael 1982, among others) has demonstrated that complexity of policy-maker articulations is, to a great extent, a function of the situational context,, such as crisis versus noncrisis. In relation to the design of DSS, it is conceivable that alternative analytical contexts—particularly the polar opposities of very low stress versus high stress environments—may shift the integrative complexity scores of users. The complexity dimension therefore can be applied to both the analyst typology and the environmental characteristics cluster of the model. Both *main effects* (the role of the dimension within each model area) and *interaction effects* (the impact of integrative complexity as a function of the interaction between the two clusters) should be taken into consideration.

The DSS Environment

The environment for a DSS is the second component of the framework. The environment in which the user operates has a profound effect on the DSS design and development process. The environment includes features of the analytical situation (particularly the distinction between low stress and crisis decision contexts and the previously noted structured-unstructured problem continuum) as well as the organizational milieu, especially the organizational climate and prevailing norms and the centralization or distribution of decision-making processes. Bonczek, et al. (1983) discuss DSS in the light of organizational decision making.

The Decision Support System

DSS characteristics also vary. Any computer-based problem-solving or decision support system involves a number of design and development choices. The variations range from hardware and software issues to questions of how to target, model, and even package the system. Six sequential design and development phases can be identified (Andriole 1983):

- System targeting
    User profiling
    Task profiling
- System modeling
    Functional model of the overall system
    Mode of processing
    Embedded type of logic system

- Software design
  - Input routine(s)
  - Display routine(s)
  - Software language
- Hardware configuration
  - CPU
  - Memory/storage configuration
  - Input device(s)
  - Display device(s)
  - Hard copy device(s)
- System packaging
  - Documentation
  - Support
- System transfer

Insights and findings from psychology are pervasive in both the generic computer-based system and DSS design and development literatures. There is a great deal of human factors research available on the subject of *software design*; many studies have appeared, for example, on when and how to use color (and when not to use color). The various forms of interactive dialog, the alternative types of input and display routines, the different ways to manage and minimize information load, and the available techniques for dealing with response time and error-handling procedures are all relevant to software planning.

The second phase, *system modeling*, yields a functional representation of how the system will operate when developed and deployed. This basic conceptual blueprint is of particular importance from the DSS design perspective. The blueprint should be based on the model in the user's head, not on the system designer's preferred model.

One core dimension of system modeling refers to the *mode of processing*: how will the system be set up to operate? A basic distinction must be made between free-flowing "what if" games versus a reliance on precise estimates and confidence intervals. Users can and do think very differently when it comes to this basic processing mode preference. Some relate very well to "what if" games (mental scenario exploration and "simulation," creatively identifying hypotheses, "playing" with ideas) and react negatively to formal methods. Others are ill at ease with these kinds of approaches, and clearly prefer formal techniques like Bayesian probabilities and correlation analysis. This antinomy is reflected in such dichotomies as games versus models and "fuzzy sets" versus constrained systems.

Along with the mode of processing, DSS designers should consider different types of underlying *logic systems*. Decision makers seem to structure problems in very different ways on the basis of how they prefer to set up and organize the problem-solving process. For example, some automatically tend to think in terms of complex causal models consisting of arrays of variables, arrows, and feeback relationships. Compare this logic system with an approach oriented around time-dependent flows of concrete events. Illustrative examples of alternative logic systems include:

- System dynamics models
- Linear programming
- Lines and boxes in chart form
- Descriptive statistical trends and patterns
- Event networks
- Causal models
- Interaction arrays and diagrams

In a DSS, system modeling refers on the conceptual level, to the user's operating epistemology. Formal epistemology focuses on "how we know." Analogously, *operating epistemology* concerns "how the user knows." How does he or she view the world? What is the dominant mode of information acquisition? How does he or she generally process information? What are the constructs that make up the user's embedded model for making judgments and decisions? How is this model structured?

Central to the entire DSS design and development process is this operating epistemology concept. Cognitive style and related variables refer to the process features of an individual's operating epistemology; the system modeling task should ideally develop a blueprint around the contents of the operating epistemology. This is where a DSS becomes fundamentally different from an MIS; strategic planning and other DSS-oriented decision tasks are compatible with an array of different operating epistemologies (within the same organization and possibly even within the same user). The uncertainty and fluid nature of much corporate decision making underline the fact that a DSS does not simply manage information. It constructs a decision model and interfaces the model with data—in support of the user. This is aided rather than unaided decision making, but it is clearly not computer-based decision making.

Environmental-situational variables also impact on the user's operating epistemology. Organization routines and procedures are independent variables in their own right. Figure 13.1 brings this all together. The user's preferred operating epistemology and task characteristics and other environmental-situational variables both shape the operating epistemology. The decision support system is the dependent variable in the model. Note that a DSS that is designed by management scientists without user involvement from the beginning of the process implicitly reverses the arrow from the DSS to the operating epistemology; the user is expected to conform to the dictates flowing from the assumptions, logic, and blueprint of an alien system. Users have been turned off in the past by MIS or CBIS designed by management and computer scientists who have failed to secure user inputs and involvement, and such a strategy would be even less sensible with respect to decision support systems.

SOME PSYCHOLOGICAL PRINCIPLES OF DSS DESIGN AND DEVELOPMENT

In making decisions, a corporate executive—or a decision maker at any level of the hierarchy—must acquire and process information and make judgments and choices. A large body of basic and applied literature has accrued in psychology on the subject of how people make inferences, arrive at probabilities, and otherwise go about the process of deciding what to do. Hogarth and Makridakis (1981) present surveys of the basic research literature and the empirical studies of corporate forecasting and planning, organizing the many analyses under the

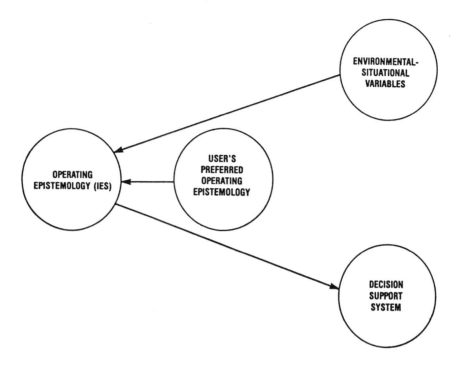

Figure 13.1   Building Blocks for the Design and Development
of Decision Support Systems

rubrics of (a) acquisition of information, (b) processing information, (c) output (the choice or decision), and (d) feedback to the
decision maker. The research generally supports the finding that
the human decision maker is an intuitive scientist who is susceptible to many biases and fallacies and has limited ability to
process information.

A lot of this kind of research has tested college students in
the social psychological laboratory. Also, many of the experimental contexts have been somewhat artificial and have not always
effectively simulated the nuances and pressures of real world
analysis and decision making. For example, in research on causal
judgments, the experiments have neglected the very important
natural causal task of encoding unstructured empirical information (transforming raw into processed data) by giving the subjects
prestructured stimulus material (Fiedler 1982)—although, it

should be noted, this can only inflate estimates of people's natural abilities by providing them with preprocessed material. In addition, the research is constantly evolving, with earlier interpretations subject to revision and refinement.

None of this, however, invalidates one of the basic findings: *that people are susceptible to a number of biases and errors in describing and otherwise dealing with empirical reality.* Human deficiencies range from the failure to understand and apply fairly complex statistical principles to concrete inference tasks to a host of more commonplace shortcomings. The inability to comprehend regression tendencies in statistical prediction is not surprising.[1] Nor is the intuitive failure to detect covariation accurately in statistical correlation problems at all shocking (or particularly troublesome, since computers can do the job effortlessly, efficiently, and instantly).

But many of the flaws are much less subtle and consideraby more disturbing. *People often insist on the superiority of a vivid, concrete case as evidence over abstract, statistical information*; what this means in the extreme instance is that a mass of statistical data can be "refuted" by one case that contradicts it. The intuitive scientist frequently remembers what is readily available in his or her memory in situations where availability (or the ease of remembering or imagining something) is unrelated to true frequency or probability; for example, more people die from drowning than fires, but the latter are usually believed to be a more frequent cause of death than the former. People cling to their initial beliefs more than is justified, and weak data can lead to unshakable beliefs. To cite just one of many illustrative examples, Anderson (1983) reports that subjects told about a relationship between fire fighter trainees' level of preference for high risk and their later success as firefighters continued to believe in the relationship even after they were informed about the fictitious nature of the original data. The belief persisted more for those given concrete data (two case histories) than for subjects presented with abstract data (a statistical summary).

As an additional general characterization of the research, it should be pointed out that not all of the experiments have been artificial. Some have involved complex and realistic tasks; others have concerned real decision situations. There have, for example, been many analyses of experts making judgments and forecasts in their areas of expertise; the expert is prone to many of the shortcomings of the layperson (Hopple 1984).

The Corporate Decision Maker

Every day, corporate decision makers have to confront multifaceted judgment and decision questions, including characterizing the environment and aspects of it (*description*), discerning relationships between inputs and outputs or other sets of variables (*covariation assessment*), inferring the causes of an event, situation, or process (*causal analysis or explanation*), or projecting the future (*prediction*). All of this is heavily dependent on theory—on the ideas, images, and models of reality that the decision maker carries around in his or her head.

What follows is a very small and not necessarily representative sample of the what-why-when and theory questions that corporate managers face. Is John Smith a good employee? What caused the plant in Akron to go out of business? Which strategic plan should be implemented? What are the goals of the organization—and why have they evolved the way they have? What will be the sales of product X in year Y? What causes productivity? What, by the way, is productivity and how do you measure it? Will a proposed organizational restructuring work? What produced the conflict situation in department X? What motivates employees? What is job satisfaction and what are its correlates? What will the external environment look like in twenty years? Why did Mary Jones quit? What theory of motivation, or the control process, or organizational creativity, or group decision making, or performance, or span of control, or delegation, or decentralization, or productivity, or . . . is valid? Where will company X or department Y be in five years? Where will I be?

The personal interview. Several examples of the corporate decision maker as an intuitive scientist will illustrate the workings of the psychology of judgment in the office. Traditionally, personnel recruitment includes the personal interview as a key facet of the hiring decision. In one's private life, we constantly "code" people. Is Bill aloof—or is he shy? Is Mary stupid—or is she only inarticulate? Is John a creative genius—or a consummate shooter of the bull? This basic descriptive task, which we employ continuously to select friends, spouses, and lovers, is at the core of interviewing job applicants (also known as position candidates).

The only problem with all of this is that interviews are invalid—and are certainly less valid than, for example,, recommendations from past employers and associates (especially if the prospective employer intentionally goes beyond the list of references provided by the applicant). Some candidates come across well in a formal interview and turn out to be terrible employees. Others give every indication of being lackluster and withdrawn, but if hired turn out to be highly motivated, dynamic employees. There is little relationship between formal interview performance and on-the-job performance.[2]

Why is this so? We judge people on the basis of samples of their behavior. A public opinion sample must be representative of the general public to be useful; if we do not draw samples in such a way that each person has an equal probability of being included, the sample will depart from a "pure random" piece of the whole population and, to the extent that it does, will not be a true mirror of the whole. Similarly, a sample of a person's behavior must be genuinely reflective of his or her real nature to be valid.

Sampling poses two kinds of issues. First, small samples are unreliable, a generalization that explains why whirlwind courtships do not predict very long marriages. By its very nature, a formal interview yields a very small sample of the candidates's "total universe" of behaviors. Secondly, a sample must be unbiased. Even an extremely large sample is worthless if it is biased (that is, if it is not an accurate reflection of the real person). Interviews often produce a dramatically biased sample of behavior because of faking, defensiveness, nervousness, and so forth.

Why do we nevertheless cling to personal interviews? Because they are (falsely) reassuring, because they are SOP (standard operating procedure), and, most importantly, because the vivid "data" generated by the process seem to be so valid and reliable. Stalin captured a very fundamental truth when he noted that "the death of a single Russian soldier is a tragedy. A million deaths is a statistic." Analogously, a personal interview is concrete compared to the abstract, pallid data on a resume, in letters of recommendation, and so forth.

Description. Description involves presenting and summarizing information. The typical briefing with reams of statistical tables and charts and dense masses of information may, according to psychology, be less effective or even totally neutral (or counterproductive?) if certain precautions are not followed. Vivid case information drives out boring statistical summaries. Sometimes this is bad if, for example, you ignore EPA mileage data and listen only to your brother-in-law's one experience with a Varoomovette 103. On other occasions, it may be good. Doctors have had a lower rate of cigarette smoking since the publication of the Surgeon General's report about smoking and cancer; interestingly, there is a clear relationship between area of specialization and smoking behavior, with lung cancer specialists (who see very vivid evidence of the effects of smoking) showing the lowest rates of cigarette consumption of all physicians.[3] The relationship is monotonic, with doctors who have specializations distant from the lungs showing increasingly higher rates of nicotine ingestion.

Nisbett, et al. (1982, 115–116) cite several examples of concrete information exerting a strange (albeit sometimes beneficial) impact. The reporters who followed McGovern in 1972 knew that he trailed Nixon in every poll—by a wide margin. Yet, they minimized his margin of losing because they had *personally* seen large, enthusiastic crowds cheer for him. The inference is clear: if you want your statistical information to have an impact, do not present it only as a dry, statistical summary. Concretize it and make it vivid in reports and briefings. This also has clear implications for the display of such information in DSS.

Probability errors. Another example concerns strategic and other forms of planning (Tversky and Kahneman 1982). People are prone to all kinds of mistakes with probabilities. One of the most difficult to resist is in the evaluation of conjunctive and disjunctive events. People tend to overestimate the probability of conjunctive events (such as, drawing a red marble from a bag seven times in a row) and to underestimate the probability of disjunctive events (such as, drawing a red marble at least once in seven tries). Successfully completing a new undertaking, such as developing and marketing a new product, is usually conjunctive in nature. For it to succeed, each event in a series must occur. Even when all are likely, the overall probability of success can be very low if the number of required events is large, leading to excessive optimism about probability of success.

All of this suggests that system designers should be aware of these findings and explicitly take them into account in the DSS design and development process. However, a DSS is more than a computer-based system for acquiring, managing, and supporting the processing of information. By definition, a DSS is also a decision-making aid, an extrasomatic mechanism for facilitating the making of choices. In order to choose or decide, the decision maker filters information through a schema or decision model, an elaborate mental construct which is already in the decision maker's head. This shifts the focus of DSS design and development to the realm of causal analysis.

CAUSAL MODELS

How does the layperson perceive causes or explain phenomena? First, we know that people have no qualms about immediately (and, in fact, apparently spontaneously) attributing an effect to one or more causes. Secondly, this is not always done in an unbiased fashion. In explaining human behavior, there is a strong tendency to favor internal or dispositional (enduring personal) over environmental-situational determinants.[4] Therefore, people expect consistency in an individual's behavior across many disparate situations, an expectation that is realized a lot less frequently empirically than it is theoretically.

Most research on causation has given subjects preestablished causal situations and categories to analyze. Only recently has there been interest in having people identify the dimensions they actually use in assessing causation (see, for example, Russell 1982; Wimer and Kelley 1982).

How good are people at causal analysis? This is a difficult question because there are rarely indisputable answers to questions about what caused something.[5] Clearly, we have at least moved beyond the magical thinking of primitive cultures and early medicine, where cures were seen as closely related to symptoms (such as, the lungs of a fox as a remedy for asthma). However, there is quite a bit of evidence that people often resort to *misguided parsimony* and seek only one sufficient explanation for something. Many other shortcomings have also been catalogued in the research literature on causal attributions.

Self-interest and especially *ideological and emotional* factors seem to lead to *biased causal interpretations*, a finding that has direct relevance to corporate crisis forecasting and management (crises are stressful by nature) and to any management situation where strong feelings are engaged. For example, research on causal attributions in international relations suggests that analysis can be flawed by self-interest and heightened ideological-emotional concerns.

Is international conflict caused by such enduring dispositions as national character (the aggressive Russians, the imperialistic Americans) or by situational factors (conflict dynamics in a relationship, irresistible opportunities for expansion)? Did the Soviet Union invade Afghanistan because it is inherently aggressive or as a result of situational pressures as perceived by the Kremlin—or both (Heur 1980)? Whatever the "correct" answer is, the respective causal interpretations of Soviet and U.S. policy makers differ dramatically.

In addition to misguided parsimony or the principle of minimum causation (find the first plausible cause and stop the search, a clear satisfying strategy), ideological-emotional biased attribution tendencies, and simplistic causal analysis in terms of a single case, the relative importance of *prior versus immediate causes* has also been examined. Often, we can envision a causal chain with early and later causes of an event or phenomenon. Vinokur and Ajzen (1982) report that people perceive prior events to be more important and assert that this tendency is culturally learned rather than required by the dictates of logic or philosophy of science. There is no "right" answer to this, as they point out; depending on the analytical situation and the needs of the decision maker, emphasis may be placed on the earlier causal forces (from a strategic planning perspective), the immediate cause or the precipitant (from a crisis management vantage point), both, or a complex network of prior and immediate causes (the path analytic answer to the question).

In a particularly interesting experiment, Tetlock (1983) examines the relationship between *accountability and the complexity of thought*. Subjects reported their thoughts on three social issues and then expressed their attitudes under one of four conditions: expecting their attitudes to be anonymous or expecting to justify their attitudes to someone with liberal, conservative, or unknown attitudes. Only when subjects expected to defend their attitudes to someone with unknown views did they engage in complex information processing.

This kind of accountability, Tetlock speculates, may reduce overconfidence (by forcing people to look for contradictory evidence) and encourage careful, unbiased analysis. We should not overgeneralize on the basis of forty-eight undergraduates at the University of California who received course credit or a $3.00 reward for participating in the experiment, but the results offer clear advice for the decision maker: to maximize the complexity of thinking that goes into strategic planning and other kinds of analysis, avoid providing cues about your position on the relevant substantive issues (especially early in the analysis or decision process). This has the nice byproduct of also minimizing the danger of the "groupthink" syndrome.

Corporate Strategic Planning

Virtually any area of corporate decision making could be used to illustrate the essential role of causal analysis. Strategic planning is grounded directly in judgments about environmental influences on corporate decisions and the operation of chains and networks of causal factors. A strategic plan is really a set of objectives anchored in the matrix of a large and complex causal model. To the extent that causal forces are misidentified or left out, the plan will be deficient.

In strategic planning, after goals have been formulated and current objectives and the strategy fleshed out, *environmental analysis* must be undertaken to determine how economic, technological, social/cultural, and political/legal forces can influence the organization (Stoner 1982, 113). Changes must be detected when they are initially emerging in order to maximize the prospects for anticipating and controlling such external causal forces, thus implying that prior causes should receive more attention than immediate ones.

Here, *multiple advocacy* policy planning, where all major institutional viewpoints are represented, can play a role of great significance. Both internal and outside experts can facilitate the process of thorough and rigorous planning and policy analysis by injecting alternative explanatory perspectives and policy postures into the system. Techniques to counteract defensive avoidance in group decision making prevent groupthink and promote multiple advocacy; SOPs can be adopted to guard against premature closure, individual myopia, simplistic analysis, and group-induced shifts toward an artificial and inaccurate (but reassuring) consensus.

Analysis of the external environment involves both direct elements (consumers, direct competitors, government agencies, and other actors who interact directly with the firm) and indirect causal factors (technology, economy, political trends). To deal effectively with either dimension, the decision maker must focus on the key aspects of the environment, singling out the most relevant and tractable features of the causal landscape (see, for example, Ahroni et al. 1978). The indirect environment generally provides early warning signals about changes that will subsequently affect the organization. Both expert assessments and formal forecasting techniques can be utilized to uncover the most critical environmental variables and clusters of forces.

DSS DESIGN AND DEVELOPMENT

Plans flow for views of the world; options are the outgrowth of perceived opportunities, constraints, and causal configurations; views of the world and perceived sets of opportunities and constraints reflect and are embedded in causal models that people implicitly or explicitly rely on in planning. These three simple propositions form the underlying assumptions for the approach to DSS design and development portrayed here.

The Knowledge-based System

The foregoing discussion on causal analysis presumes a DSS that draws on work on knowledge-based systems (KBS) or expert systems in artificial intelligence. Such a DSS would be a genuinely interactive and dynamic system as well as an intelligent KBS rather than an expert system that mimics (and could eventually replace) the problem solver. The KBS-DSS should be capable of generating the user's generic causal structure or schema, interacting with the user to embellish the individual's cognitive map of the problem domain and offering "advice" about how to expand or refine the schema. The generic schema would be created, refined, stored, and updated or revised as necessary. Depending on scenario-driven changing causal parameters and constraints, the dynamic form of the schema would be capable of varying its contents and even structure. The envisioned aid would thus genuinely marry the expert and the expert system, creating an active KBS midway between a "naked expert" and a passive, automated expert system.

In both decision analysis and causal modeling, structuring or specifying the model invariably turns out to be the most difficult, time consuming, and crucial part of the analytical process. Although several formalized approaches are available in the management science literature for problem identification and problem cause/analysis (for example, Cause and Effect Diagrams and Control Data Corporation's Alpha Omega technique), problem identification and formulation or problem structuring is typically done in an experiential, intuitive fashion. The analytical process of causal inference can and should be tackled in a more systematic and explicit fashion.

The extensive research on how people perceive and assess causation provides a considerble amount of useful advice for designing and implementing such a knowledge-based system to represent the planner's causal model or cognitive map. The popular causal schema concept, which embodies the idea that people use preexisting knowledge structures (mental models that range from simple event-scripts or stories and person-scripts or stereotypes to abstract, formal schemas) to integrate and react to stimulus information, underlies much of the research on causal attributions.

Of critical importance to such an approach is the maintenance of a balance between mechanically imposing the findings of experimental and social psychology (condescendingly telling the user how to build his or her KBS-DSS) and simply letting the decision maker transfer the schema from his or her head to the computer. For example, the KBS can be taught about such crucial distinctions as the one between schema of multiple sufficient causes (MSC) and schema of multiple necessary causes (MNC), using this information to query the user and suggest alternative ways of structuring the world causally. But the system will be designed to be an intelligent assistant operating in an interactive problem-solving mode, not an expert system surrogate for the human planner or decision maker.

Rules and Guidelines

The substantive knowledge base will provide the foundation for creating, refining, and storing a user's generic schema profile. The other major component of the expert system will be a set of rules and guidelines for causal analysis. These principles will be of three forms: "mandatory" logic and inference rules; "recommended" rules; "advisory" rules.

The *mandatory rules*, the smallest part of the causal rule system, will be comprised of simple error checks. For example, if the user asserts that constraints a and b lead to situation c, when the knowledge base knows that a and b lead to d, this will automatically be communicated to the user.

The *recommended rules* involve situations where research in social psychology demonstrates fairly convincingly that a precept is valid. For example, it is well known that people are prone to all kinds of mistakes with probabilities, particularly with respect to the evaluation of conjunctive and disjunctive events. People tend to overestimate the probability of the former and underestimate the probability of the latter. Analogously, a causal chain which involves a new undertaking, such as a dramatic shift in market planning, is typically conjunctive in nature, which means that each event in a series must occur for it to succeed. Even when all are likely, the overall probability of success (or the overall credibility of the schema) can be very low if the number of required favorable causal factors is large. In this case, the user will be so advised and will have the option of modifying the schema if he wishes.

The *advisory rules* refer to causal analysis stratagems for which the evidence is murky in nature compared to the above, but where there is an empirical research foundation to support the idea of "advising" the user to think about the issue. Positing a single cause versus contributing causes (the MSC versus MNC problem in attribution research) provides an illustration. Another concerns the relative importance of prior versus immediate causes. Often, a causal chain with early and later causes of an event or phenomenon can be envisioned. People seem to perceive prior events to be more important, a reaction which is mandated neither by the dictates of logic nor philosophy of science. Depending on the nature of the situation and the needs of the user, emphasis may be placed on antecedent causal forces (from a long-range strategic planning perspective), or the immediate precipitant (from a crisis management vantage point). The smart causal rule system will advise the user of this through prompts and queries when he or she initially structures the schema, but will do so only as an "advisor."

Through the substantive and causal rule system knowledge bases, the DSS will be able to elicit and represent the user's cognitive map. Once the schema is displayed, there will also be automatic queries to revise or enhance the aid before the final mental model is stored. The schema can also be updated as the user's thinking changes.

CONCLUSION

It has been estimated that 95 percent of all computer power has been devoted thus far to record keeping and to large-scale scientific and engineering computations. With the proliferation of a host of computer-based information and decision support systems and aids, there is the potential for exploiting the unique configuration that results from the marriage of electronic computers, knowledge-based systems, and the still emerging field of decision science. The generic KBS-DSS sketched out above in a very embryonic fashion provides one illustration of what is possible. The failure to follow the guidelines of psychology, however, will neither improve the decision-making process nor guarantee the enthusiastic support of the user. More egregious would be the failure to involve the user at every point of the design and development process; a decision support system assumes a genuinely symbiotic relationship between the biocomputer and the electronic computer.

NOTES

The author wishes to give a special note of thanks to Wendy A. Shepherd for her indispensable assistance in the preparation of this chapter.

1. Statistical regression refers to the tendency for estimates to regress toward the mean; a student tends to do well on one exam and less well on a second, sons tend to be somewhat shorter or taller than their fathers, etc. The tendency is nonexistent if two variables are perfectly related (a correlation of + or − 1.00), which of course is rare. But people consistently display nonregressive prediction tendencies.

2. This generalization does not necessarily apply to assessment centers, where the candidate participates in a wide range of simulated activities; see Stoner (1982, 540–541) for details.

3. The EPA and smoking examples both come from Nisbett and Ross (1980).

4. Locke and Pennington (1982) refine the internal-external or dispositional-situational distinction somewhat by distinguishing between internal reasons (psychological or situational) versus other internal causes.

5. In the dispositional-situational studies, people generate judgements about the causes of success or failure on an exam or some similar individual effort. People tend to overrely on personal causes. People also expect personal consistency across situations even though such consistency is empirically low for traits like aggressiveness or honesty. But this causal interpretation reflects the theories of social psychologists and behaviorists (although not all theories are wrong, of course). A Freudian psychologist, to cite one example, would disagree.

REFERENCES

Aharoni, Yair, Zvi Maimon, and Eli Segev. 1978. Performance and Autonomy in Organizations: Determining Dominant Environmental Components. *Management Science* 24 (May): 949–59.

Anderson, Craig A. 1983. Abstract and Concrete Data in the Perseverance of Social Theories: When Weak Data Lead to Unshakeable Beliefs. *Journal of Experimental Social Psychology* 19: 93–108.

Andriole, Stephen J. 1983. *Interactive Computer-Bases Systems: Design and Development*. Princeton, N.J.: Petrocelli Books.

Blanning, Robert W. 1983. What is Happening in DSS? *Interfaces* 13 (5 October): 71–80.

Bonczek, Robert H., Clyde W. Holsapple, and Andrew B. Whinstone. 1983. Computer-Based Support of Organization Decision Making. In *Decision Support Systems: A Data-Based, Model-Oriented, User-Developed Discipline*, ed. W. C. House, 291–323. Princeton, N.J.: Petrocelli Books.

Fiedler, Klaus. 1982. Causal Schemata: Review and Criticism of Research on a Popular Construct. *Journal of Personality and Social Psychology* 42 (June):1001–13.

Heuer, Richards J., Jr. 1980. Analyzing the Soviet Invasion of Afghanistan: Hypotheses from Causal Attribution Theory. *Studies in Comparative Communism* 13 (Winter): 347–55.

Hogarth, Robin M., and Spyros Makridakis. 1981. Forecasting and Planning: An Evaluation. *Management Science* 27: 115–38.

Hopple, Gerald W. 1984. Prophets and Profits: Expert-Based Corporate Crisis Forecasting Systems. In *Corporate Crisis Management*, ed. Stephen J. Andriole. Princeton, N.J.: Petrocelli Books, pp. 123—146.

Locke, Don, and Donald Pennington. 1982. Reasons and Other Causes: Their Role in Attribution Processes. *Journal of Personality and Social Psychology* 42 (February): 212–23.

Nisbett, Richard E., Eugene Borgida, Rick Crandall, and Harvey Reed. 1982. Popular Induction: Information Is Not Necessarily Informative. In *Judgment under Uncertainty: Heuristics and Biases*, ed. Daniel Kahneman, Paul Slovic, and Amos Tversky, 101–16. Cambridge: Cambridge University Press.

Nisbett, Richard E., and Lee Ross. 1980. *Human Inference: Strategies and Shortcomings of Social Judgment*. Englewood Cliffs, N.J.: Prentice-Hall.

Ragan, T. J., K. T. Back, V. Stansell, L. J. Ausburn, F. B. Ausburn, P. A. Butler, and K. Huckabay. 1979. *Cognitive Styles: A Review of the Literature*. Norman, Ok.: University of Oklahoma.

Raphael Theodore D. 1982. Integrative Complexity Theory and Fore-casting International Crises. *Journal of Conflict Resolution* 26 (September): 423–50.

Russell, Dan. 1982. The Causal Dimensions Scale: A Measure of How Individuals Perceive Causes. *Journal of Personality and Social Psychology* 42 (June): 1137–45.

Schroeder, H. M., M. Driver, and S. Steufert. 1967. *Human Information Processing.* New York: Holt, Rinehart and Winston.

Stoner, James A. F. 1982. *Management.* 2d ed. Englewood Cliffs, N.J.: Prentice-Hall.

Streufert, S., and S. Streufert. 1978. *Behavior in the Complex Environment.* Washington, D.C.: V. H. Winston.

Tetlock, Philip E. 1983. Accountability and Complexity of Thought. *Journal of Personality and Social Psychology* 45 (July): 74–83.

———— 1984. Cognitive Style and Political Belief Systems in the British House of Commons. *Journal of Personality and Social Psychology* 46 (2).

Tversky, Amos, and Daniel Kahneman. 1982. Judgment under Uncertainty: Heuristics and Biases. In *Judgment Under Uncertainty: Heuristics and Biases,* ed. Daniel Kahneman, Paul Slovic, and Amos Tversky, 3–20. Cambridge: Cambridge University Press.

Vinokur, Amiram, and Icek Ajzen. 1982. Relative Importance of Prior and Immediate Events: A Causal Primacy Effect. *Journal of Personality and Social Psychology* 42 (May): 820–29.

Watson, Hugh J., and Marianne M. Hill. 1983. Decision Support Systems or What Didn't Happen with MIS. *Interfaces* 13 (5 October): 81–88.

Wimer, Scott, and Harold H. Kelley. 1982. An Investigation of the Dimensions of Causal Attribution. *Journal of Personality and Social Psychology* 43 (December): 1142–62.

V

FUTURE DECISION SUPPORT SYSTEMS TECHNOLOGY

INTRODUCTION

What will future decision support systems look like? How will they behave?

The last chapter in this book deals with the future. It suggests what future hardware will look like, how software will operate, and how the office of the future will deal with the changes that automated and computer-assisted decision making will precipitate.

14

Next Generation Decision Support Systems

Stephen J. Andriole

The design and development of decision support systems will change dramatically over the next five to ten years. In fact, next generation decision support systems will bear very little resemblance to the systems available today.

The way decision support systems of the future will be used will also be very different. They will play much larger roles in our professional lives. In some instances, they may well manage our professional lives, executing major and minor decisions on our behalf.

This chapter explores this new territory. It looks at the hardware and software challenges, as well as how future decision support systems will challenge and alter professional environments.

It is important to remember that the next generation of decision support systems will benefit from a technology push now visible across the entire realm of computer, management, and behavioral sciences. Decision support systems designers will benefit from this push, but will have to direct it toward the development of truly effective decision support systems. This is the real challenge.

THE NEW PERSPECTIVE

Early on in this book, perspective was discussed as a way to distinguish between the different kinds of decision support systems available today. The point was made that for many, decision support has a narrow definition, while others regard it very broadly. The new perspective on decision support will be extremely broad, reflecting the capabilities of new systems that will be broad, integrative, and functional on many levels. Future decision support systems will permit decision makers and information managers, resource allocators and administrators, and strategic planners and inventory controllers to all improve their efficiency.

The broad perspective will be permitted by the new technology (see below) that will emerge over the next several years, and a centralization in the corporate and governmental workplace, a centralization that will not be ideological but rather driven by the same technology that will permit the design and development of more powerful decision support systems. In all likelihood, the movement toward *technological* networking and system integration will translate into new imperatives for the management of information and decision making. In short, the office of the future will transform itself because new technology will permit the change and, significantly, because it will demand it.

What will be driving what? Will new corporate and governmental requirements suggest new decision support system requirements, or will new decision support systems suggest new requirements? Would next generation decision support systems look the way we expect them to look if they were conceived in an applications vacuum, or is the interpretation and anticipation of applications driving the form that future decision support systems will take?

The questions are relevant to all parts of the information and manufacturing economy. In the automobile industry, for example, robots are arriving in order to solve specific requirements *and* because robotic technology has finally evolved into a cost-effective alternative to human labor. Word processing is now cheap and efficient. But has computer-based word processing changed, eliminated, or reduced requirements? It is interesting that many social theorists have argued that the development of the office copier has dramatically changed the way information is produced and distributed. Some argue that copiers have triggered a paper explosion that has oversatisfied the need for information. In other words, copiers—just because they exist—now satisfy far more requirements than can actually be identified. Will decision support systems suffer a similar "success?"

While definitions of decision support will grow, so too will our understanding of computer-based problem solving. Decision support, while very broad in concept and application, will nevertheless be subsumed under the general rubric of computer-based problem solving.

HARDWARE

The hardware that supports decision support systems technology today is "conventional." There are turnkey systems as well as generic hardware configurations that support the use of decision support systems. CPUs, disk drives, keyboards, light pens, touch screens, and the like can be found in a variety of decision support systems. There are also microcomputer systems, as well as systems that require larger (minicomputer) hardware configurations.

Next generation decision support systems will be smaller and cheaper, and therefore distributed. They will be networked, and capable of up-loading and down-loading to larger and smaller systems. Input devices will vary from application to application as well as with the preferences of the user. Voice input will dramatically change the way decision support systems are used in the future; voice-activated text processing will expand the capabilities of decision support systems by linking decision support to word processing and report preparation in a "natural" unobtrusive way.

Many decision support systems will have embedded communications links to data bases, other systems on decision support networks, and the outside world via conventional voice communication systems. IBM's recent acquisition of Rolm suggests that the merger between computing and voice systems is well underway. Future decision support systems will have voice input capabilities, conventional headset communications, deep data base linkages, and a "place" on a much larger decision support network.

Briefcase- and smaller-sized decision support systems will become widespread. The embedding of spreadsheets in popular portable microcomputers suggests that decision support chips will be developed and embedded in future hardware configurations. In fact, not unlike some of the more powerful calculators of the 1970s, future decision support systems will permit you to mix-and-match decision support chips within a single decision processor. The chips will be sold independently by decision support vendors.

Future decision support systems will also be integrated with video display systems of several genres. There will be video disc-based decision support systems as well as packaged systems that integrate powerful computer-generated imagery capabilities. The cost of both video options is falling dramatically, and the decision support system consumer of the future will be able to select the one that best serves his or her needs.

It is safe to say that video will become integral to future decision support. But it will be integrated directly into the system, not an optional afterthought to your purchase. Behavioral scientists have just about convinced the design community—via the amassing of much evidence—that information, both statistical and conceptual, can be communicated much more effectively via graphic, symbolic, and iconic displays. Decision support systems that do not have these and related capabilities will often fail.

requirements. There is a real possibility that AI will oversell its capabilities and thereby undermine its application potential. Nevertheless, the tools and techniques of AI can make important contributions to decision support systems design and development.

Some future decision support software will be generic and some will be problem-specific. Vendors will design and market generic accounting, inventory control, and option selection software. They will sell this software in chip or disk form. Nearly all of it will require some graphic interface that is directly manipulable by the user. Other software will be very problem-specific, tailored to routine problems and organizations.

It is extremely important to note the appearance of decision support system development tools. Already, as noted, there are packages that permit the development of rule-based expert decision support systems. There are now fourth-generation tools that are surprisingly powerful and affordable. These so-called end-user systems will permit on-site design and development of decision support systems that may only be used for a while by a few people. As the cost of developing such systems falls, more and more "throw-away" decision support systems will be developed. This will change the way we now view the role of decision support in any organization, not unlike the way the notion of rapid application prototyping has changed the way application programs should be developed.

APPLICATIONS

Decision support systems will be used very differently in the future than they are today. They may well function as clearinghouses for our professional problems. They may prioritize problems for us, and they may automatically go ahead and solve some of them. They will become problem-solving partners, helping us in much the same way colleagues now do. The notions of decision support systems as software or hardware, and users as operators, will give way to a cooperative sense of function that will direct the design, development, and application of the best decision support systems.

Decision support systems will also be deployed at all levels in the organization. Today, decision support is targeted at the mid-level and high-level manager; tomorrow all levels will be supported by powerful interactive, adaptive systems. The distribution of decision support systems will permit decision support networking, the sharing of decision support data, and the propagation of decision support problem-solving experience (through the development of a computer-based institutional memory of useful decision support "analogs" that might be called upon to help structure especially recalcitrant decision problems). Efficient organizations will actually develop an inventory of problem/solution combinations that will be plugged into their decision support networks.

Decision support systems will also communicate with systems in other organizations in other parts of the world. Falling satellite communications costs will permit global linkages, and contact with data bases, expert systems, inventories, and the like, thereby multiplying the capabilities of inhouse decision support systems by orders of magnitude. This global networking is not decades away, but only five to ten years away.

Finally, next generation decision support systems will bridge the gap between our professional and personal worlds. Because they will have capabilities to manage our professional lives, they will also be capable of managing our personal lives. Since future decision support "delivery systems" will be expandable and inexpensive, the integration of personal management modules will be inevitable. This blurring of the traditional lines between our professional and personal worlds may not be desirable, but it is likely. Again, the technology will drive such changes to a significant extent, technology that will trigger changes because of its capabilities not necessarily in response to real requirements. In other words, there is a technological destiny built into our forecasts about the role of future decision support systems.

CONCLUSION

The net effect is awesome. Decision support in the 1990s will be enormously broad and powerful. It will be distributed and networked. It will be "intelligent" and inexpensive. The effects of this reality are difficult to precisely predict, though a number of the ideas expressed above are in fact inevitable. Have we given enough thought to the direction in which decision support technology is taking us? Have we assessed the desirability of the direction? Have we determined the impact that next generation decision support systems will have upon the office of the future? Will they define the office of the future? Or will the office of the future suggest a role for decision support? We have clearly avoided these and other tough questions. If we are to manage and exploit the new technology, we need to address all of the pertinent questions as soon as possible. When we do, we will be able to inform and direct progress so that the next generation is as capable and responsive to real needs as it possibly can be.

CONCLUSION

This book has dealt with a number of important decision support systems issues and problems. It has also provided a snapshot look at the field, especially as it has been manifest on microcomputers, at a particular point in time. The changes that will occur during the next decade are almost impossible to list. The likelihood is that decision support as we know it today will give way to a whole new concept in design and application.

Like all dynamic fields, decision support is changing so fast that it is very difficult to maintain a working perspective or to keep abreast of the most recent developments. This book has attempted to impart some information, but the real work lies ahead. If we are to design, develop, and prudently apply microcomputer-based decision support systems then we need to not only master progress, but direct it as well. The real challenge lies here and in the mangement of what has become an eclectic and interdisciplinary field of inquiry. If we succeed, then decision support may well become the standard for designing many other computer-based problem-solving programs.

CONTRIBUTORS

Leonard Adelman received his Ph.D. in psychology from the University of Colorado. He has taught courses on individual and group decision making and reviewed papers for publication in *IEEE Transactions on Systems, Man, and Cybernetics*. He has published research on factors affecting the learning of complex inference tasks; the utility of decision support systems for clarifying expert judgments; the relative effectiveness of different structuring, weighting, and discussion techniques for group decision making; and factors affecting the successful evaluation and subsequent implementation of decision support systems. Dr. Adelman is currently the Manager of the Decision Sciences Section of the PAR Technology Corporation.

Stephen J. Andriole is the President of International Information Systems, Inc. He was formerly the Director of the Defense Advanced Research Projects Agency's (DARPA's) Cybernetics Technology Office, where he also served as Program Manager. He is listed in Who's Who in Engineering, Finance, and America, and has served on several ADP utility working groups and panels for government and industry. He is the author, coauthor, editor, and coeditor of seventeen books and several hundred articles and papers, including *Applications in Artificial Intelligence, Invitation to Artificial Intelligence, Interactive Computer-Based Systems Design and Development, Corporate Crisis Management*, and the *Sourcebook on Artificial Intelligence*. He earned an M.A. and Ph.D. from the University of Maryland (College Park) in 1973 and 1974.

Stephen W. Barth received his B.S. degree in mathematics in 1975 and his M.S. degree in computer science in 1980 from the University of Illinois, Urbana. He then served as a consultant for Intelligent Terminals Ltd., and part time staff member at the Machine Intelligence Research Unit of the University of Edinburgh under Professor Donald Michie. While at Edinburgh he was primarily responsible for additional development and knowledge engineering with the AL/X expert system as applied to fault diagnosis on North Sea oil production platforms. Currently he is a senior staff member with PAR Technology Corporation where his responsibilities include design and knowledge engineering for several expert systems applications.

Authella M. Bessent is Associate Professor of Operations Research and Codirector of the Educational Productivity Council at the University of Texas at Austin. She has been a leader in the application of operations research methods to productivity assessment in public sector organizations both in the United States and abroad. Her research has been published in a variety of journals including *Management Science*.

Wailand Bessent is Professor of Educational Administration at the University of Texas at Austin, and Codirector of the Educational Productivity Council. His current research interest is the development and testing of an efficiency measurement model for public sector enterprises. He is past president of the University Council of Educational Administration and a consultant for educational planning in South and Central America.

Charles T. (Terry) Clark received his B.A. in mathematics from Pan American University in 1963. In 1972, he received the M.S. degree in systems analysis from the Air Force Institute of Technology. He received his Ph.D. in operations research in 1983 from the University of Texas at Austin. He is currently a Lieutenant Colonel in the U.S. Air Force serving as an Assistant Professor of Logistics Management at the School of Systems and Logistics, Air Force Institute of Technology, Wright-Patterson Air Force Base, Ohio.

Allene K. Cormier is a Principal and Senior Consultant of System Strategies, Inc. of Potomac, Maryland. She has ten years of office and information systems consulting experience with major corporations and government agencies. She has presented and published several papers discussing her work, and has been invited to speak at both national and international forums sponsored by management science and information systems societies. She was appointed head of the IBM user's group for office systems including both host-related and stand-alone systems, and served in this capacity for two national meetings. Ms. Cormier has an M.S. in information science from the University of Washington in Seattle.

Michael L. Donnell received his Ph.D. in mathematical psychology as well as M.A.s in mathematics and psychology from the University of Michigan, Ann Arbor. Dr. Donnell is Assistant Vice President and Manager of the Military Analysis and Interactive Systems Department at Science Applications International Corporation (SAIC). He was formerly the manager of PAR Technology Corporation's Decision Sciences Section. During the last seven years he has designed, developed, and evaluated many micro- and mini-computer-based decision support systems, including an enemy course of action evaluation aid, a Bayesian aid for updating intelligence estimates, and a target prioritization aid. His latest project is an AI-based real-time advisory system for use by Naval command and control officers.

Joyce J. Elam is an Associate Professor of Information Systems at the Graduate School of Business, University of Texas at Austin. Prior to joining the faculty at the University of Texas, she was an Assistant Professor at the Wharton School of the University of Pennsylvania. She has consulted with a number of large corporations and government agencies on the design and implementation of information systems in such areas as manpower planning, distribution and logistics operations, and productivity assessment and analysis. She has published in the professional literature in such journals as *Information and Management, Mathematics of Operations Research,* and *The European Journal of Operations Research.*

Janice Fain is a leader in the field of computer-based problem solving. Dr. Fain has designed and developed many interactive systems targeted at a variety of problem areas, including crisis management, option selection, and data base management. She has pioneered the development of microcomputer-based decision support systems for industry and government. She has also developed a number of interactive simulations for industry and government, many of which have been productively used for over a decade.

Gerald W. Hopple is a Senior Analyst at Defense Systems, Inc. of McLean, Virginia. He was previously a Professor at the Defense Intelligence College where he taught courses on advanced analytical methods for intelligence analysis and production. He has designed indications and warnings (I&W) systems for government, and is currently at work on the design and development of an expert system for M1 tank diagnosis. He has published extensively in professional journals, has presented numerous professional papers, and is the author, coauthor, editor, and coeditor of eight books, including the *Sourcebook on Artificial Intelligence.* Dr. Hopple earned a Ph.D. from the University of Maryland (College Park) in 1975.

Paul E. Lehner is Advanced Senior Staff Member of the Decision Sciences Section of the PAR Technology Corporation. He holds a Ph.D. from the University of Michigan in psychology, which he earned in 1981. He is the technical director of a variety of efforts involving research and development in the application of AI to computer-based decision support. In addition to publications in this area, he has published in the fields of mathematical and decision theory.

Robert F. MacLean holds an M.Ed. in education from the Pennsylvania State University and a Ed.D. in mathematics education from Temple University. His doctoral dissertation was in the area of computer-assisted instruction (CAI). Dr. MacLean is currently directing the Computer Sciences Corporation research and development project in user-system interfaces. He has over seventeen years of technical and managerial experience in the development, implementation, and testing of computerized systems.

Ruth H. Phelps is the Team Chief for the Learning Technology Team of the Instructional Technology Systems Technical Area of the U.S. Army Research Institute for the Behavioral and Social Sciences (ARI). She is formerly a member of the Battlefield Information Systems Technical Area of ARI. Dr. Phelps received her Ph.D. in 1977 from Kansas State University, where she specialized in decision-making and cognitive processes, models, and training. She has contributed to professional journals in these and related fields; she is also the Chairperson of the Behavioral Decision-Making Section of the IEEE Systems, Man, and Cybernetics Society.

William B. Rouse received his Ph.D. from the Massachusetts Institute of Technology. He is currently Professor of Industrial and Systems Engineering and Director of the Center for Man-Machine Systems Research at the Georgia Institute of Technology. He is also cofounder and President of Search Technology, Inc., a firm specializing in systems engineering approaches to research and development in computer-based training and decision support systems. He is the author and coauthor of numerous articles and reports and has written *Systems Engineering Models Human-Machine Interaction, Human Detection and Diagnosis of Systems Failures,* and *Management of Library Networks: Policy Analysis, Implementation, and Control.*

Andrew P. Sage is the First American Professor of Information Technology and Associate Vice President at George Mason University in Fairfax, Virginia. He received the SMEE degree from MIT and the Ph.D. from Purdue in 1960. He has been a faculty member at the University of Arizona, the University of Florida, and Southern Methodist University. He was the Lawrence R. Quarles Professor of Systems Engineering at the University of Virginia from 1974 to 1984. He is a fellow of the IEEE and the American Association for the Advancement of Science. He has received numerous professional awards, is on the editorial board of several major journals in systems engineering and information technology, and the editor of three: *IEEE Transactions on Systems, Man, and Cybernetics; Automatica;* and *Large Scale Systems.* He is the author and coauthor of hundreds of published papers and research reports and several books.

John W. Sutherland received his Ph.D. from UCLA in 1967, concentrating in management and system science. He has taught these and related subjects at UCLA, CUNY (Bernard Baruch), and Rutgers. In addition, he has served as Chairman of the Department of Administrative Sciences at Southern Illinois University and as Dean of the W. Paul Stillman School of Business at Seton Hall University. He is currently Senior Professor of Information Systems at Virginia Commonwealth University in Richmond, Virginia. He is the author of six major books in the system sciences, and has published numerous papers in professional journals.

Bennett Teates is the head of Command and Control Programs at Georgia Institute of Technology's Engineering Experiment Station. He is also a Senior Research Engineer with the Electronics and Computer Systems Laboratory of GIT, and was the director of the project to develop the concept and approaches to accelerated transfer of off-the-shelf decision support systems technology.

BOB KIRCHGESNER